THE WAY UP

THE WAY UP
The practical psychology of success

AINSLIE MEARES

Souvenir Press

First published 1970 by Souvenir
Press Ltd., 95 Mortimer Street,
London, W.1, and simultaneously
by The Ryerson Press, Toronto 2,
Canada

ISBN.0.285.50290.5

Printed in Great Britain at
The Grange Press
Southwick, Sussex

PREFACE

As you pick up a book of this nature, the first thing you ask is, 'What does this man know about it? On what authority does he presume to advise me?' So I shall explain my position. I do not speak from personal experience of some remarkable material success. I am a psychiatrist, and I speak from knowledge of the experience of others. I have seen as patients many men and women who were on the way up. They were in trouble. That is why they had come to see me. Some were just plain irritable, tense and anxious because they had not learned how to calm their tensions from the stress of the way up. With some it had gone further, and they had the headaches, ulcers and rising blood pressure which is the price of success for those who have not captured the knack of dealing with problems with inner ease. Others have come knowing that they have real ability, but have been failing to make the grade. And of course there are the successful ones, who have come to me, startled and shocked to find that on the way up they have lost so much of other things, of family, friendship, culture, and even parts of their own personality that the fruits of success have turned sour in their mouth.

You ask if I have helped these people. The answer is unequivocable. Yes, I have helped them, and they have advanced on the way up towards both material and inner success. It has all been a matter of understanding and coping with people. You must be confronted with similar problems. That is why I think I can help you.

AINSLIE MEARES, MD
45 *Spring Street, Melbourne*

CONTENTS

[vii]

INTRODUCTION

You are on the way up, so you are busy. Time is short, and there is not much leisure for reading. I shall remember this, and I shall be concise, but read this introduction as it explains how it is that I can help you.

The way up. By this I mean the way to something better. It is the way to success. But success has many facets. We shall deal primarily with material success; but this can never be complete or even satisfying without corresponding success in other aspects of living. So we shall consider these too, particularly as they stand in relation to material success.

Now, right at the beginning, I shall ask you to agree with me in three basic propositions. First, let us agree that almost all of us, you and I and the others, do in fact have the capacity to proceed a little further on the way up. And of course, there are many of us who have the capacity to go a great deal further. I am sure you will agree with this.

Secondly, there are these other aspects of living which we must master if our material success is to have any real meaning. This is really self-evident. If a man destroys himself in attaining his success, it is no success at all.

The other proposition which I ask you to accept is equally straight forward. It is simply this – that psychological factors play a very important part on our way up. In other words, it is our ability to use our native talents to best advantage which counts. This of course is a psychological process. It means that we must understand ourselves as well as we can, so that we can use our strength to best advantage and at the same time avoid exposing too much of our weaknesses. Perhaps even more than this, we may discover potentialities within us which we never before knew existed. In the same way we learn to assess the personality structure of others. We are then in a position to influence them, and if our understanding is deep enough, we can come to influence them in an easy natural way without them really being aware of what we are doing. This is applied psychology. It is the way we cope with others and come to influence them; and to do this successfully we must learn to cope with ourselves. This is an integral part of the way to material success. But if in writing this little book I felt that I was merely giving a few rising executives an advantage over others, I would not think that I was contributing much to the sum total of things. However, there is more to it than that, and I believe that such a study transcends the individual. You and the others like you are part of an elite. You will influence others. Coping with people in a way which leads you to your own material success is really only another facet of the great truth which links man and man. Things run more smoothly, so all are benefited. As a psychiatrist, many people discuss these matters with me. Now I shall talk to you about them just as if you were sitting here with me in my consulting room.

1

Your personality characteristics and how to use them

Our success in life depends on the way in which we use what talents we have. In the material sense this is obvious. Every businessman knows that he must make full use of his material resources. He knows if he fails in this he is not on the way up. The same applies to the resources of our personality. This is what I want to discuss with you. It is a matter of finding the way to use our personality to best advantage. This is probably one of the most important factors in determining our success in life in whatever field we might be.

We shall discuss the various characteristics of our personality. These are aspects of ourselves which together make us what we are. Most of us have all these characteristics in some degree; but the degree to which they are present in each of us varies from person to person, and so contributes to the unique individuality of each of us.

These personality characteristics are normal. They are only abnormal when they are present in very great degree. It is perfectly normal to be a little extraverted or to have some obsessive traits in our personality. These are things within us which we can use to advantage. People have often said to me, 'I am an introvert', as if they had some disease. It is no more abnormal to be introverted than it is to be tall or short, or blonde or brunette.

We ourselves have these personality traits, and so do all those around us. It is the understanding and practical use of these traits, both in ourselves and in others, which can make such a difference to our material success of life.

Our personality characteristics are a defence against tension. At times we have all been insecure in ourselves. This is inevitable. As children we are small and vulnerable; grown-ups are big, and to children the world often seems threatening. So the child, who of necessity experiences some insecurity, builds up ways of coping with things, and so comes to evolve a pattern of behaviour to relieve his inner tensions. One child copes one way and another child in a different way. One will withdraw and cling to mother's skirts, another will become boisterous and self assertive, another will solve the same problem by having a tantrum. These ways of coping develop into our adult personality characteristics. In a general way they follow fairly set patterns, such as extravert and introvert patterns of behaviour. We can analyse these different ways of coping, and see how they can best be used in ordinary life. In doing this we must apply the same principles to ourselves as we do to those around us. It is often much easier to see these characteristics in others than in ourselves.

Our personality characteristics are both our strength and our weakness. They are our strength because they reduce our general level of anxiety. In this way they help us to greater inner security, and reduce our feeling of nervous tension. They give us inner freedom so that we can work and love and create. They help us to be more effective and more productive. But on the other hand, these same personality characteristics in another way tend to reduce the free functioning of our minds. They tend to make us rather one sided, so that we do not get a really clear image of what is going on. An extravert and an introvert look at the same problem. But because of their different personalities, their minds interpret the facts differently. They see things as if they were wearing slightly different glasses, and the image is distorted. Our success in life depends very much on the way in which we use the strengths of our personality characteristics to best advantage, and at the same time minimize the effect of their weakness.

Extravert personality characteristics

The extravert is a doer. He likes to do things, and get on with the job. This is his approach to life. He does not sit and ponder the matter. He goes straight to it. He is realistic and practical. There is no great concern about the remote consequences of what he does. The activity of his mind is directed outwards, towards the world in which he lives, and away from the mental processes of his own inner life. In fact the inner life has little attraction for the extravert. He does not feel it. He does not understand when others talk of it. He sees little meaning in it. For him life is factual and realistic. He sees it clearly and knows what has to be done.

The extravert is gregarious. This is the second important characteristic of the extravert. He likes people. Men and women, young and old, he is at ease with them. Being with people fulfils an inner need so that he is at his best in the company of others. As a consequence of this he likes parties and games. He mixes readily; fun comes easily. Holidays and weekends are a round of social activity. Rather than spend an evening at home by himself, he visits some friend, or if that is not possible, he renews acquaintances at the local pub. The same easy friendliness pervades his life at work. He has a few words with the typists and is equally at ease with the boss. This is his way of life.

Extravert characteristics are a way of adjusting to life. There are many things within us – our doubts, fears and uncertainties – which spring from life itself, but which can be very disturbing to us if we let them occupy our minds too much. When this happens our general level of anxiety is increased, and we become aware of it through the feeling of nervous tension. Extravert characteristics protect the individual from anxiety of this nature. By being a doer rather than a thinker he is saved from this tension; and by his gregarious nature he keeps himself surrounded by friends, and long periods of isolation in which these uncomfortable thoughts and feelings might intrude are avoided. But we must remember that the process is unconscious. The person with these characteristics does not behave in this way purposely. He does it unconsciously because he likes it. For this is the pattern which he has evolved to cope with the realities of life and to avoid his own inner tension.

Other factors are also involved. The doer obviously makes himself more materially comfortable in all aspects of living.

[3]

This in itself reduces inner tension. And his inner need for friendship brings others around him which is biologically protective. In this way an individual develops extravert personality characteristics as an unconscious adjustment to the material facts of life and as a way of maintaining peace of mind.

Extravert characteristics suit the individual for an active rather than a passive occupation. Remember that the extravert capacity for doing includes mental doing as well as physical. But the mental doing is always related to outside reality, not to one's inner feelings. It is the doing of realistic planning and organizing. This may involve sitting at an office desk all day, but it is still the type of 'doing' which the extravert does so well. By an active rather than a passive job I do not mean that the person with extravert characteristics should not work in a subordinate role. This does not matter so long as the work is active doing, either mentally as in planning, or physically in manual work.

Conversely, a person with these extravert assets is not likely to be on the way up if he allows circumstances to direct him into the more thoughtful or philosophical occupations such as art, music or psychology in which there is less scope for him to use his native abilities. Rather he should cultivate an interest in these other matters as a side line or hobby in order to broaden his personality.

Decision-making comes easily to extraverts. Extravert characteristics make us doers. This in turn brings with it a capacity for making decisions. This comes about through the extravert way of looking at things. He sees things as black or white. A matter is right or wrong. It is a question of doing this or doing that. There are no shades of grey between the black and white. This gives the extravert a great ability to make decisions, and of course this is very important for those on the way up. He has a directness and simple straight-forwardness, which allows others to follow his reasoning with ease in a way that provides a valuable quality in an executive.

So if you have this type of extravert characteristic, keep yourself in a decision making job. If you have to choose, do this at a low level rather than work at a higher level in a routine

[4]

job. You will be successful in the decision making job and soon graduate to something better.

Extraverts should use their gregarious friendliness to advantage. The natural friendliness of the extravert is a great asset. You should work in occupations which bring you into contact with people. A job in personnel, public relations, or in sales gives an individual scope to use this aspect of his personality to full advantage. Someone with these assets would not be using the full capacity of his talents if he allowed himself to get into a job where he was working in an office by himself all day. Working in the company of others is satisfying to such an individual, but this is not using this aspect of his personality to full advantage. To be on the way up he needs to use his gregarious friendliness in the work that he is actually doing. This means work which involves making fresh contacts with people. The extravert's success in such a role is almost assured.

Learn to delegate your work. This of course is a first principle for anyone on the way up. As the extravert is practical and un-complicated, he does not worry or fuss about work that he delegates. It comes more easily to him than to others, and this can be a very valuable asset. Introverts and perfectionists are always uneasy about delegating work because of their basic insecurity. But the extravert is not troubled this way. A further important consideration is the ease with which the extravert deals with people. This makes it easy for him to get on well with those to whom he delegates his work.

This important asset of the personality can, of course, become over developed so that it is then no longer an asset, but becomes a hindrance to further progress. This occurs when the extravert, through these aspects of his personality finds that he can delegate work very easily. He falls to the temptation. He does too much of it; and soon finds himself on the down grade.

Extravert characteristics allow risk-taking. The way to the top involves risks. Some people are better suited to taking risks than are others. The extravert is very well suited. This comes about from the fact that he is a doer and not a philosopher. He is not inhibited and held back as others are. Adventures suit the extravert. And don't forget that there can be real adventure in doing things that are new even though they are within the four walls of an office.

There is the calculated risk and the gamble. It is the calculated risk which is often so important on the way up. The extravert is good in this area because he is practical, and assesses the proposition realistically. And because he is realistic, and unlike the gambler, he always has some plan to follow if the risk-taking venture should not come off.

The extravert should avoid too much gregarious activity. Our strengths are also our weaknesses. Western culture favours the extravert approach to life. There is a premium on being a good fellow, a good mixer, and all that goes with it. The business world can be a very happy place for the extravert with his easy social contacts. But we should note that this western approach to life does not obtain everywhere. In Buddhist and Hindu societies people generally regard the introvert adjustment to life as the more desirable. They look down on the, 'hail fellow and well met', approach of the extravert. It is considered brash; and a higher social value is placed on the inner experience of the mind.

A great weakness of the extravert approach to life is that the individual may be so successful at it that his progress on the way up is halted. It is simply that too much social activity, too much time with one's fellows just does not leave sufficient time for the very intense study which is so necessary for those on the way up. This proposition seems so absurdly obvious that I am hesitant to discuss it with you. But intelligence, social status or success in our career are often little protection against this weakness of the extravert character. The chairman of the board can fall to it, and come to the meeting insufficiently prepared just as easily as the first year extravert commerce student is distracted from his studies. This is a real weakness. Guard against it.

Overconfidence is a pitfall for extraverts. In general, extraverts have a lower level of anxiety and nervous tension than do other people. Their practical outlook and way of doing things enables them to cope with most of the problems of life without too much tension, and so leads them to an easy and natural self-confidence. Their general lack of inner life with its doubts and fears saves them from the loss of confidence which this induces in others. So the extravert has a sense of confidence in himself which most other people lack. This in itself is a great asset. He goes forward without the restraint of inner doubts, but in so doing, it is easy to go too far and verge on to the dangerous area of over-confidence.

Other factors contribute to the extravert tendence to over-confidence. Our society prizes the extravert way of life. We like our children to be good mixers, good team members and good at social occasions. All this comes naturally to the extravert personality and may lead him into over-confidence.

The extravert tendency to over-confidence is further facilitated by his lack of introspection and self examination which results from the relative absence of inner psychic activity in his mental make-up.

Remember that things are not all black and white. The extravert turns to reality. He is practical. This gives him a very great advantage over others in making decisions. But because of these very same characteristics, the decision may come too quickly. The practical way of looking at things in itself leads one to ignore the subtlety of the situation. This applies particularly when a decision will affect other people. Because of the paucity of his own inner subjective life, he has little appreciation as to how others feel. So he may make a decision with little considera-tion as to how it will affect others either materially or emotionally. A neglect of this aspect of the decision may reflect badly on the individual at a later date. This situation arises quite commonly in the present-day vogue of take-overs in business.

Be practical and decisive but not ruthless. I can hear you say, 'But business is ruthless'. Let us accept the intense competition in the society in which we live. This is natural. It is part of our biologi-cal heritage stemming from the aggressive element of our personality which is so essential for survival. But the point I wish to make is that the executive with extravert characteristics often acts more ruthlessly than he realises. This comes about

B   [7]

because his practical outlook tends to reduce his capacity to fully appreciate how his decisions affect others.

I recently saw one of the victims of a business take-over as a patient. He is a quiet, sensitive man who had built up a successful family business over a lifetime. The stress of being taken over by a ruthless extravert competitor has broken him, and most of his staff who had been with him for years are without a job. The interesting point is that I happen to know the extravert competitor, and from what I know of him, I feel sure that he is quite unaware of the effect of his take-over on the people concerned.

Extraverts should have a few introvert friends. This is important. The great weakness of the practical extravert approach to life is that there is a lack of sensitivity as to how others feel about things. The extravert has turned away from his own inner feelings to the practical matters of the external world. He is not concerned with inner feelings, in fact he unconsciously denies them. As a result he loses the ability to appreciate what is going on in other people's minds. This of course is a grave short-coming to the individual as a person; but it also reduces his chances to make the way up because so much of business success concerns an appreciation as to how others feel.

How do we overcome this? A very obvious way is to learn from those around us, to learn from association with people who have the capacity to understand how others feel. This means introverts. But the extravert tends to shy away from introvert friendships. He feels the introvert is too complicated. He is poor company; he is no good at parties. Besides this, the extravert is often mildly ill-at-ease with the introvert because he does not quite know what to do with him or say to him. In fact he finds him rather a bore. So the extravert tends to associate with extraverts, and to gather them around him as his friends. But if you have marked extravert characteristics you can gain from association with a few introvert friends, and greater understanding as to how others feel will come of it.

It broadens the extravert personality to cultivate some artistic interest. This may seem strange advice. Extravert people are practical and are generally not interested in matters of art.

Remember I am giving this advice with the object of helping you to broaden and deepen your personality, and not from any social motives that are often associated with a pseudo interest in art.

The extravert has unconsciously come to understand the psychological aspects of practical living. This is his adjustment to life. But he lacks full understanding of the inner life. This is his weakness because it stops him understanding people. If you can increase your understanding of your own inner life, you will understand others so much the better. But there is something very important here. It is not a knowledge of art that I am asking you to acquire, although this would be a step in the right direction. It is the learning to experience a feeling in connection with art which is significant. This is a subjective experience, and helps us to understand the inner subjective life of those around us.

There is just one further point about this. Let this venture into the field of art be something that you like doing. It is not a chore. It is something that you can like, something to which you can look forward. This approach is necessary if it is to have the desired effect on your mind.

Make a conscious effort to understand how others feel. This is a small exercise in self discipline. The extravert is not always good at self discipline, but try this.

Please do not ignore this point, and say to yourself, 'I understand well enough how others feel'. This is the typical extravert response. The truth of the matter is that the extravert, with his mind on practical reality, simply has no idea at all as to what goes on in the mind of more introverted people. Without this understanding he will always be at a loss in the successful management of introverted members of his staff. And of course the extravert is always liable to misjudge things with an introverted superior unless he has learned to understand how others think.

The matter of understanding how others feel has reached a new significance in business in recent years. The time has gone when management could control employees simply by the cold exercise of authority. Now things have to be done rather more subtley. And this is where the extravert with all his practical ability and decision making aptitude is most liable to fall down.

You have been talking to someone. When he leaves, try to work out what he was thinking and feeling. If you commute into the city by train, you can try to discern what is in the mind of the person sitting opposite. This little exercise can be quite good fun; and with a little practice you will be surprised how much more you understand about the people around you.

Extravert individuals should make a conscious effort to pay attention to detail. Because of his relative lack of inner life he is not held back by complexes. He is not inhibited. He is able to see the big picture. He sees the practical problems, but again rather on the grand scale, and not in detailed setting. The junior should guard against this problem by watching himself about details. Get into the way of consciously making yourself consider the details. Do it so that it becomes a habit, and the weakness of your extravert personality will be strengthened.

With the senior executive it is rather different. He can often cover up this weakness by having a subordinate take care of the details, and thus leave himself free to use his extravert assets in the grand planning.

To get the best out of others, be direct in dealing with extravert persons. This follows from what we have said about the extravert adjustment to life. He is practical, and his appreciation of a situation is not obscured by complicated feelings from his inner life. This allows a direct approach. If you have to tell him something bad or unpleasant, you can rely on him being practical about it. He will adjust to the new situation in a realistic way, and will not brood about it in the way that others might.

Use the friendliness of the subordinate extravert. Because the extravert is himself a friendly person he expects others to be likewise. A good relationship with one's subordinates is highly desirable for anyone on the way up. To achieve this with extraverts you must offer them some degree of friendliness. I am not suggesting for a moment that you should reduce your status as his superior. You can keep this, but at the same time make some show of friendliness. The extravert does not like a superior who keeps himself remote. This is foreign to the extravert's own pattern of life. He does not understand it; and the superior loses his chance to have a good relationship with his subordinate.

Introvert personality characteristics

The introvert is shy and sensitive. He is complicated in his interpersonal relations and is often ill-at-ease in the company of others. He tends to avoid social gatherings. There is a diffidence, lack of confidence, or timidity about him. He is quiet and unassuming. He can enjoy things, but he does so in a rather subdued fashion. He would prefer to be quietly by himself rather than the centre of a noisy party.

The introvert is preoccupied with his inner feelings rather than the outside world. He is a thinker rather than a doer. His inner life is just as real as that of the life of external reality, and what is more, it is just as satisfying. So he likes to sit and think. He likes to let his imagination run, and he enjoys the products of his phantasy in day-dreams in the way that others enjoy their creations in the external world.

As I write this, it is mid-December. In Australia it is the custom with many firms to hold a Christmas party. In the last week I have seen two introverts of junior executive status whose main problem in life is their intense apprehension about attending the office Christmas party. They cope with things all right in their ordinary office work, but any social occasion evokes this abnormal anxiety.

Introvert characteristics are a way of coping with life. It is not hard to understand this. When we are very young the world often appears a strange and threatening place. At the same time the child has an active imagination. Most of us can remember little incidents concerning our imagination of childhood days. If the parents do not give the child the emotional security which he needs, the world will appear all the more threatening. This may be further aggravated by a natural sensitivity of the nervous system. When this happens the child may turn away from the hostile external world to these other pleasures of the inner world. The introvert characteristics of adult life are the result of this process, and thus provide the individual with a pattern for coping with life. We have seen how the extravert turns outward, and so saves himself the stress of worry from this inner world which he soon comes to deny. On the other hand, through various circumstances, other children find the external world the more threatening and turn inwards to develop introvert characteristics. The big competitive world of reality is a difficult place. The introvert finds it rather frightening so he seeks his pleasure in thought and imagination rather than in doing.

The introvert withdraws to avoid being hurt. The introvert is very sensitive, and this is increased by his preoccupation with his own inner feelings. Because of his sensitivity he is easily hurt. He may feel slighted when no slight was intended. To save himself from this situation, he withdraws. He gives up the boisterous company of others. He avoids parties and social gatherings and thus saves himself from inner tension.

Many young introverts manage like this. They do their work and get on in the firm. But if they are on the way up a stage is reached when they become involved in social contacts. It is common for the young executive to be sent overseas on a business' trip. This often necessitates meeting others at a social level. The introvert can no longer defend himself by withdrawal, and until he is able to overcome this defect of his personality, his progress on the way up is halted.

The introvert withdraws inwardly as well as physically. He withdraws physically from the hurly-burly of life, but he also withdraws in another way. There is an inner withdrawal. When he does go to a party or social gathering, he may withdraw into himself. He is at the party, but is not of it. This of course is done unconsciously to save hurt to his inner feelings from contact with people whom he does not understand.

We can see the effect of the inner withdrawal in another way. He is often frightened of becoming too involved emotionally. This is an unconscious defence against being hurt because he is so sensitive. So he withdraws his emotions. The effect is that his feeling towards his friends, or any project comes to lack any real enthusiasm.

The introvert is inhibited. His feelings are held back. The easy flow of normal emotion is checked so that fun and laughter come only grudgingly. This is another psychological defence. By unconsciously holding himself in, he does not expose himself so much to the slights of the external world, and his sensitivity is saved from further hurt.

Use the advantage of your introvert personality. Our society looks to extravert characteristics. It is these that are prized and sought after, for they are considered good and desirable. In consequence of this, persons with introvert characteristics are likely to think that these facets of their personality are nothing but a handicap in life and have no desirable aspects at all. Introvert patients talk to me like this every day. This is not true. The introvert characteristics bring with them many assets. It is important to realize this, so that these unrecognized assets can be used on the way up.

Use your introvert sensitivity. This sensitivity is a great problem and tends to make you withdraw. But it is also a great asset. It lets you in to the whole world of artistic and cultural life which the extrovert finds so hard to understand. These are areas in which you are well suited to work.

The introvert's sensitivity enables him to appreciate subleties of feeling and thought which completely elude the extravert with his black and white, good or bad approach to things. He is thus more aware of minor changes in interpersonal relations, and so can make appropriate changes before things become too involved.

The introvert has a capacity to understand how others feel. There is a paradox here. The extravert is friendly and easy with people; but it is rather on the surface and his lack of inner life prevents him from really understanding how they feel. On the other hand, the introvert through his sensitivity understands how others feel, but at the same time he is inhibited and held back from being openly friendly. In general, the professions rather than commerce or industry give the introvert better scope to use this capacity. He is well suited for the academic life. Occupations relating to art, medicine, psychology, teaching and literature suit introvert persons.

Use your introvert imagination creatively. The introvert in turning away from the material world becomes preoccupied by thought and imagination. He can let his thoughts range without limit. In the wide sweep of his imagination there is nothing to constrain his thinking. It has quite a different quality from the realistic planning in the thought of the extravert. This wild imaginative thinking of the introvert can be tamed and used creatively. One sees this process in its most obvious form in the introvert's artistic expression. But the same process can have a place in the business world. The creative idea comes from the free use of imagination. It must now be put to the test of practical reality. This is the part which the introvert finds difficult and which you must train yourself to do. The introvert executive in the higher eschelon can circumvent this difficulty by having a practically minded extravert subordinate whom he can use to test the reality value of his creative phantasy.

The introvert must avoid withdrawing. I know that it is easy to give advice, and it is often hard to follow it. The individual with introvert characteristics likes to withdraw because it reduces his nervous tension. But remember that too much withdrawing has a bad effect on the development of our personality. We need contact with others to develop our full maturity. Remember that our personalities are not nearly so fixed as psychiatrists used to think. I have known many introvert persons of middle age make quite dramatic changes in this respect.

In asking you to avoid withdrawing, I am not inviting you to mimic the extravert type of behaviour. That is something quite different. The aim is to continue in contact with people in the quiet and restrained fashion which is part of the introvert adjustment to life.

People with introvert characteristics like their solitary hobbies and pastimes. Keep these. They are a part of your particular life in your own individuality. But do not let them occupy your life to the exclusion of other activities of a more gregarious nature.

Don't become a pseudo-extravert. People unconsciously do this. They see that the extravert approach to life is more socially advantageous. The young introvert is liable to feel that if he could only meet people freely and easily it would help him on the way up. So he makes himself behave like an extravert. He laughs and jokes and slaps people on the back. But it is all rather forced. People sense that he is not behaving naturally and it all tends to fall flat.

Yesterday I saw an airline pilot who showed this reaction to a marked degree. He is a very good and efficient pilot, but on the ground he is shy and awkward. He is particularly conscious of it because of the contrast with the easy social manner of his wife. He came into my room talking and joking, but at the same time he was tense and jittery because this was out of character with his introvert personality. We must be true to ourselves; and the introvert must aim to be a mature introvert not a silly make-believe extravert.

Persons with introvert characteristics must avoid bluntening their feelings. If you are very sensitive, as introverts are, you may have a tendency to try to blunten your feelings. This is a way of protecting one's self. To be very sensitive is to be easily hurt. So let us make ourselves less sensitive and we will not be hurt so much. This is a psychological defence against anxiety. It is a very bad defence and quite destructive to the personality.

'I'll make myself wooden, and then I shall not be so worried by all these things.' But such a course bluntens the feelings and soon leads to apathy. This is the introvert on the downhill path heading for dissolution of his personality and perhaps schizophrenia.

For the future development of his personality the introvert must aim to retain his precious gift of sensitivity. He must not allow himself unconsciously to blunten it or blot it out, to make life easier. On the contrary, he must learn to cultivate it, and control his inner tension by ease of mind rather than by psychological moves to reduce sensitivity.

Introverts must learn to avoid day-dreaming. The way up demands that we are practical and realistic. It is easy for introvert persons to waste hours in the pleasure of day-dreaming. This leads nowhere, except when it is pronounced and then it is often a first step towards schizophrenia.

Day-dreaming is an escape from the present-day problems of life. Others may escape with a few drinks, but the introvert habitually turns to day-dreaming. So it is when things are not going well that we must be particularly on guard. It may be problems at work or domestic difficulties; the introvert tends to escape into day-dreams.

Day-dreaming differs from quiet thought on realistic subjects. This of course is valuable. It is the basis of creative enterprise. Introverts are good at it. But don't let it deteriorate into uncontrolled day-dreaming.

Again, day-dreaming differs from the periods of quiet reverie when we just let our mind wander for a few moments. These moments are good for us. They serve a useful purpose in reducing our general level of anxiety. Persons who are habitually very tense lose the ability to have moments of normal reverie and their nervous tension becomes further increased.

The introvert should cultivate the use of authority. Because he is sensitive, the introvert is inclined to be timid. This makes it hard for him to use authority. In addition to this, his sensitivity makes him fully aware of any hurt or unpleasantness that his orders may cause to others. If one is on the way up it is necessary to acquire some skill in the use of authority. This comes by experience. When little opportunities arise for taking charge in some small way, take the opportunity, and use these occasions in a firm positive way to develop this aspect of your personality.

The introvert should cultivate a practical attitude towards decision-making. With his active inner life the introvert is inclined to become philosophical about things. This impairs decision-making in the practical world of business in which the decision is really not a matter for any abstract philosophy.

Because of his tendency to be philosophical, the introvert is liable to procrastinate. He defers decisions. Of course it is wise to give oneself time to think; but the introvert tends to avoid the decision because of the anxiety that he feels in dealing with it. As a result, introvert executives tend to allow things to accumulate in the 'too difficult basket'.

[16]

The introvert should appoint some extravert subordinates. The introvert finds it easier to cope with people who are themselves a little introverted. He can understand them better. He is more at ease with them. But as with so many things, the situation which makes us most at ease is often not the best for us either in ourselves or in our productivity. An extravert subordinate by his different attitude towards things can unconsciously do something to make up for the deficiencies in the personality of his superior. At the same time contact with the extravert has some maturing effect on the other.

The introvert is not well suited to ruthless competition. We have seen that the introvert is essentially a sensitive person. This makes him well suited to all forms of artistic activity. But the same sensitivity which is such an advantage in the field of art makes the introvert very vulnerable in the ruthless competition of big business. He is inclined to be too sensitive, too easily hurt. As a result of being sensitive he can feel how others feel. In more extreme cases he is inclined to worry as to how his business opponents feel. In this way he may be too soft for the ruthless competition of big business. In such situations the introvert is best used as a backroom man providing ideas for the business which are put into effect by his more robust extravert associates.

I have recently seen an intelligent young introvert of twenty-six. A few years ago he became factory manager in a family business. He does the job well, but his sensitivity tortures him. He had an expensive car, but kept feeling it was wrong driving past the workers. So he sold it and bought an old one. There was some petty thieving in the factory, and he could not call the police although he thought he knew who was responsible. 'His wife has just had another baby.' On another occasion he told me, 'I can't bear working there and going home to my comfortable house while they live in places little better than slums.' He has recently decided to give it up and buy a country property. This, of course, is an extreme example. If you are a little introverted you will understand how he felt. If you are a real extravert you will think, 'What a fool'.

Another example comes to my mind. One of the top flight

men in medical research consulted me. He said he was rather tense and this became more of a problem when he was called upon to give a formal lecture. Then he added, 'I have another trouble; I can't say "no!".' Juniors would ask his advice and assistance and he would spend a great deal of time helping them himself instead of directing the research, and having others supervise the juniors! This apparently was a result of the sensitivity of his introvert personality. It made him a very nice person, but at the same time left him with an unrealistic approach to his role in life. The introvert can mature past this, and attain a realistic approach to life without discarding his sensitivity. In fact this man has progressed a long way in this direction.

The introvert matures more slowly than the extravert. Remember this; it is very important. We do not all mature at the same rate. This applies both to our bodies and our minds. The extravert schoolboy is much more mature than his introvert counterpart. In this way the captain of the school and the captain of football are almost always extraverts. But your strength is still to come. The extraverts whom you have envied as a boy come to the full maturity of their personality in their early twenties, while the introvert continues to mature into his thirties.

Be yourself. If you are an introvert, don't try to be an extravert. Aim to be a mature introvert. This is something fundamental. There are many people, whom you know, who are in fact introverts, but who try to ape the manners and behaviour of an extravert. This is very sad. It comes about simply because our present culture puts a premium on extravert behaviour. These are the pseudo-extraverts. They are really behaving in a way that is foreign to their true selves. Because of this their behaviour does not ring true. The casual observer just senses it as a little strange. 'He's an odd fellow.' Even if we are not consciously aware of it, we somehow sense this incongruity between the real person and the way he is behaving. His cheerfulness is forced. His gregariousness is unnatural. It is all false. And somehow people come to look at him as false, and his progress on the way up is halted.

Let us be what we are, and accept our introvert characteristics, and bring our introvert personality to its full maturity. This means that we develop our mature sensitivity and keep our active inner life. But we do this without anxiety and without withdrawing, and in full and active contact with the world of reality. This is not as difficult as it may at first seem. Remember we have great capacity to change and mature. This is much greater than we ordinarily think. One of the main reasons why people do not more often change for the better in the way of integration and maturity of personality is simply that they do not try. They accept their present very imperfect patterns of reaction and approach to life, and do not try to do any better. This attitude is not good enough for anyone who is on the way up. We must do more, and as I have said it is not as difficult as it might seem. An important point in your favour is that introverts mature slowly and are less set in their personality structure than others.

The introvert can improve his social aptitude by experience. The introvert's ineptitude on social occasions is a true handicap on the way up. The real trouble is that introverts like to withdraw and save themselves the tension of these situations. But the man on the way up can do better. He can bring himself to learn. And the way he learns is by experience. Thinking about it; talking about it and regretting it is no help. This is something that needs facing, quietly and easily. But it must be done.

The key to success, the thing which opens the new life to the introvert, is to learn to manage one's anxiety at the same time as one experiences the social situation. It is this that makes the therapeutic experience possible, and in fact not too difficult or unpleasant. The way in which you control your anxiety is clearly set out in the next chapter.

Introverted persons should aim for greater inner freedom. I do not mean greater freedom of thought or imagination. The introvert already has these in marked degrees. I mean an inner freedom so that one can act freely. Because of his sensitivity the introvert tends to become inhibited and held back. He is denied the free flow of doing and feeling. This is an internal inhibiting process. It is protective. He simply feels that something will happen if he lets go.

If you have this trouble you must learn to overcome it by

experience. You come to let go. Do it little by little. Participate in things more freely. Don't aim to do it all at once. Do it gradually. But you must do it. It is necessary for you as a person, and it is essential if you are on the way up.

Aim to reduce your general level of anxiety. The introvert's sensitivity makes him feel slights and hurts which others simply ignore. But more than this he is sensitive to the way that others feel, and from this experience he is aware that they often suffer. This comes to him in a way that is foreign to more extraverted persons. The same process applies to the wider aspects of life. The introvert is often painfully aware of the paradoxes of living, of life and death, of now and then, of have and have not. This is part of his inner life. As a result of all this the introvert tends to have a high level of anxiety. This applies particularly to the introvert who has not yet matured. Use the methods for dealing with anxiety as set out in the next chapter.

A young man told me, 'I am just tense, terribly tense, and it is holding me back'. What he said was painfully true. Besides his difficulty at work, his girl friend had found him so tense that she had recently jilted him. He was so upset by it all that he had deliberately injured himself. But he learned to relax. He has now been promoted and has a new girl. Every week I see examples, such as this, of the importance to the introvert of reducing his level of anxiety. For the introvert it is the most important thing in the world, for it is the key to the further maturation of his personality.

It means this. Retain your sensitivity whatever you do. Don't try to blot it out. You know you are vulnerable. You feel the hurt of these things. But you understand. You understand deeply, and the hurt is without pain. You are calm and at ease, and sensitive too.

This little book is not the place to elaborate this discussion. You who are introverted know what I mean. This is more important to you than the rest of the book. It just goes to demonstrate very clearly the way in which our too fixed patterns of thinking and feeling tend to limit our comprehension of basic human experiences of others not quite like ourselves.

The introvert subordinate is easily offended. We have seen that

[20]

the introvert is inclinded to be shy and sensitive. This makes him easily offended. This is likely to happen when no offence was intended. As he is shy he does not say anything about it, but suffers the imagined slight in silence. His more extraverted and less sensitive superior may be aware that something has gone wrong in their relationship, but he does not know what it is. This type of situation is very common in commerce and industry. It may easily arise when a friendly and uncomplicated extravert superior makes some joke at the expense of his introvert inferior. An introvert is often not sufficiently robust to take jokes made at his expense. He is too complicated and inhibited so that he lacks the extravert ability to react freely and naturally. As a result he withdraws, and the relationship between the two deteriorates. Extravert superiors should learn to imagine that they can see, 'handle with care', written on their introvert subordinates.

Show the introvert subordinate that you understand how he feels. This idea is best communicated by doing something rather than by trying to say it in words. If something goes wrong with the introvert's job and you do something to lighten his load, the introvert because of his sensitivity will appreciate the fact that something has been done for him. Your action is felt by the introvert as a communication. In similar circumstances an extravert subordinate would be inclined to accept your action just as a matter of course. But to the introvert your action had meaning. 'He gave me a hand when I was in a jam.'

The introvert is sensitive, so don't be too harsh on introvert subordinates. The introvert is likely to take any criticism or reprimand very much to heart. This is simply the result of his being a very sensitive person. As his superior you wish to correct his fault; you do not want to punish him or humilate him, or your relationship with him will deteriorate and his work output will fall off. So it is, 'kid gloves', with introverts.

Remember that people respond differently when fault is found with their work. Extraverts, because they are practical and matter of fact, take criticism well and their output is increased. People with a paranoid tendency often become surly, and there is little change in output. On the other hand some introverts become confused and bewildered from lack of support and their output falls off.

Please do not think that I am going too far in this. Don't just say to yourself. 'I give the orders, introverts and extraverts alike, and they are there to do what they are told.' This approach is not good enough. I am writing this little book for those on the way up. If you are on the way up, you must get the most out of your subordinates; and the 'kid gloves' approach will surely pay off in your management of introvert subordinates.

Obsessive personality characteristics

The obsessive is a perfectionist. He likes to have everything just right. He is meticulous and careful. He pays great attention to the details of anything that he is doing. His desk must be tidy and so must his house, and those that work with him in the office and his wife and family at home. If the others are not tidy in the same way that he is, he is inclined to feel tense and ill at ease. This makes him fuss over things which do not seem important to the others.

This perfectionism pervades the whole life of those who have obsessive characteristics. They are often very particular about cleanliness. This may extend well beyond the bounds of normal healthy hygiene, and the obsessive may frequently find himself washing his hands quite unnecessarily. The same tendency is seen in the neat and tidy way in which he wears his clothes. Likewise his manner of speech his precise, and his handwriting may show the same perfectionistic tendency with each letter being clearly formed.

At work his perfectionism shows itself in his punctuality, and the way in which he has everything correct and in order. In the office he is known for his thoroughness. His work is detailed and accurate. The others know they can rely on him for he will never let them down. In a way this makes him vulnerable, and the others may come to trade on his conscientiousness and exploit him to do work that they themselves should do.

The obsessive has compulsive tendencies. This really means that he sometimes tends to do things in response to an inner urge rather than a practical logical reason. This tendency may show itself in little things. He washes his hands. Then he feels he should wash them again. If he does not do so, he feels uneasy, so he does it. He may feel that he must tidy up the office, even though he knows that this is not really necessary. He develops odd habits, such as touching certain things or not touching them. Door-knobs, hand-rails toilets and taps are common objects of minor compulsive acts. These things worry the obsessive, and reduce his efficiency. If he resists them he feels tense from an increase of inner anxiety. So he usually does the little compulsive act. He then feels less tense but at the same time he is rather annoyed with himself because he fully appreciates the illogical nature of the compulsion. On the other hand if you ask him about his compulsion, he rationalizes, 'there are always germs about'.

The obsessive feels he has to check things over. It is really more than that. The fact is that he has to check over things even when he knows that everything is all right. He shuts the safe, and starts on another job. Then he worries if in fact he shut it properly. He knows he did; but he feels himself getting tense about it, so he goes back to check it. But he really does this to relieve his inner tension rather than see if the safe were closed. This is so, because all the time he really knows that everything is in order. This compulsive checking over may involve the obsessive in all manner of small things. He may find that he has to add up every column of figures twice or perhaps three times just to relieve his feeling of inner uncertainty and tension. Interestingly enough, if you ask him about it, he always rationalizes, and gives a sensible reason, 'I might have left the door open'. 'I might have made a mistake in adding up.' But it is his inner tension rather than the reason he gives which makes him go back and check things over.

Rigidity is another characteristic of the obsessive. People with obsessive traits in their personality often find it hard to understand what psychiatrists mean when they speak of rigidity. The obsessive who has never experienced real freedom in thinking and feeling does not believe that he is rigid.

It shows itself in the way in which he gets an idea into his head and sticks to it. This characteristic leads to very desirable qualities in the way of determination. But if it is carried just a little further the same rigidity becomes mere stubbornness. Sometimes the rigidity shows itself to the person concerned by his being rather painfully aware that a certain thought keeps recurring to him, or if the condition is more pronounced he may be bothered by not being able to get some thought out of his head. On the other hand, the individual may not be aware of the way this process works. But his friends notice and are often irritated by the way in which the obsessive keeps bringing the conversation back to the same topic. He can't let the matter drop, but goes on and on hammering the same point. If looked at from another point of view, it means that the obsessive lacks the normal ability to maintain a free flow of thought from subject to subject. In this way the obsessive's thinking may become constricted.

As one would expect, this rigidity shows itself in action as well as in thought. There is a tendency to do things the same way each time. In this way it is very easy to fall into a routine for all kinds of things. When one's clothes are taken off, they are always folded and put away exactly the same way. When the individual arrives at the office he greets the others exactly the same way each morning, and then proceeds to arrange things on his desk exactly as he does every other morning. Of course, routines like this are helpful in that they save the mental energy involved in making new decisions, but the individual who relies too much on established routines loses flexibility of action.

The obsessive is highly ethical. He must have everything just right not only in the affairs of practical life, but morally as well. He is conscientious to the point of being over-conscientious. In this way he may suffer from what the church knows as scruples. If he promises something he carries it out to the smallest detail of what he has promised, even when it is much to his own disadvantage. He does this to an extent which goes beyond what would be expected in fulfilling the spirit of his promise. This is

[24]

the same as in everything else. The emphasis is on the detail rather than the idea as a whole.

Following on his highly ethical propensity, the obsessive is frequently religiously minded, and in as much as he likes things to be well ordered and to follow a routine, he usually finds the more formalized and ritualized religious services the more satisfying.

Obsessive characteristics work to reduce anxiety. The individual unconsciously feels that if he can have everything just right, there can be nothing to worry about. So he is unconsciously driven to pay great attention to details and to check things over scrupulously. By this means he aims to have everything just right, and he feels that he will then be free of worry and free of nervous tension. So this becomes his way of doing things and he develops the perfectionistic way of life of the obsessive.

In a similar way the other obsessive characteristics are also ways of warding off anxiety. We can see this in his routines. If we do something once, and it goes all right, we can be pretty sure that if we do it again exactly the same way it will again be all right. There is less uncertainty, so inner anxiety is reduced; and the obsessive unconsciously falls into the way of doing things by routine so as to save himself from unnecessary anxiety.

In a similar way he reduces anxiety by developing a rigidity of personality. By avoiding new ideas and new patterns of thought anxiety is reduced, and the obsessive is able to carry on with a lower level of nervous tension.

The obsessive approach to life starts in early childhood. Parents fuss over their children. This is natural enough. We all want to do what we can for our children, and bring them up to have as good a life as they can. So we are inclined to fuss. Sometimes mothers are particularly bad in this respect, and the degree to which they fuss about the toilet training of the child seems to be particularly important; and it seems that the seeds of an obsessive approach to life are often sown at this early stage of our childhood. But in later childhood and early adolescence over fussy attitudes of parents can still have their effect. Obsessive patients have often said to me, 'My parents have taught me to be meticulously tidy'.

The obsessive way of dealing with anxiety may fail. The idea of having everything exactly right lacks moderation. In actual fact we can never attend to all the details so completely as to exclude every possible chance of things going wrong. We live with uncertainty. Life itself is uncertain. The obsessive is inclined to overlook this. Instead he checks over the details again and again, more and more. Soon a state of affairs is reached in which the checking over becomes a worry in itself; and the obsessive pattern of doing things, instead of relieving anxiety, comes to have the opposite effect and actually increases the individual's anxiety. When this happens there is no let up from it, and the inner tension drives the obsessive progressively to a more and more constricted way of life.

The obsessive must have the right kind of job. Success or failure, whether one makes the way up or not, always depends to a large extent on the individual having a job that suits him. But this is more important for persons with obsessive characteristics, than it is for others. This is due to the rigidity of the obsessive personality which often makes adjustment to change difficult. Furthermore, the obsessive characteristics are very definite. There are no two ways about them. So the obsessive is not in doubt as to whether the job suits him or not. If it does, he is happy in it; if it does not suit him he is acutely aware that it is not the job for him.

Obsessives do well in positions requiring attention to detail and personal trust. Most of the successful men in accounting and banking have marked obsessive characteristics in their personality. These occupations allow the obsessive to use the strengths of his personality to full advantage. So does any field which requires a great store of detailed knowledge. The obsessive is happy and successful in any job which gives scope to his perfectionism.

It often happens that we choose some area for our basic professional training without sufficient consideration for these aspects of our personality. For instance an individual with marked obsessive characteristics may qualify in engineering, which is a field that is usually more satisfying to the practically minded extravert. When this happens it is often wise for the engineer obsessive to move more into the administrative aspects of the firm rather than follow up too closely his original training as an outdoor engineer.

I have seen several very successful men with obsessive characteristics make a serious mistake quite late in life. In the eyes of many, one of the last steps on the way up is to acquire a farm or country property. In a way this is considered by the successful business-man as a transition into a higher social category. If in fact he has already come a long way up during his life time, this final move to land-owning status may seem very important. But there are dangers in this. The successful executive with his background in business is usually aware of the obvious danger that he is not experienced in running a country property. As he is aware of this, he seeks advice or employs a manager. But the successful obsessive is usually not aware of the degree to which he will find difficulties from his own personality. His approach to life has been to try to have things just right. In fact this has been the key to his success. He has always aimed to have things under control. But with a country property it is all so different. It is often impossible to have everything neat and tidy. In fact neatness and tidiness are qualities of man not of nature. And with activity dependent on the weather and season it is not possible to control matters in the way to which he has been accustomed. The new situation of running the country property really requires a deal of adaptation to circumstances rather than controlling them. The obsessive is weak in this area because of his rigidity. In a number of success-ful executives this final step on the way up has been a great disappointment. Instead of enjoying life in the country, they have become tense, anxious and irritable in sufficient degree as to seek my professional help.

Obsessives need the right kind of vacations. We have noted that persons with obsessive characteristics usually have a fairly high level of anxiety. They are usually tense. In this respect it is interesting how often obsessives tell me that they are really less tense at work and more tense at home in the weekends. The psychiatrist can easily fall into an error here, and assume that husband and wife do not get on, or that there is some other conflict in the home. This is not necessarily so. The obsessive is most comfortable when he has something definite to do. This relieves his tension. On the other hand, a leisurely Sunday afternoon with no definite plans makes him restless and ill-at-ease.

The same principle applies even more so to vacations. With his obsessive difficulties about trying to get everything just right, the obsessive executive becomes tense. He wants to relax but can't. So he does the obvious thing. He goes for a holiday where he will be away from all his business worries, and where he can be quiet and relax with nothing to do. He pictures himself lying, relaxed just sunbathing on the beach. It simply does not work. He goes down to the beach. The others are at ease and deeply relaxed lying in the sun. But the obsessive is restless. His mind seems to be too active. He can't lie still. Instead of relaxing he becomes more tense. So he tries again the next day. But it is just the same, perhaps worse. I have heard this story very often. He returns to the city more tense than when he went away, and comes to see me.

A vacation, as with other things in life must be considered in relation to the individual's personality. The obsessive needs something to do on a holiday. He then relaxes unconsciously, and returns to work the better for it. If he goes to the beach he is better boating, sailing, or fishing rather than sun-bathing on the beach. If he goes to the hills, he is better playing golf, tennis or walking rather than looking at the view and hopefully trying to relax.

The obsessive does not like to delegate tasks. You cannot be sure that everything is just right if you leave it to someone else. So the obsessive tries to do it all himself. By doing it all himself, even if he has to work unduly long hours, he feels better because he knows it is just right. This may be a very laudable attitude of mind for a junior clerk, but it is far too constricting for a young executive who is on the way up. So in this respect the individual with obsessive characteristics must take himself in hand, and consciously bring himself to practise delegation of tasks. This is foreign to the obsessive's way of doing things, so it is inevitable that at first he will experience some degree of inner tension in doing this. But stick to it, and you will minimize one of the serious weaknesses of the obsessive personality.

If you have obsessive characteristics, be careful not to supervise others too closely. This is a very common failing of the obsessive. It applies particularly when some task has been delegated. It is the second line of defence. The first line is to do it all yourself; the second line is to supervise it to such an extent that you might as well be doing it yourself. And don't forget that this over supervision, which is a characteristic weakness of the obsessive has a devastating effect on the person who is subjected to this over supervision.

The same tendency is seen in the way in which an obsessive individual often repeats his instructions to an inferior when there is really no need for the repetition. This is merely another aspect of the obsessive's need to check things over just to be quite sure. It has the effect of reducing tension in the obsessive, but it irritates the other person and so increases tension in him.

Decision-making is often difficult for obsessives. We noted that the introvert also has difficulty in making decisions. His trouble is that he is likely to get waylaid by a mist of philosophical considerations and the clear vision of decision is obscured. With the obsessive the problem is quite different. His trouble is that he sees both sides of the question, and then cannot make up his mind. This is particularly pronounced with important decisions such as marriage and future employment. In these matters the obsessive often has the greatest difficulty in making up his mind. The same difficulty arises in connection with problems at work. With his characteristic thoroughness he works out all the arguments both for and against. Then he comes to a decision. But he goes back over it in his mind just to be quite sure he is right. And as soon as he does so, the arguments for the opposite decision come to him with increased force. He may reverse his original decision, only to find the same thing happen again.

If you suffer from this obsessive weakness, you must discipline yourself. Think the problem over and consider the arguments for both sides. Then come to a decision and stick to it. This first decision is the right decision. Use this knowledge to make it easier for yourself to keep to it. There must be no going back.

Obsessives should avoid jobs that are untidy, either physically or mentally. This follows from all that we have said before. The obsessive is never really comfortable working in surroundings which are of necessity untidy. Similarly, the obsessive is not well suited for work which involves him getting dirty. In these circumstances he may be continually plagued with the feeling of wanting to wash himself.

The obsessive works best in clean and orderly surroundings; and he is also best adapted to a job which involves an orderly mental approach. This allows the obsessive to exploit to his own advantage his natural tendency to do things in fixed patterns and routines.

Last year a fifty eight year old man consulted me. He was a senior executive of a large firm. He had suffered from nervous tension all his life, but it had been crippling over the last twelve months since his firm had been taken over by a still larger firm. He feared that his new masters would consider him redundant and he would be put off. I think his assessment of the situation was quite realistic. Through his obsessive personality he was driven to meet the threat by ever increasing attention to detail. To be quite sure that his new board could find no fault with him, he checked and re-checked everything he did. This made him slow with his work, so he stayed on every night after the others had gone as well as taking home work to do at night and in the weekends. His anxiety became greater and greater so that he was virtually incapacitated, not by his work but by the over-activity of his obsessive reactions. I was able to show him how to relax and gain some degree of inner freedom. After an interval of some months I saw him again, and he was really coping quite well.

Persons with obsessive characteristics should aim to avoid unnecessary detail. It is the compulsion to worry about details which so often holds back the obsessive. In this respect there must be a conscious effort to establish a freer pattern. Learn to avoid unnecessary details at home in the ordinary matters of living, and then the same pattern will gradually follow into work at the office. At first this will probably produce some increase of nervous tension, but tolerate this as it will soon pass off; and better still, cope with it through the relaxing mental exercises which I shall describe later.

Obsessives should cultivate the habit of looking at the big picture. With his attention focused too much on detail the obsessive is liable to lose sight of the overall plan. He is apt not to see the wood for the trees. Those on the way up need a wide and distant vision of things. If you have some detailed job to do, do it in the detailed way which is necessary, but at the same time keep in mind how it fits in with the big plan. Obsessives often fail to do this, and keep all their attention on the immediate small task in front of them. So cultivate a wider vision and improve your capacity for large scale planning.

Obsessives can become more effective by cultivating a greater freedom of thought and behaviour. This is to offset the constriction and rigidity of the obsessive personality. Keep doing new things. This is important for all of us, but it is particularly important for those with any marked obsessive characteristics in their personality. If you are in a subordinate capacity, it may be hard to do new things at work. But obsessives tend to avoid the opportunity to do new things even when the opportunity is offered. They do this because the routine of the old job keeps anxiety low, and a move to something else would necessarily increase anxiety until the individual has settled in to the new situation. If your job allows some freedom of action, don't be content with the old routine. Experiment a little. Do a few new things. Cultivate this type of outlook and it will have a noticeable maturing effect on an obsessive personality.

Whatever the situation at work, there is always scope for doing new things in one's domestic life. New faces, new friends, and companions with a new outlook all help. The theatre and the films can also help, but these must be different types of shows, and not just the routine affair that the obsessive goes to year after year. By these experiences in your private life, a greater flexibility of mind is produced which will show to advantage in your work.

[31]

People with obsessive characteristics need to learn to compromise.
The obsessive does not compromise on moral principles. This of
course is right and proper. Keep to it. But the obsessive through
his rigidity is often unable to compromise on everyday business
matters in which there is no moral issue involved at all. This
attitude of mind makes discussion and negotiations difficult. It
really means that the obsessive must have it all his own way or
lose out on everything. As it is extremely difficult to get it all
our own way, it is likely that the uncompromising obsessive will
suffer a complete loss.

Remember that we live in a world which is imperfect. The
obsessive with his ingrained perfectionism is likely to forget this
basic fact of life. We must be realistic. We must make allowances.
We must remember that others may not be able to attain the
same degree of excellence as we do ourselves. Strive to make
things better. But to try to insist on absolute perfection in areas
where perfection is impossible is not being realistic. Things do
not get done and progress is impeded.

Games are good and help to free the obsessive personality. Some
sporting activity is good for all of us, but it is particularly
beneficial to the obsessive. Those with obsessive characteristics
like golf because it unconsciously fulfils the need for accuracy
and routine. In a similar way obsessives like bowls, figure-
skating on ice, and if they ski they do so with neatness and
precision. It is much better for the obsessive to be active in one
of these sports rather than to play no games at all. But other
forms of sport which allow a greater freedom are of greater
value from the point of view of helping the obsessive to maturity.
In this respect tennis is better than golf because of the greater
freedom it allows.

Do not depart from your high standards but be realistic. Do not in
any way interpret my desire for your greater freedom of mind,
as an invitation to lower your moral or ethical standards. No.
Preserve these. Cherish them. But temper them with realism and
understanding.

At different times I have seen a number of young obsessives
who have had trouble of this nature at work, and have consulted

me on account of their nervous tension. A new boss has wanted them to do their work in a slightly different fashion. The obsessive has taken offence at this feeling that any change from his usual way of doing the job is morally wrong. This of course is ridiculous. The trouble is that the obsessive's rigidity makes him feel that his way of doing the job is the only right way.

Remember this; what is to your subordinate's advantage is also to your own. For instance, it would not be for your ultimate advantage for me to discuss weaknesses in the obsessive personality purely from the point of view of showing how more work could be extracted from the individual. Rather we must use our psychological knowledge to make things easier for those for whom we are responsible. To really be on the way up we must manage subordinates so that they work more easily, more comfortably within themselves, and with less tension and anxiety. When this happens, it follows that they work more harmoniously, more efficiently; and the resulting increased productivity is to the advantage of all concerned.

Give the obsessive subordinate very definite instructions. We have seen that he is an accurate and precise person. He likes to be treated as he would treat others. When this happens he is less tense, he is freer, and works more effectively. So detail his job to him. Give him a definite frame of reference. Set him limits, so that he knows how far he should go and where he should stop. The obsessive cannot work effectively with vague instructions. You can tell an extravert 'See what you can do about this', and he will produce something useful. But the obsessive with his detailed approach simply does not know where to start. He just gets tense and muddled, and nothing happens. You must tell the obsessive, do this and this and this; and then he will do it very well indeed.

Use the obsessive in positions of personal trust. He is meticulous, reliable and conscientious to the point of being over-conscientious. If you diagnose your subordinate as obsessive, you can trust him. He will never let you down. What is more, he works well in a position of trust because it fits in with the basic elements of his personality. He likes it.

[33]

Obsessives also do well in routine work without supervision. In fact, they often work better if not supervised at all. This follows from what we know of the obsessive personality. It fulfils both his liking for routine work as a way of reducing anxiety, and the absence of supervision satisfied his inner need to show how reliable he is.

Avoid having very extraverted persons working with obsessives. One might think that the presence of a good extravert might do something to bring the obsessive out of his shell. But no, it has the other effect. The rather casual, untidy way of doing things of the extravert conflicts with the neat orderliness of the obsessive. It irritates him. He can't stand it. The level of his anxiety is increased, and his work output falls off.

As opposed to this, it is wise for the obsessive to cultivate a few extravert friends. Contact with them can help him towards greater freedom. But one only sees a friend for relatively short periods. The obsessive can tolerate this. On the other hand, working with an extravert is often too much for the obsessive. There is no let up. He can't get away from him. His nervous tension mounts; and the extravert does not understand what all the fuss is about.

Don't give obsessives messy jobs. You might say that no one likes a messy job. That might be true enough. But some people by nature of their personality are better able to cope with some situations than are others. The individual with obsessive characteristics is at an extreme disadvantage when given a messy job. It is just like picking a physically weak man to do particularly heavy manual work. The obsessive by virtue of his personality is not suited to the task. This applies to physical work which is dirty or untidy, and to mental work which concerns a lot of loose ends.

Last year a man consulted me because he was having a nervous breakdown. He was an obsessive, and had been particularly successful in running a large milk bar. His obsessive cleanliness and attention to detail had been a great help in this. He decided to live in the country and run a dairy farm. But here his obsessive personality was a great disadvantage. He could not stand the dirt of the cow yards, and he broke down with severe anxiety symptoms.

Although the obsessive cannot tolerate a messy occupation, he can do some messy jobs of short duration very well indeed. He cleans everything up and makes it all spick and span. He likes doing this because he likes tidying up and there is an end to it. But he cannot tolerate this as a permanent job.

In managing an obsessive, go half way to meet him. This is probably a good principle for most situations; but it applies more in our dealing with the obsessive than with others. He is rigid. He is likely to get stuck in fixed patterns and grooves of thought. We, ourselves, have a much greater degree of flexibility. If we insist that the obsessive has to make all the changes, things will go wrong for the simple reason that he has not the capacity to do so. This principle applies equally in getting the obsessive junior clerk to change his way of doing something as it does to top level negotiations. Don't just dismiss the matter with the thought, 'The man's just stubborn, he is a fool, you can't deal with him'. If he is obsessive remember that his thought processes are slightly different, and that we must use a rather different approach to him.

Don't change the obsessive's job too frequently. Remember that he works best in a well established routine. This allows his level of anxiety to remain low, and all goes well. With frequent changes of job he does not have time to establish easy routines. Anxiety is high, and work is poor.

On the other hand, if you are on the way up see to it that you don't get stuck for too long in some job simply because you have become accustomed to it. When you think to yourself, 'I have got into the way of it', the probable reason is that you have established routines which have reduced anxiety and made the job seem easy. If you are on the way up, this is the stage when you should move on.

The obsessive likes formality. When a setting is formal everything is in its proper place; people know their status and their roles. Everything is just right. This is what the obsessive likes and what he needs. In fact the concept of formality is an unconscious obsessive approach to inter-personal relations so that everything happens in an ordered fashion. The obsessive feels, 'Everything is just right, there can be nothing to worry about'. So he regulates his life, both at home and at work, on clear-cut formal lines. Everyone knows where he stands. In the office the superior-inferior relationship is clearly defined; so is the parent-child relationship in the home. Casual interpersonal relationships are avoided as the obsessive does not know where he stands, and becomes uneasy. This is one reason why obsessives are often ill at ease with the casual mannered extravert.

These principles have their obvious application for those on the way up. In business we deal with obsessives, whether they are our superiors or inferiors, in a rather more formal way than we do with others, and things run so much the more smoothly.

Negotiating with an obsessive may be difficult. We should always approach any negotiation with due regard to the personality structure of the other person. This is particulary important with an obsessive because of his rigidity. If we put forward some plan to an obsessive, we can be sure that he will want to know all the details as to how it can be put into action. If you cannot supply these, he will reject your plan. This is a common sequence of events even when the negotiations are still in the initial phase, and the stage has not yet been reached for detailed planning. It arises because the obsessive has developed a pattern of living in which he does not look at the general picture, but turns immediately to the details. Even if the general concept of the project is weak, so long as the plan of action is thoroughly detailed, the obsessive may accept it.

Hysteric personality characteristics

Hysteric characteristics occur in men as well as in women. In the minds of many people, including some psychiatrists, hysteric characteristics are associated almost exclusively with women. This is wrong. Hysteric characteristics are quite common in men. It is just that these characteristics take a rather different form in men and women. The female personality with its passive-receptive qualities allows easier display of emotion than does the masculine-aggressive personality of the male. This situation is strengthened by cultural factors which allow women much freer expression of feeling. Thus if a woman gives vent to her emotion it may be considered quite normal and appropriate by those around her; but if a man were to express his feelings in a similar way it would be considered out of place. This social taboo works to prevent a man from manifesting his hysteric characteristics openly.

The hysteric is a rather dramatic person. With the hysteric everything is slightly exaggerated, so that sometimes we get the feeling that he is acting a part in his ordinary life. There is exaggerated speech with florid use of words, and a hectic display of simile and metaphor. At the same time, he emphasises his points with exaggerated expressions and gestures. This is the hysteric way of dealing with things, to make his point, to convince others, and to command attention from those about. But this approach sometimes has an unreal quality about it. It really smacks of the stage.

Most of us have a mixture of personality characteristics. In order to make it easier for you to identify the individual with hysteric characteristics I am describing this type of personality in its fully developed form. I am over emphasizing, exaggerating a little, in fact being slightly dramatic in order to make my point with you. In other words this communication to you has hysteric characteristics. As you read, you will notice that I also disclose other personality characteristics. The orderly way it is set out with a repetition of similar types of headings represents an obsessive approach in that I am trying to be quite sure that you will not miss the point. In a similar way you will have noticed that I write about the way people feel in different situations. This matter of having the feelings of others intrude into one's own mind is, of course, an introvert characteristic. Extravert tendencies are, I think, less marked, as I have less of this approach within me. But the book itself is a realistic project and represents a practical approach to life so this in essence is an extravert function of the mind. I mention these things merely to illustrate that these personality characteristics are not in any way abnormal in themselves, and that most people display a mixture of these characteristics. It is only when they are exaggerated to the extent of constricting the full development of the individual that they become pathological.

The hysteric seeks the limelight. His rather dramatic way of talking and his behaviour in general has the effect of focusing attention on the hysteric. If you watch him closely you will see that a lot of this is clearly purposive in its attention seeking. Although the purposive action is obvious to the observer, the hysteric himself is often quite unaware of what he is doing. He has grown into this pattern, this approach to life, so that he does it naturally and without thinking about it. It has become part of him.

Why should the hysteric seek the limelight when the introvert does everything he can to avoid it? These are just different patterns of dealing with the same problem. This is anxiety. The introvert withdraws from the situation to save himself being anxious. The hysteric seeks the limelight to bolster up his confidence and in this way also avoids anxiety.

The hysteric expresses emotion very freely. With hysteric women there is laughter, then suddenly tears, then back again to laughter. Men smile and laugh, then hostile and aggressive; then it is laughs again. These quick changes of emotion add dramatic colour to what the individual is expressing. But they change so quickly and so easily that the observer is left with the impression that there is little depth to the feeling which is expressed all too readily. But we must remember that this free expression of emotion is not consciously contrived by the hysteric. It just happens because this is the pattern of behaviour which he has evolved for coping with life situations.

The hysteric communicates by expression and gesture. There are other means than words for getting our meaning across. The hysteric habitually uses exaggerated facial expressions and elaborate gestures with his hands to emphasize what he is saying in words. This process is often in such degree that it would seem that the expressions and gestures are much more important than the words. This is so because the expression of emotion is so important to the hysteric, and this is more effectively communicated by expression and gesture than by words.

He also uses his behaviour to communicate. If we tell a junior to do something, he may do it without comment. But by the way he does it, he may tell us quite clearly what he thinks about the task he has been told to do. This is communication by behaviour. Hysterics are unconscious experts at this. It gives them advantages in many situations. For example, if we have an important meeting with someone, it is not so much what we say when we greet him that is so important, but rather it is the way we greet him. Acts speak louder than words. This is an important part of the hysteric's way of communication, only like everything else, he does it in an exaggerated fashion.

The hysteric tends to exploit others. You may say that these are hard words. But they are true. The hysteric has this ease of expressing his feelings in dramatic fashion. He tends to use his ability to his own advantage. If he is not well, he uses this way of dramatically expressing his feelings in order to enlist sympathy. But it usually goes further than this, and you will see that he uses these dramatic ways of communicating in order to bring others to do tasks which he might well have done himself.

We all know this sort of person. There is the woman in the office who gets such terrible headaches. She has to hold her head in her hands and she takes her pills in front of the others for all to see how bad she is. She then has them all helping her in a way that would be impossible if she bore her pain more stoically. The same thing happens with men. The hysteric executive who does not like flying feels off colour on the day of the flight, and is so able to send a substitute.

Hysteric characteristics are a way of coping with anxiety. We are all insecure. This is fundamental, as life itself is insecure. Insecurity is a basic cause of anxiety. If we can do something to bolster up our ego, to make ourselves more confident, we will feel less insecure and less anxious. Hysteric characteristics work towards this end. By being dramatic, by exaggerating and over stating what he says, the hysteric unconsciously gives himself more confidence. By using his behaviour and manner of speech

D [39]

in a way that focuses attention on himself, he gains an inner sense of importance. These things reduce his feeling of anxiety. He feels better, more at ease and more comfortable in himself. This, of course unconsciously motivates him to continue the hysteric approach to life.

Hysteric characteristics are aimed to make people like the hysteric. We feel it important that people like us. The more insecure we are, this tendency is so much the greater. This feeling is often quite deep-seated within us, and we are not always fully conscious of it. But it is there, present in all of us.

The hysteric unconsciously brings us to like him by expressing his emotions very freely. If he is sad, he does not cover it up, but he lets his feelings go. We see how sad he is. We are sorry for him, and friendly to him. If he is happy, there is no reserve about it. His smiles and laughter let us know. We become happy with him and like him for it.

This is part of the hysteric way of coping with life. It is something very basic. The child at kindergarten brings flowers for teacher. Then she will like him; and when she likes him, she will be nice to him. The hysteric is unconsciously striving to make people like him; then like the child he uses them to his own advantage. Hysterics habitually use sickness or any other misfortune in this way. They use it as a means to make people like them, and then use it to make these people do things for them. In this way hysterics become unconscious manipulators of people. Soon a second phase develops. The others gradually become aware that they are being used. At this stage the hysteric characteristics come to have the reverse effect of what is intended. Instead of making people like the hysteric, they come to make people dislike him, and in fact people soon grow to be extremely hostile to him.

Hysteric characteristics are a cover-up. We all have some sort of facade. This is necessary as a kind of self defence in the rough and tumble of the world in which we live. If we were to expose our innermost selves we would be too easily hurt. This is natural enough. But the hysteric has a very dramatic kind of facade which he uses in order to disguise and protect his inner self.

Let us remember that the reaction is unconscious. It is a way of coping with life which the individual has evolved to make things easier. He is really quite unaware of the inner meaning behind it all. Perhaps I can explain what I mean by an example. Hysteric women usually have quite a sexy, flirtatious manner and way of behaving. They frequently dress rather sexily, and have a way of vamping men. Their whole manner is sexually seductive. The fact that is relevant to our present discussion is that most hysteric women have a very poor sexual response. In fact most hysteric women are frigid. So we have the strange phenomenon that this group of women, who are least successful sexually, behave in the most sexy and seductive fashion. This is the facade. This is the hysteric cover-up. It is a disguise for inner inadequacies. We see it in other things. The hysteric who is not doing too well at the office often covers up with enforced good humour and jollity.

I remember a man of thirty-five who came to see me about increasing nervous tension. He was an hysteric with a very good social manner as a facade. In fact he presented himself very well indeed. He had recently had interviews for a very good job. By means of his facade he was able to convince the employers that he was much more competent than he really was. He got the job, but had broken down with anxiety because the work was far beyond his capability.

The hysteric is good in acting, demonstrating, selling and public relations. These are occupations in which the hysteric can use his natural tendencies to full advantage. If you have these characteristics to any marked degree, these are fields in which your personality can help you to success. Most successful actors and actresses have marked hysteric elements in their personality. This allows them to express emotion on stage and screen in a dramatic and convincing fashion without themselves being upset by feeling too deeply the emotions they are expressing. In a similar way the hysteric has a natural aptitude for demonstrating things in a dramatic, attention-seeking fashion which is often most successful in commerce. His initial ability to make people like him can find rewarding outlet in sales and public relations.

Don't be too dramatic; it irritates others. This would seem obvious. Yet the individual with hysteric characteristics is unaware of it because it is a part of his habitual approach to life. At different times I have had several men come to me for advice, saying that they had all the qualifications and they seemed to be doing their work well, but they were making no progress on the way up. These men had hysteric characteristics, and were unconsciously using their over dramatic approach in a way that irritated their superiors. This is particularly likely to happen when things have gone wrong. The hysteric is then likely to exaggerate the situation in a dramatic way aiming to enlist the sympathy and help of others. But if his reaction is too dramatic, too histrionic, it turns the others against him. The important point, and the one which I wish to emphasize, is that the hysteric can be quite oblivious of the fact that he offends in this way. So, if you have hysteric characteristics, watch yourself.

The flirtatious approach can lead to trouble. In the office men have to deal with women, and women have to deal with men. At work we like to think that sexual feeings do not come into the situation. This is not true. Our attitude to a woman differs from our attitude to a man. Let us recognize this. It is natural and it should not complicate matters. But for the hysteric it is very important to be liked, so he falls into a way of using sex to bring people to like him. He develops a flirtatious approach to women. It is quite innocent. He is the same to young and old; or he may even be more flirtatious with older women as he is safer with them. It is just his approach. The girl hysteric does the same thing. There is nothing improper. But the man senses the mildly seductive undertone, the shadow of a smile, the glance that lingers. It is all quite innocent. It is just the hysteric way of getting along with people. But it can go wrong. The hysteric does not realise that others are more sensitive than he is. The introvert spinster book-keeper may misinterpret things; so may the young executive when his secretary was only trying to get along with him.

Don't unconsciously use your hysteric characteristics to exploit others. Guard against this. It can happen at all levels. It is not an uncommon story for a young hysteric to join a new firm, and to get away to a particularly good start. This arises from the hysteric's charm in bringing people to like him. He really seems set on the way up. Then things go wrong, and he can't understand it. The others have become aware that he is using his charm to exploit them. He puts things so nicely to them, and with such an engaging smile that they can't help doing things for him. Then they realise what is happening and they become hostile to him.

Last year a young man of thirty came to me with this very problem. 'I have been in this new job for about a year. At first it went very well. Now they don't seem to like me.' He was aware that he had become unpopular, but he was not aware how he had caused it. In fact, he attributed his unpopularity to the jealousy of the others on account of his early success. But this was not so. He had been using the assets of his personality to exploit the others. Here was a man who had made a good start on the way up, but who had lost it all through being unable to manage his basic personality characteristics.

If you have hysteric characteristics, cultivate the experience of feeling rather than the expression of it. Those with hysteric characteristics live on the surface. The expression of feeling seems more important than the feeling itself. This is a kind of defence. We do not want to be wracked by feelings that disturb us too deeply.

We have seen how the introvert defends himself in similar situations by bluntening his feelings, and the extravert by becoming boisterous. But the hysteric approach with its expression of feeling which is not fully experienced, is shallow and not quite genuine. For the personality to improve and mature, the individual must aim to be genuine in himself. He can then use his hysteric characteristics on the way up without being caught in the pitfalls which we have discussed.

But the search for the genuine in one's self may be an elusive goal for the hysteric. It is all so intangible. Where does one start? If you have these characteristics, start here and now. The hysteric avoids self examination. Now is the time for it.

Let the hysteric subordinate use his personality assets. This means placing him in a job where his dramatic approach and his ability to bring people quickly to like him, can be used to advantage. We have mentioned selling, demonstrating, and public relations.

The hysteric works best with an audience. He is not a back-room boy like the introvert. If he can let people know what he is doing, he does it all the better; and if his audience is a mixed one, it is so much the greater stimulus for him. The hysteric girl with her charm and ability to make instant friends is an excellent receptionist where she has many brief contacts with people. But these same qualities would irritate, if she were your personal secretary.

Guard against being manipulated by the hysteric subordinate. I mention this because the process is insidious. At the start neither you nor the hysteric is aware of what is going on. You don't suspect it; and the hysteric does it unconsciously because it is a part of his habitual adjustment to life. Every doctor has fallen for this. We have an hysteric as a patient. He has a charming manner, and we are sorry for him because he is sick. Then we suddenly realize that he has involved us in interfering with his relatives on his behalf.

I have had senior executives as patients who have come to me with anxiety symptoms as a result of being manipulated in this way by a charming hysteric subordinate. Once the process has got under way, it is very difficult for the executive to call a stop to it because he has already allowed precedents to develop.

Other personality characteristics

THE HYPOCHONDRIAC

The hypochondriac is preoccupied with his bodily functions. We have seen how the extravert's interests are directed to the material things of the outside world, while the introvert is preoccupied with things of the mind. The hypochondriac on the other hand is preoccupied with his body and the way that it functions. He makes mental notes about the frequency and nature of his bowel actions; and it is the same with the function of his kidneys. He is inclined to check his pulse rate, and he likes to have his blood pressure taken from time to time.

We have seen how extravert, introvert, obsessive and hysteric characteristics each in their different ways works as a defence against anxiety. The same is true with the hypochondriac. 'If I keep a check on my body there can be nothing to worry about.'

How do we manage hypochondriacal subordinates? If an employee suffers from genuine physical or nervous illness, we do what we can to help him by allowing generous time off for recovery. Besides being humanitarian this pays in the material way of staff relations. But with the hypochondriac it is rather different. Because of his mental preoccupation with his bodily functions, he is liable to take time off for very trivial conditions which others would simply ignore. It is not in the interests of the hypochondriac or of the firm that he should be indulged in this way. It is to the hypochondriac's advantage that he be kept at work during these periods of worry about his health. He may then profit by the experience and come to learn that he can work through the bad phases and nothing terrible happens. If this pattern can be initiated, he at least has made a start towards a more healthy state of mind.

Senior executives sometimes develop hypochondriacal characteristics. This is rather strange. The man of robust personality has made the way up and now becomes preoccupied about his health. The condition is sufficiently common to warrant discussion. A number of factors comes into this. The individual may have had minor hypochondriacal characteristics all his life. With advancing age, continued business stress and perhaps some impairment of physical health, these previously dormant traits of his personality become active. With others it may be that the intensity of the struggle of the way up has been the individual's one absorbing preoccupation. Now he is there, he relaxes. His mind is no longer so intently interested on his business, and now becomes focused on his health. He has friends who have suffered coronary attacks and others have died of cancer. He is aware that he is rather overweight, and that he smokes too much. These factors all predispose towards some hypochondriacal preoccupation. The answer is a check-up with a competent and sensible physician, and the development of later life interests to take place of the lessening interest in the business.

PARANOID CHARACTERISTICS

The paranoid individual is the fellow with a chip on his shoulder. He feels that he is not being treated fairly. People are trying to exploit him. They are against him. It was clearly favouritism that he was passed over for promotion. As a result of these beliefs, he becomes suspicious of those about him. He is inclined to examine every incident to see if it has some veiled meaning directed against himself. In this way he comes to add up two and two to make five; and he concludes that the others are in fact hatching little plots against him. Personal relations with those around him become strained. The others feel on edge because of his suspicious attitudes, and the smooth working of the group is disturbed.

The paranoid attitude is a psychological defence. By blaming the other person all the time, the paranoid individual absolves himself from blame and guilt. He always convinces himself that it is the other fellow's fault, and in this way anxiety is reduced.

If the others are ganged up against him, it is a very good reason why he is not getting on very well. This helps him not to feel so bad about it. In other words the paranoid attitude is just another pathological reaction to reduce nervous tension.

In considering paranoid attitudes we must remember that they often have a basis in fact. It often happens that the paranoid person is not well liked, and that others are in fact rather against him. The factor which makes his condition paranoid is his reaction to this, his suspiciousness about it, his unreasonableness, and the way in which he adds up little matters of pure coincidence in order to prove his case.

The paranoid individual disrupts the firm. His tendency to blame others has a bad effect on other employees. His blame is usually centred on some superior. These matters often grow out of a factual situation. It may well be that the superior is partly to blame in not having handled the paranoid person wisely. There are often others who are rather disgruntled and not too happy in their job. The paranoid person is liable to infect these others with something of his own disquiet, and the unrest grows.

[46]

There is no easy way of coping with the paranoid individual. Generous offers by the management are accepted, but are incorporated into his system of paranoid attitudes. 'It is only a confession of their guilt.' 'I forced them to do it.'

Senior executives sometimes develop paranoid traits. Paranoid attitudes are more common in older persons. The senior executive has made the way up. There is not long to go before he retires. Others are waiting for his retirement all ready to step into his shoes. They want him out. This is the factual situation on which paranoid attitudes are so often based. The paranoid attitude commences when he begins to wonder whether they might be plotting to get him out before his allotted time. He begins to become suspicious. He is less open and frank with the others than he used to be. His work deteriorates; and soon moves are in fact made to replace him.

This has been the unhappy sequence of events in the last phase of the way up of several senior executives whom I have seen as patients. It is a reaction of insecurity and anxiety. I think the most practical way of guarding against such a situation is this. When it is nearing time to step down, it is very important that we have somewhere to step to. If we have some satisfying plan for the next phase of our life, the idea of stepping down is no longer a worry. But if we realise that we are stepping down into a vacuum, as it were, our anxiety level is high, and paranoid attitudes are more likely to develop.

How does one negotiate with a paranoid individual. Business men have consulted me on this point on a number of occasions. There is no easy answer, but there are some guiding principles. The first thing to remember is that the paranoid person is normal outside the area of his paranoid attitudes. So he may be functioning quite effectively in his job. But within his paranoid area he is really insane. This is so because the paranoid idea is wrong in fact, and he does not change his mind about it in response to any logical argument which others would accept as proof that the idea was wrong. From this it follows that it quite useless to try to talk the person out of his paranoid idea by any form of logical discussion. This is quite hopeless. The only way to cope with the situation is at a non-logical level. If you

[47]

can bring the paranoid person to like you, there is a chance that he will do what you want because he likes you. This is really the only hope. But even this is very difficult because the paranoid person is also suspicious. So it is very important that the attempt to befriend him is made very cautiously, slowly and indirectly. This is best achieved by keeping the initial phases of the negotiations to generalities, and avoiding at all costs any head-on collision with the paranoid person.

PSYCHOPATHIC PERSONALITY

The psychopath is a person who does not have a properly developed conscience. This is the opposite condition to that of an obsessive, who really has a too active conscience, so that he fusses about scruples and cannot get on with the realities of life. There is none of this with the psychopath. He just does not care. He does not mind whom he exploits. There is no problem as to whether any course of action is right or wrong; the only criterion is whether or not he will benefit from it. He is quite ruthless. There is no feeling of remorse for those who suffer at his expense. He is cold and unfeeling.

On account of his utter ruthlessness, the psychopath may be quite successful in a material way. But this is usually short-lived. Others see how he operates and will have nothing to do with him.

As he has an imperfect conscience, he breaks the law if he thinks he will go undetected. In other cases the psychopath simply does not look ahead, and he does things which must inevitably bring him into conflict with the law. He is convicted and punished. But because of his inherent lack of conscience, he does not profit by his experience. He repeats the offence, and has further convictions.

Psychopaths often come from broken homes. An important factor in forming our conscience is the way in which we identify with our parents and take into ourselves their moral and ethical values. In the case of the psychopath it often happens that the parents have separated, and during his early formative years the child was brought up by various relatives. In these circumstances he may not have had sufficient contact with a stable adult with whom to identify, and in this way comes to grow up with a defective conscience. But this is not always the case, and some psychopaths seem to have been brought up in quite good circumstances, but have still developed this disastrous personality characteristic. In these cases it seems that the psychopathic characteristics are developed simply as a pattern of coping with life on a purely selfish and short-term basis.

Avoid dealing with people who have psychopathic characteristics. Generously minded people often think, 'He had a bad start in life. I must give him another chance,' or perhaps they just feel, 'He has a bad reputation, but he will be all right in this deal with me.' He won't. He would slip you up like he has the others. So avoid dealing with a psychopath.

In similar way it is easy to be sorry for a person who has been in trouble. You have the opening. You could give him a job. Give him another chance in life. I am sorry to have to warn you against such idealistic and humanitarian motives. The real psychopath does not respond to kindness. He will let you down.

THE HOMOSEXUAL

The homosexual has an effect on others working in the firm. From this point of view we must consider three different classes of homosexuals as their effect on others in the firm is rather different. There are people who are known in psychiatry as latent homosexuals. These are individuals who have the homosexual tendency, but it has never been evoked, and the individual himself is quite unaware of it, although perceptive observers can sense the tendency in him. Then there are persons who are aware of their homosexual tendency but do not practise it; and there are practising homosexuals. Female homosexuals are usually known as Lesbians.

Many male latent homosexuals are shy, timid, introverted people. They are often ill-at-ease in the company of men, and when working with men develop a high level of anxiety which reduces their work output. This may be particularly marked if the latent homosexual has to work closeted in an office with a single male companion. The individual can give no explanation of his disquiet. All he knows is that he feels anxious. He is

[49]

more at ease in the company of women. In fact women often get on well with the latent homosexual. They sense his trouble at some level less than clear awareness. They feel safe with him; and it is not uncommon to find some older woman rather mothering him. Within these limits his employment does not raise undue difficulties.

As with the latent homosexual, for the most part other people are usually unaware of the condition of the practising and non-practising homosexual. There may be just one person who is perceptive enough to recognize the problem, and he spreads the gossip among the others. This may have a disturbing effect on other employees. Some react with open hostility to the suspect, while his presence provokes anxiety in others. Those who react most violently are often latent homosexuals themselves. The net result is that the homosexual has a disturbing effect on his workmates. In these circumstances it is interesting to note that a practising homosexual is usually less anxious in himself than is a non-practising one.

On the other hand, in general, the presence of Lesbians on the staff does not have the same disruptive effect. In fact many career women are Lesbian, either latent or practising, and fit into the business world very easily and very effectively.

Intelligence

Intelligence differs from the personality characteristics which we have been discussing. It is an inherited ability. Psychological and physical factors may prevent us from using our inherited intelligence to the full, but we can do nothing to add to it. Intelligence also differs from the personality characteristics in that it is not a psychological defence to help us cope with life in the same way that they are.

Intelligence concerns one's ability to produce the idea most appropriate to the particular situation. It is a matter of the right idea at the right time. There is an aptness about it. Intelligence is that function of our mind which allows us to do this.

When we are presented with an idea, another idea comes to

our mind in response to the first idea. This is the process of thought. With some people the second idea is not only particularly apt to the first idea, but is apt to it in the context of the particular circumstances in which it is used. This process is the basic function of intelligence. In ordinary life we do not analyse it quite like this. But the sequence of ideas which a person offers us in ordinary conversation make some impact on us. If the ideas have this particular aptness, we are left with the impression that the individual is bright. In other words we have made an unconscious assessment of his intelligence.

There are different types of intelligence. But this principle does not go quite as far as popular belief would lead us. The idea that some people are exceptionally gifted in some particular area, and dull in other respects, is a popular misconception. The usual situation is that the individual, who has some special gift, also has a high ability in other areas as well.

Nevertheless, from the practical point of view we can distinguish these rather different classes of intelligence. There is intelligence which shows itself mainly with figures. This is a mathematical ability. Others have intelligence which shows itself in mechanical ability which concerns apt ideas about space and form. A third general form of intelligence concerns abstract thought. It is obviously important that we should work ourselves into a position that gives us scope to use the particular type of intelligence which we have in greatest degree. The same principle, of course, applies in alloting jobs to our employees.

Don't confuse intelligence with knowledge. Knowledge is really the store of facts which we carry in our mind. But there is a proviso to this. Knowledge is the store of facts in our mind to which we have access. All of us have many more facts in our minds from past experiences of learning and observation than we can recall. These other facts can often be made accessible by hypnosis or other techniques of psychiatry, but they do not form part of our knowledge in the ordinary sense. Knowledge does not measure our intelligence. But it gives our intelligence the material on which it can work to full advantage. To be on the way up we must have considerable knowledge. Unlike intelligence we can easily increase our knowledge. We do this by close observation. We do it in study; and in study it is a matter of reading both widely and deeply.

Wisdom is attained when intelligence is tempered with experience. The intelligent individual is not necessarily wise. Experience is necessary for intelligence to exercise proper judgment. But the individual must not only have had the experience; he must also have integrated it into the functions of his mind so that it comes to join with intelligence to produce wisdom.

A record of achievement is a good guide to intelligence. When running a business it is obviously important to know who on your staff is intelligent, and who is not. If this is not done, your manpower cannot be used to best advantage.

In general, in our competitive society, those who achieve success are intelligent. The reverse is not true. Intelligent persons may be held back through lack of training or opportunity, or they may not be able to use their intelligence on account of disorder of the personality. In spite of popular stories to the contrary, most people who have succeeded are intelligent. So the school, and university records, as well as the degree of success in earlier employment are quite a useful guide.

The intelligent person catches on to new ideas. Watch how different men succeed in new jobs and in new situations. Observe also the way in which they grasp any new ideas that you bring up in conversation. By observing the way people 'Catch on' as we talk with them, we can make a good estimate of their intelligence without their being aware of what we are doing. These are the people that you should use in implementing the new methods, and new processes which are a part of any progressive business.

A person's manner of speech discloses his level of intelligence. On basing a judgment on this principle, care must be taken to evaluate the individual's manner of speech with his educational standard and social background. Intelligent but poorly educated persons often use similes and metaphors in their conversation more aptly than better educated but less intelligent persons. In fact we can get a very good idea of an individual's general intelligence simply by observing his use of simile and metaphor as he talks to us. Casual conversation may disclose the degree to which the individual is observant of everyday matters. One should never be misled by those who use abstruse words. This is pedantry, and is a sign of the pseudo-intellectual rather than the intelligent person.

The intelligent individual makes appropriate casual comments. They are apt and relevant to the circumstances. This is independent of education. In assessing these, they must be distinguished from the slick, gimmicky, platitudinous, socially acceptable comments which form such a part of ordinary conversation. These are conventional modes of speech and are not related to intelligence. In a similar way many people cover up their lack of intelligent thinking by using popular stereotyped expressions. I would not rate anyone who speaks of something as, 'being a challenge' or 'a meaningful experience' too highly. Clichés such as these are frequently used by unintelligent but well educated persons as an unconscious cover up for their lack of original thought.

Are intelligence tests any good? Yes, they are very good; but they must be used sensibly. Our success with any particular project, or for that matter our success in life itself, depends very much on our intelligence. But there are other important factors too. Our personality, our determination and our drive are also very important. The most common error of those who administer and report on intelligence tests is to advise too exclusively on the basis of pure intelligence without giving these other factors adequate consideration. Thus an individual with a very high I.Q. may be advised to embark on some project or course of study which is in fact quite beyond him on account of immaturity of his personality. In a similar way persons of average intelligence are often advised against tertiary education whereas in fact they might be quite well suited for it, as determination and a well integrated personality may well compensate for their marginal intelligence.

We want a job in which we can use our intelligence. This is obvious. If we are blessed with the gift of intelligence, and we are on the way up, we must be sure that we are in a job which gives us full scope for our natural ability. This may mean shopping about for the right job. And changing jobs is always chancy. But those on the way up must take chances. Then you might ask, 'How do I know when I have a job that suits my intelligence?' The answer is that you feel satisfied in the work itself, independent of any dissatisfaction with those with whom you work or the salary, although these dissatisfactions may be sufficient to make the job unsuitable. But if you find the actual work not too easy, and not hopelessly difficult, and at the same time satisfying, you have s good guide that it suits your level of intelligence.

Anxiety inhibits the full use of intelligence. This is one of the most important factors with which we must contend if we are on the way up. The problem arises at all levels. The anxious student unconsciously uses psychological mechanisms to control his nervous tension. There is a reaction to inhibit the anxiety; but this may induce a general inhibitory effect which tends to damp down not only the anxiety but all his mental processes as well. He then complains of a blank feeling. He can't concentrate. He can't get on with his studies. He can't do anything. This is all due to the body's attempt to inhibit his anxiety. I have seen many such lads as patients. Their concentration and ability to study returns when they are shown how to let their mind experience the natural ease of things again. The executive may develop similar troubles. A chronic anxiety condition may prevent the full use of his intelligence and his progress on the way up comes to a stop. As with the students, I have seen many such men who have been able to resume the onward march when their anxiety has been relieved.

Marked personality characteristics prevent the full use of intelligence. The obsessive, who is so perfectionistic that he keeps checking things over to be sure that they are right, cannot use his intelligence to full advantage. He may find that he even has trouble in reading because he feels that he must go back over what he has just read so as to be sure that he has grasped all the details. As a result he can only function at a level far below his full potential.

Nor can the shy introverted individual gain full use of his

intelligence. He is so tensed up on account of his extreme shyness that he has to use much of his mental capacity in controlling himself, and there is little left to deal with the problem in hand. In a similar way the extravert is diverted by his gregarious needs, and is unable to settle down sufficiently to use his intelligence to best advantage. Similarly, it is easy to see how other personality characteristics, the hysteric, the hypochondriac and the homosexual may also impair the full use of intelligence.

Our drive largely determines how well we use our intelligence. This is our motivation. It is the force within us that gets us going. It is the will to succeed and also the energy to attempt it. In the material world of reality, intelligence without drive means nothing. It remains only a force latent within the individual, a potentiality that he is unable to use. But for him, who has drive, it is different. His intelligence is motivated into action, and he moves from idea to idea, from project to project. On the other hand, those who have not learned to manage their personality characteristics, will lack drive because the mental energy which should be used in drive has to be used to cope with their personality difficulties.

Have an occasional 'think-in'. We can use our intelligence easily enough in the routine matters of our job. But we want more than this. We want to be able to use it creatively. This requires time and opportunity for our intelligence to work things out. In this respect, I am sure that the idea of a quiet 'think-in' is most valuable. There is some project on hand. We have done a lot of reading about it. There have been full discussions, and we have a lot of figures. What we now want is the bright idea, the concept that will make the project work. We let ourselves be at ease. We are quite relaxed. Our mind wanders, this way and that. We just let ourselves go more and more completely with it. There is a profound relaxation and a kind of effortlessness with it. In this state of mind our intelligence is quite uninhibited. It has free rein. And in this state of being our intelligence will often come up with the solution of a problem that has defied hours of intense logical thought.

Don't be superior about your intelligence. This is a common fault of the academic, and it has done much to alienate him from those of equal ability who work in commerce and industry. It is not long ago that a class of people believed that the state owed them a living in virtue of their privileged birthright. This mantle has now fallen on the pseudo-intellectual who so often cries to the state to support a similarly indolent pattern of life.

An intelligent young man had recently returned to a very prosperous family business after a period at the Harvard School of Business Administration. Personal problems became to acute that he sought my advice. He had become so superior about his intelligence that the people who had founded the very successful business had found it impossible to work with him. The problem was as simple as that!

We must not expect others to be like ourselves. Much of our difficulty with subordinates is due to our lack of appreciation of their level of intelligence. If we are in the upper group of management, it is likely that we are more intelligent than the general run of the firm's employees. As a result of this difference of intellectual level, they think in patterns of thought which are rather different from our own. I do not refer to the different point of view which is determined by the disparity of social position. I mean the rather different pattern of thinking between the highly intelligent and those of average or less than average ability. It means that we must make allowances, and we must also remember that these people, who are less intelligent than ourselves, can also make a contribution because they offer a point of view different from our own.

Don't promote people beyond their capacity. This is a common failing at all levels of commerce and industry. Don't forget that the dullard may be quite presentable in both manner and appearance, so that his lack of intelligence is not at all obvious. This situation is common in persons of below average intelligence, but who have been well educated, and who have learned the social niceties of manner and speech. These people may disguise their lack of intelligence very successfully. I have seen as patients a number of men who have been promoted beyond their capacity in this way, and have subsequently broken down with anxiety symptoms because they have found the strain too much.

There is another situation of which executives should be beware. The intellectually dull but socially sophisticated young man may present himself very well on the golf course or at a social gathering. Beware of these encounters, and do not let them influence you too much. He may perform much better at the golf club than at the office.

Give dull employees clear instructions. Because of his lack of intelligence, the dull employee does not comprehend your instructions as clearly and quickly as others. An explanation that would be more than adequate for yourself or someone like you may be hopelessly inadequate for someone a little less intelligent. We must not assess the merit of the instructions which we give in terms of them being clear and concise. The only criterion is whether or not they are fully understood by the other person. This means that instructions for the same task must always be expressed appropriately for the particular person receiving the instrctions.

Don't talk down to less intelligent employees. When one is aware of these problems, it is easy to make the opposite mistake, and over simplify instructions to the extent that the other person realises that you are treating him as if he were not too bright. This of course is exactly what you are doing. Only it must be done without the other person being aware of it.

We can profit here from the everyday experience of psychiatry. If I have to give instructions to an unintelligent patient or to a patient whose intelligence is temporarily impaired by nervous illness, I always have a few casual words with him first. This establishes a friendly relationship, and he then does not feel that I am talking down to him when I express the instructions in very simple language.

Let dull employees stay in the same job. The person with rather less intelligence does not adapt to change too well. His power of adjustment is reduced. Another man can change from job to job without stress. In fact, the higher his intelligence the more he likes changes, as this gives him opportunity to use his intelligence and saves him from the boredom suffered by intelligent persons doing routine work. But for the dull, the reverse holds true. Changes increase anxiety, and performance of work falls off on account of nervous tension.

Don't employ intelligent persons in routine jobs. They don't do them well. It is too easy. They are bored. They become restless. They don't maintain attention; and they don't do the simple job as well as a less intelligent person.

A few years ago I saw a schoolboy whom I believe is so intelligent that he is almost a genius. But he could not pass his school exams! The work was so easy that he simply could not pay attention. The same principles apply to the intelligent young man in business or commerce.

Of course, there is an exception to this rule. The highly intelligent person, who cannot use his intelligence on account of problems of his personality, can only be employed in routine work. In most cases he is not very happy in it, as he knows that he ought to be doing better, but at the same time realises that he can't.

Give intelligent subordinates experience in different jobs. These are your future executives. The more effective they are, the better for yourself. They need experience in width as well as in depth. Without experience in width, the bright young man with possibilities becomes a specialist. This may be rewarding enough. But if he is really to make the way up in its fullest sense, he needs variety of experience.

Avoid getting anxious when instructing persons more intelligent than yourself. This can be quite a problem with the executive who is himself introverted. The extravert executive rides over this situation, and for him there is no problem. But with the introvert it is different. His sensitivity plays tricks on him. He feels embarassed by awareness of his subordinate's higher intelligence. His anxiety is increased, and he acquits himself badly in the discussion.

The situation is often aggravated by the intelligent junior manipulating the discussion so as to bring into evidence his own superior intelligence. This is a part of the interpersonal manoeuvring of individuals in any organization.

In dealing with the situation, the less intelligent senior must avoid simply squashing the intelligent junior with authority. If he does this, the junior has in fact won. There are better ways. In his sensitivity the introvert senior must not forget that other factors beside intelligence have combined to give him the position he holds. And if you have this kind of trouble, do all you can to keep down the general level of your anxiety in the way set out in the next section. With a lower level of anxiety we can cope with extra stresses without them worrying us.

2

Coping with ourselves

Anxiety

Anxiety impedes our progress. In fact, I would think it probable that anxiety, manifested in one form or another, is the most common cause of failure of otherwise competent persons to make the way up. Anxiety is such a widespread phenomenon that we tend to overlook the crippling effect that it has on us. We make a terrible mistake. We become so accustomed to the experience of anxiety that we come to accept anxiety as normal. This point was brought to my mind very vividly not long ago. A surgeon from another State sought my help after he had developed a stutter. During the interview I made the comment that he was very tense. However, he strongly denied this, 'I am not tense at all. In fact my colleagues consider me a most relaxed person.' I just let the matter drop. A little later, when he had seen me five or six times, he came back to this incident. 'When I first saw you, I simply did not know that I was tense. I had become so used to it that it had become normal to me. Now that I am more relaxed, I can see how much better things can be.' I think there are a lot of people like this man, who simply do not know that life could be so much better. The same idea was presented to me again only last night. I was at dinner, and was seated next to a barrister whom I did not know. He said he had read my book about relaxing. Then he added, 'But everyone is tense. I take a pill before appearing in court, and half the barristers I know do the same.' I think I spoilt his dinner by explaining that there are different levels of living. People too easily accept an inferior level. We should set our sights higher than this.

Anxiety shows itself in many ways. There is the feeling of nervous tension, and with it there may be tension in the muscles themselves. There is often a feeling of apprehension. We have to be on the alert, on the look-out, because we have some vague feeling that something bad is going to happen. These feelings intrude more forcefully into our mind when we are suddenly faced with a difficult task. Our heart thumps. There is a sinking sensation in the stomach, and the feeling that it is turning over. We catch our breath, and perhaps feel we want to breathe more deeply. These are common manifestations of anxiety. And when we have had it for some time, work becomes more difficult. We can't concentrate; we can't remember things. We are irritable, not only at work when things go wrong, but also at home, and this makes us feel bad. We are restless; we find it hard to get settled, and we don't sleep too well at night. Headaches make things worse; and in general life is not what it might be.

Anxiety makes us timid. And of course there is no place for the timid on the way up. Everyone knows this, so people who are anxious often react against their timidity by making a display of courage. It is false courage. There is something incongruous about it, and it does not ring true. This was a reaction which was observed quite frequently in situations of danger during the war. A similar reaction can be seen in the executive whose anxiety makes him timid. His mind is alert and logical. He reasons things out that some bold policy or manner of action is required. But underneath he is fearful and wants to avoid such things. As a result he over reacts, and embarks on some policy which goes too far. It is not sensibly bold, but foolishly so. What is more, his associates quickly recognize it as wrong because it is so incongruous with the anxiously timid person's general way of life.

Of course a boss who undermines the confidence of a young man makes him anxious, and in those circumstances he is likely to become timid. But a more common cause of timidity at work comes from a man's personal life. The young man who is jilted or the older man whose wife is unfaithful may suffer an extreme loss of confidence in the office.

Different stresses combine to produce anxiety. There is a kind of adding up of stresses. It is a summation effect. There are stresses at work and at home, stresses from indifferent health, poor sleep or too much alcohol, and stresses from unconscious childhood conflicts which have not been resolved. All these combine to produce a stream of nervous impulses to our brain. If these impulses reach a certain level of intensity, they are not properly sorted out and integrated in the brain, and anxiety results. I mention this to emphasize that anxiety is the product of multiple stresses. Of course it often happens that some particular stress, a major problem at work, or some serious domestic discord at home, is a major factor. But this major factor always works on a background of many other less significant stresses.

Stresses at home reduce our efficiency at work. This follows from what has just been said. Sometimes people like to think that their domestic life and their business life are water-tight compartments quite independent of each other. This is simply not true. We live life as a whole. Tensions and anxieties which arise in one part are carried over to the other.

There are a number of practical applications of this principle. If you have set your sights high for the way up in the business world, you should aim to achieve as stable a domestic life as possible. If you are assessing the potential of some young man for promotion, you cannot completely disregard his private life. You cannot say to yourself, 'His personal life is his affair; it is no concern of mine.' In a way it is your concern, because everybody brings to work with him the nervous tension which is created in the home.

Nervous-tension reduces our ability to think clearly. When we are tense we are unconsciously using a lot of our nervous energy to control our tension. This reduces our efficiency in every aspect of life. It particularly affects our ability to think clearly. The easy flow of thought is lost. The right idea won't come. Our mind wanders from the task we set it to do. Our thoughts are restless, and with it there is a physical restlessness. We keep shifting our position in the chair. We pick up our pen and put it down. If we smoke, the cigarettes follow one after the other. It is no good. Thoughts won't come. Our thinking has been inhibited by our anxiety.

There are really three different ways in which nervous tension prevents us thinking clearly. There is the restlessness which makes it hard or impossible to keep our attention on the subject in question. There is the over-alertness which makes us react too strongly to ideas so that the smooth flow of thought is lost. And then there is the body's attempt to inhibit the anxiety, which has the undesired side effect of also inhibiting other mental activity.

Nervous tension reduces our manual dexterity. If our job involves some precision work with our hands, we soon become aware how our efficiency is reduced by anxiety. We notice it even in such simple things as writing a memo. Our fingers are stiff. The free movement of the pen is lost. On these occasions we dread our secretary bringing a pile of cheques for signature. Our writing goes in fits and starts and little jerks. If there is someone watching us, our anxiety is further increased, and our manual dexterity is reduced still further.

We notice the same phenomenon in other areas. The person with nervous tension walks differently. He is stiff, and the smooth naturalness of his gait is lost. His golf swing loses its ease; it is the same in tennis. If he skis, his muscles are tense and he can't understand why he has been falling. I can't help telling you a story which is relevant to this. I have been seeing a woman who plays a lot of golf. In fact, golf is an important part of her life. She is a rather tense person. She had read my book about relaxation, and she thought I might be able to help her to a fuller life. I have seen her about half a dozen times. She came in again yesterday, and I asked how she had been getting on. To my horror she answered, 'I've lost all my friends since seeing you'. With a sinking heart I asked 'How is that?' Then she explained that the previous day she had beaten her golf handicap by ten! I am now re-reading the manuscript some two months later, and I can report that she has had her handicap reduced by nine! This has been possible simply because her manual dexterity had been impaired by nervous tension due to anxiety.

Anxiety in the mind effects the muscles of the body. A quarrel at home, and it takes longer to sign the cheques in the office.

[63]

A set back from the boss and one's sexual response may be impaired. Anxiety can seep through our whole life. This is second rate living. We must do better than this.

Our nervous tension makes us edgy and so effects others. We can do all we can to disguise it. But it is no good. Those who work with us are aware of our nervous tension. Remember that emotional states are very catching. In a situation of danger, if we are with someone who shows his fear, we become frightened too. If we are with jolly companions, we too feel happy. In the same way anxiety affects others. And if it is the boss who is anxious the effect on the others is so much the greater.

Sometimes this is a conscious process on the part of the others. The signs of anxiety, the slight impatience, the gruff voice, the quicker manner of speech, the restlessness, the reluctance to deal with the problem, these things are observed; and the others are fully aware of our nervous tension. They talk about it among themselves. But sometimes it is a more subtle process. They just avoid us. Somehow they just have the feeling that this is not the right time to approach us on a difficult problem. In either case our anxiety has a disturbing effect on the smooth working of the organization.

Don't believe that a little anxiety is good. People frequently put this proposition to me. They say that a certain amount of anxiety spurs us along and helps us to get things done. My answer is this. People do things from different motives. Some give to charity because they want to help those in need, others do the same thing in the hope of some other reward. Some are honest because they feel that way about things; others because they are afraid they might be caught. In a similar way a feeling of nervous tension motivates some people to do useful things. But it is second class motivation. Let us be clear about that. There are better reasons for getting going and doing things than the uncomfortable feeling of anxiety.

Don't try to cope with your own anxiety by belittling the other person. I may not have thought to mention this, if it had not been for an incident yesterday morning. A very anxious, very highly intelligent professional man came to see me. He was really intensely jittery. He came into my consulting room, looked around him, and said, 'Why can't you get some decent pictures'. In addition to his professional qualifications, he is, in fact, a first class artist himself. So he may have thought that this gave him some right to act as an uninvited critic. But it soon came out that this was his way of coping with anxiety. If we reduce the status of the other person, we somehow think we will feel better ourselves. Further enquiry showed that he is a lonely isolated man, who would very much like the companionship of friends, but he has not got any, and the reason would seem obvious enough.

I have seen junior executives make the same mistake. Not only is business itself competitive, but there is also an unexpressed, but often quite intense, competition between the junior executives of a large firm. This is a situation which encourages the pattern of belittling the other person in order to reduce one's own nervous tension. Don't let yourself unconsciously fall into the way of doing this.

The loudly spoken executive may be covering his own anxiety. We all know him. His voice resounds around the office and the club-room. His speech is loud, his manner is loud and his way of dressing is loud. It all goes to show in a very blatant fashion what a superior person he is. But you and I know that if anyone is unconsciously driven to show how superior he is, then underneath it all, he is surely an anxious person. I can think of a man who shows this reaction in extreme. He became chairman of a large company by virtue of the fact that his wife's family were the major shareholders. I would think that he was inwardly insecure in this situation; but his unconscious reaction is such that he is generally regarded as one of the most confident, or over confident, men in the city.

There are two reasons why this type of reaction is common in senior executives. In the first place, it is a reaction which suits the extravert personality, and we have seen that the extravert's capacity for action and decision-making often helps him to high executive office. In the second place, the choice of our unconscious defences against anxiety are influenced by our social milieu. Loud mouthed behaviour is possible for a top executive, but the social milieu makes it impossible for the junior clerk, and he evolves some other way of dealing with his anxiety.

A pleasant, smiling manner may also cover up anxiety. As I have explained, I am a psychiatrist. I see patients during the day, and the evenings I enjoy writing as I am now. It seems to happen that in the day I very often see examples of the very condition that I am writing about. So it was today a young executive came to see me on account of his chronic nervous tension. He was intelligent, pleasant and smiling. My previous patient had been a very difficult man, and I remember thinking to myself how nice it was to see someone openly pleasant for a change. Then I noticed that when we came to discuss the cause of his anxiety, he became still more smiling and still more pleasant. In other words his smiling manner became more marked with increased anxiety. Then I realised that there was something incongruous about it. Something phoney. It did not quite ring true as the real smile of the person experiencing happy thoughts. The patient, of course, was quite unaware of all this. His manner was the defence which he had unconsciously evolved to help him cope with situations of stress.

How can we reduce our nervous tension? I have discussed the problem in detail in my book RELIEF WITHOUT DRUGS*. If you are troubled with nervous tension, I would strongly advise you to get the book and quietly practise the mental exercises which I describe. I cannot emphasize too strongly that anxiety with its nervous tension is one of the commonest barriers to a full and successful life.

Tranquillizers don't help much, and reduce your efficiency. The taking of tranquillizers is a second class method of coping with one's anxiety. I say this quite definitely. It is second class. I know that a great number of people do take them. Some of these are simple people who accept a low standard of life without much thought. Others are people who do not seem to

*RELIEF WITHOUT DRUGS
Hardback: American edition by Doubleday
Paperback: American edition by Ace
Hardback: British edition by Souvenir Press
Paperback: British edition by Fontana

be aware that there is an alternative way of dealing with nervous tension which is effective and not too difficult to master, and which is free of all the unpleasant side effects and mental dulling of tranquillizers.

To learn to relax is much better than taking drugs. If we come to think of it at all seriously, it becomes obvious that the body must have a natural means of coping with anxiety. We would expect this from the simplest biological considerations. And of course it is true. We have the natural means of managing anxiety, the problem is that we have lost the knack of using it. With our increasing sophistication and preoccupation with the material aspects of life, we have lost the art of coping with our tensions through the body itself. The medical profession has been little help in this. It is much easier to prescribe tranquillizers than to show the patient how to let himself be more relaxed. Instead, the profession has followed the lead of the materialistic society in which we live, and has concentrated its attention on bigger and more powerful tranquillizers.

The point that I would emphasize to you is this, that it is not difficult to learn to use the body's natural means of controlling anxiety. If you are rather tense, the little time spent on this will bring rewards in increased productivity at work and fuller life in general.

Practice letting your mind experience the natural ease of things. Do it for ten minutes a couple of times a day. Sit quietly. Just let yourself be. You don't have to make yourself relax. It is all quite effortless. It is natural. You just let yourself be, and the relaxation is there because it is natural to you. Don't be sceptical. It works. This is beyond doubt, as I have shown some hundreds of tense patients how to do it. People ask, 'What do I think of?' 'What do I do with my thoughts?' When you have learned to do it, you will find that you have very little thought at all. While you are learning, it is a good idea to think about the natural ease that you experience as you sit there doing it. You can feel your arms relaxed and legs relaxed. Experience the feeling of this all through you. It comes all through the whole of you; it is in the mind itself. Remember that it is only the experience of it that helps. Reading about it, talking about it, discussing it, is of no value in reducing your nervous tension. But let yourself learn to experience natural ease, and you will find that the level of your anxiety is soon reduced.

Bring yourself to experience natural ease in your ordinary life. You learn to experience the feeling of profound and natural ease, sitting in your chair, just letting yourself be. You can look upon this mental exercise in the same way as others look upon physical exercise. Many of us do rigorous physical exercises to keep physically fit. If you are a little tense, I am asking you to do some mental exercises to keep yourself mentally fit.

Once you have mastered the mental exercise, and you can experience natural ease, the next step is to let the natural ease come into your ordinary working life. As you walk down the street let yourself feel the same ease which you have learned to capture sitting in your chair. It is natural. It feels good. It is good. And you encourage the natural ease more and more into your working life.

There are just two further points. When practising it, don't make yourself too comfortable. If you are too comfortable, you relax very completely, but much of this relaxation is coming from your bodily comfort. This is not what we want. We aim for a relaxation which comes from the mind itself, irrespective of physical bodily comfort. So do not make yourself too comfortable when you practice it. To sit in a straight backed chair, or to lie on your back on the floor is good. The other point I wish to emphasize is the effortlessness of it all. There is no making yourself do it. It is just there, all natural, and utterly effortless. Don't be put off by the simplicity of this approach. It has lead many people to an extraordinary increase in effectiveness and productivity.

Being relaxed increases efficiency and output. I have had those who run big business come to me as patients. They have been rather tycoon types, and mostly very tense. When I talk to them about being more relaxed, they always say that if they were relaxed they would lose their punch, and would never be able to get through all their work. When I have persuaded them to go along with me, and reduce their anxiety through experiencing mental ease, they have all found that their work output has been increased. There has been no exception to this. And after all it is what we should expect. Nervous tension holds us back. Without it we do things more smoothly and more efficiently.

Hostility

We become aggressive when we are thwarted. This is a natural biological response. It is a protective mechanism which is ingrained into us. It is an automatic response to help us cope with life situations. It is a very good reaction for life in primitive conditions, enabling the individual who is thwarted to reply with aggression against those who have thwarted him, and so, perhaps, turn the tables on them. But our psychological responses have not kept up with our evolutionary development in other areas, and this primitive type of response is quite unsuited to life in our complex modern society. When we are thwarted in business there are better ways of coping with the situation than being hostile and aggressive. In fact, success on the way up demands that we learn to control this primitive reaction which still lies latent within us.

Aggressive feelings reduce our efficiency. This is common experience. We have a dispute with someone and our aggression is mobilized. In this state of mind we do not acquit ourselves well. If it were a matter of a physical fight, all would be well as our aggression could help us. But in a business battle it is no good. In this situation our aggression only muddles us, impairing our ability to think logically and reducing our capacity to handle other people. Furthermore, when the incident is passed, and we move on to our next task, the mobilized aggression is still there. We feel it in us. We are disturbed in ourselves. We cannot get on with the matter in hand.

Such a sequence is all too common with most of us. It is not good enough. If we are on the way up we must do better than that.

Others sense our hostility without us saying or doing anything. Instead of our aggression being suddenly mobilized as in a dispute, it may smoulder in a chronic form. It is often turned against some individual or group of individuals. They are not our friends. We don't see eye to eye with them. They irritate us and irk us. We feel a primitive urge to take some action against them. But we are civilized, and we can't take any open action. So it all just smoulders within us. This is hostility.

In these circumstances our own efficiency is reduced because we have to use mental energy to control our hostility; but equally important is the effect of our feelings on others. I emphasize that others around us are affected by the way we feel. We try to control and disguise our feelings, but the hostility shows through in the almost imperceptive minutiae of our behaviour. As a result, those around us sense how we feel. The awareness of our hostility provokes defensive psychological responses in them, and the situation deteriorates.

Don't excuse yourself by thinking, 'I have not done anything. I have not said a word.' The hostile emotion within you not only reduces your efficiency but that of others around you as well.

Hostile feelings are easily transferred from one person to another. This is everyday experience. The man has a bad time at work. He is frustrated and hostile; but he controls his hostility because his job depends on it. But at home his wife makes some minor slip and all his hostility is vented on the innocent woman. Similarly an executive may be frustrated at home, and vents his pent up anger on some junior at work. It is all so simple; but it happens so frequently. And it is just because people have not learned to cope with themselves.

Hostility is extremely destructive. If we are on the way up we must learn to manage it.

If we are relaxed we can tolerate frustration without becoming hostile. This is the key to handling this primitive aggressive response. Remember that we can manage our aggressive impulses at two different levels. We can control our impulses after our aggression has been mobilized. This of course is better than giving vent to our feelings. But it is an inferior way of coping because of the nervous energy wasted in doing it, and also because of the bad effect of our controlled aggression on others. The better way, the only really effective way, is to learn to experience frustrating situations without the primitive aggressive response. This is not as hard as you might think. It is a matter of learning to be relaxed in your mind so that you can handle the frustrating situation calmly and effectively. This can be achieved by practising the relaxing mental exercises as described in the last section. I know beyond all doubt that this approach is effective, as a number of previously aggressive executives have reported great changes for the better in this respect.

Don't make decisions while you are feeling aggressive. If you dictate a letter while you are hostile, hold it until the next day, and before posting it, read it again. For those given to hostile feelings, there should be no exception to this. If you catch yourself thinking, 'I'll give him what he deserves', this is the time to be sure to read it again tomorrow.

Depression

A depressed executive casts a blight over the whole firm. This is the reverse of leadership, which aims to inspire enthusiasm and confidence. A major difficulty is that the executive may not be aware of his condition. We can be psychologically depressed without experiencing much subjective depression in the way of sadness. A depressed executive is not only unable to do his own work effectively. but he casts a gloom around him which effectively stills any enterprise in his subordinates.

The feeling that things are difficult may be due to nervous depression. It is just hard to get going. The natural ease of things is lost. There is a feeling of pessimism; the good times may not last.

I have mentioned that the executive may not be aware that he is depressed. He may also be quite unaware that he has become pessimistic. There is great danger to the firm in this. The executive's judgement is unconsciously distorted with pessimism, and enterprise is lost. Perhaps another executive questions him about it. But this does little good. The depressed person always rationalizes, and gives logical reasons for his decisions. These reasons are logical in themselves, but at the same time are distortions due to his prevailing pessimism.

How can we recognize nervous depression in another? First of all there is a change in the person. He seems rather different. He is not his old self. He does not like a joke in the same way as he used to. He is more inclined to keep to himself. He does not go to his club for lunch, but eats quietly in a cafe. If you ask him out, he is inclined to make excuses not to come. In fact he would prefer to stay at home. You may notice that he is rather slower at his work. His pessimism is noticeable in other things besides the business. He thinks his son will probably fail his exams this year, although he has done well in the past. Jokes that would have made him laugh now irritate him. These are all little things, but they spell the diagnosis of nervous depression, which is quite a serious condition on account of its effect on the individual's judgement.

Well, if I am depressed, what do I do? First and foremost, if you have this difficulty in getting going and this pessimism about you, ask your local doctor to refer you to a psychiatrist because he can help you. But there are also things which you can do to help yourself.

There are two different types of nervous depression, and they need a rather different approach. In one type the depression results from the frustrations of life. These may be due to problems and difficulties at work, or conflicts and misunderstandings at home. Nervous depression which results from frustrations at home may show itself primarily in pessimism at work. In this type of depression which arises from frustration either at work or at home, we can help ourselves by learning to be more relaxed in the way that I have described. This reduces our level of anxiety, and allows us to cope realistically with the frustrations of life with less inner disquiet.

The second type of depression is different although the signs are very similar. It arises from causes within our body rather than in the frustrations of our life; and it can be helped by medication with anti-depressant drugs. That is why it is wise to see the doctor.

[72]

Don't change jobs or make important decisions while you are depressed. Guard against this at all costs. It is most important. Every week I see patients who are depressed and who have resigned from their job feeling that it was too much for them. In a few weeks their depression has gone. They are perfectly well again, but without their job. In matters of work be very careful of any decision which you are about to make that involves downgrading either yourself or your firm, as your judgement may easily be distorted by nervous depression.

Drive

Drive is the force that spurs us on; it is our motivation and our energy. In the man who has drive, the mind is searching and probing. There is pressure of thought so that ideas come quickly and forcefully. This characterizes his thinking. There is purpose about him. We are aware of it from the way he speaks. There are no vague abstractions, no use of empty phrases to fill the need for the social niceties of the occasion. His ideas come too quickly and forcefully for that. We cannot sit restfully in quiet conversation with such a man. His stream of ideas commands our attention. On account of this we often find his company stimulating, but if we ourselves are tired, we find him overpowering, and our sense of fatigue is increased.

The drive within him, which stimulates this pressure of thought from his mind, produces a similar activity in his body. He is on the go. He does one thing and then another. This is not just the restless activity of an anxious person. There is purpose behind it. There is no stopping with the job half finished. His drive gives him energy and determination, so that his projects are brought to fruition.

Drive inspires others. This pressure of activity in mind and body has the quality of enthusiasm. It affects others. We are taken along with it. Our own thoughts are stimulated to keep pace with the rapid flow of his ideas, or if we are engaged in physical activity, we find that we unconsciously follow the pace he has set us. This is the hallmark of leadership. And if we are on the way up this is what we need.

[73]

Can we increase our drive? Yes. We can in two ways. First we must free ourselves from those factors which inhibit drive. Anxiety and depression are the most important. Anxiety makes us tired, and our mental energy is wasted controlling it. So there is no mental energy left for our drive. Nervous depression slows up our reactions, and our drive is damped down. We have discussed ways of alleviating anxiety and depression; and there are also positive things we can do to increase our drive. Awareness is one. The very fact of being aware of this state of mind and its importance to our success is a help. We can cultivate this habit. We do it consciously at first, and then it comes naturally to us. We can prod ourselves into active thought and active doing. The purposive cultivation of this attitude of mind is particularly helpful to introvert persons whose drive is liable to be inhibited by their sensitivity.

Drive results from the transformation of aggression. This is the process of sublimation. We have within us the primitive, animal, propensity of combativeness which we know as aggression. This has contributed to our success as a species and as a race. In the past, in primitive conditions, it has contributed to the success of the individual. But in civilized society there is little outlet for primitive aggression. If we do in fact vent our aggression, it is likely to land us in trouble with our fellows or the law. But by sublimation the primitive aggressive force can undergo a psychological change, so that it is transferred into something useful that can help us in a socially acceptable combative fashion in civilized society. This is the psychological process by which our drive comes into being.

Beware lest your drive deteriorate into aggression. Just as drive is derived from our aggressive urges, in the same way, given the right circumstances, the psychological force of our drive can deteriorate, and again manifest itself in primitive aggression. Watch yourself for this. The executive who becomes more and more driving, may soon find that he is treating opponents with open and uncontrolled aggression. This is a debasement of his drive which is forceful but controlled, and hence a useful component in his personality.

In other cases, the executive with well developed drive uses it

[74]

advantageously in all circumstances except when he is thwarted. He then 'blows up' and shows an aggressive violence which is contrary to his usual driving but controlled manner of behaviour. This is merely a further illustration of the close relationship between drive and aggression.

Drive is greater in men than in women. This is what we should expect. The masculine-aggressive aspects of a man's personality contrast with the femine-passive traits of a woman. There is less basic aggression in the personality of the mature woman, so there is less of the force to be transformed into drive. The woman who is conspicuous for her drive lacks something in feminity. This means that in general women are not suited to positions in commerce and industry which require a high degree of drive. If they are working in a field requiring drive, better that they work with a male associate to provide in his personality what they lack.

Self discipline

Discipline is a part of the way up. Like it or not, this is true. And there are the two aspects of it. The external discipline which is exerted on us from without and the internal discipline which we impose on ourselves. Industrial firms are big and complex organizations, and their efficiency depends on the maintenance of reasonable discipline. If this is the structure within which he is going to work, it is important for the young man to adjust to it just as soon as he can; and it is important that this adjustment be as complete as possible. If this is not so, anxiety results from conflicts of the young man's aggressive drive with the frustrations of discipline. He must learn to go along with it.

The recent university graduate often has difficulty with discipline. I have seen a number of young men as patients who have been caught in this situation. They have been tense and anxious through conflict with the discipline of authority, and on account of their inability to make progress. Those who have come to me like this have nearly all been young people who have recently graduated from the university, and have only a short time ago taken their first position in commerce or industry. In other words it is a condition to which those just out of university are particularly vulnerable. They have had a few years on the campus with very great freedom. They have grown accustomed to it. Any restraint is now felt as irksome and irritating. They are so used to talking about individual freedom that they feel any discipline as unnecessary restraint. 'I should not have to tolerate this. I won't.' And if they are not careful they are looking for another job. I have heard this story many times from young graduates, whereas the lad who goes to work without going to the university seems to escape this particular difficulty.

Beware the lack of external discipline. Nobody likes to talk about discipline. It reminds us too much of home and school. But if you think back, you will remember when discipline was first relaxed just after leaving home and school, that you and your friends had a phase of rather foolish and unruly behaviour. This is a part of growing up. Strangely enough this phase may have a counterpart in later life.

In the lower eschelons of the firm we are subjected to quite a degree of direct and indirect discipline. Most of this is unspoken, and comes to us rather indirectly through the structure and customs of the firm. We are rarely very conscious of it, but at the same time we know that it is there. It constrains us, and influences us so that our behaviour conforms with the standards of the firm. But when we make the rather abrupt change to senior executive status, we are suddenly relieved of this external discipline. All at once, we are much more our own masters. It is like leaving school again. We feel the freedom of it. Both pleasure seeking forces and aggressive drives are liable to be given uncontrolled expression. It is uncontrolled because the individual has not replaced the external forces of discipline with something from his own personality.

Avoid a too rigid self discipline. People very greatly not only in the degree to which they are self-disciplined, but also in the way in which they achieve their self-discipline. This point has

[76]

become very clear to me through psychotherapy with patients. Sometimes the self-discipline is very harsh, while others attain a similar standard of behaviour with very little effort. Harsh self-discipline is a feature of people who have obsessive characteristics in their personality. And of course persons with masochistic traits often exert a very severe discipline on themselves so that the discomfort of it fulfills their psychological need to be hurt and feel satisfaction in it.

There are others whose harsh self-discipline comes from their intense determination. They are set on making the way up. They drive themselves, and they discipline themselves. I have seen many such men as patients. Their approach to life is so demanding of themselves that they have a very high level of anxiety which makes them irritable and difficult. This usually shows at home rather than at work where they assert terrific efforts to control themselves. But at home their tension shows through. They are irritable and make life impossible for their wife and family. We should all aim to drive forward and discipline ourselves; but there are better ways of doing it than this.

Cultivate an effortless self-discipline. This idea may at first seem a contradiction in terms. This is not so. It is something very real for those who are fortunate enough to attain it. This is something very important. Please go along with me.

We are inclined to think of discipline as a kind of struggle. It appears to us as a contest between our wish to do something and the forces, both internal and external, which would stop us; or it may be that our wish is not to do something, and these other forces work on us to make us do it. It need not be like this. There are people who know what has to be done, and they just do it. These are persons of mature personality. There is no struggle. It is effortless. They do it just naturally. They are not tired out by the constant exercise of self-discipline as others are, nor are they made tense and anxious by the struggle. This is first class living, and this is what we should aim for.

How can we attain effortless self-discipline? First, let me stress the point that this is not just an idealistic phantasy. It is something realistic, it is something that can be attained. I have seen people as patients who have made great strides in this direction. A low level of anxiety is a necessary part of the background. It is shown in a relaxed body and mind coupled with a general feeling of natural ease. The relaxing mental exercises of which I have spoken can be a great help in this direction.

Then there is the way in which we deal with the problem itself. There is the task facing us. On the one hand we would procrastinate, and on the other, we would take ourselves in hand and make ourselves do it. Both are wrong. This is akin to those polarities of thought such as, good and bad, body and mind, management and staff. Let us transcend these polarities of thought. Let us think at a different level. Here is the task. The question of procrastination does not arise. Nor is there any need to make ourselves do it. We just do it, and the process is effortless.

Don't discard this idea as impracticable. There is every likelihood that it can help you. Just give it a chance, and don't expect it to come all at once.

Prejudice

Prejudice can ruin our chances on the way up. This happens more frequently than we might care to admit. Within the firm we do not choose our workmates. We are usually thrown together with others of very different background and interests, and with values which differ from our own. We often have to work closely with some such people. If we are given to prejudice our relationships are strained, and we simply do not function as affectively as we should. The same applies when we come to negotiate with others outside the firm. If we have a prejudice against that sort of person, our aggression is mobilized; we control it, but our hostility is sensed by the other person and successful negotiation is jeopardized. Thus, those who have the responsibility of appointing negotiators should always consider their representative's personal prejudices. For instance, if the other person is a Jew, it would be foolish to appoint a representative for negotiation who is prejudiced against Jews.

Because of his prejudice, he is emotionally involved and his judgement is distorted.

The seeds of prejudices are sown in early childhood. There are two common situations which lead to prejudice. In general the child takes on the attitudes, modes of behaviour and moral standards of his parents. This process is known as introjection. If the child is brought up in a home where racial prejudice is the rule, he is likely to grow up with the same prejudice.

We also develop prejudices as a result of specific childhood experiences. A sensitive working-class boy who through scholarships is sent to an upper class school, and who is humiliated by the thoughtless teasing of other boys on account of his social status, may easily develop a prejudice against upper class people. Similarly, an upper class boy in a state school may develop a prejudice by being teased or bullied by the others. As we would expect, in psychotherapy prejudiced patients commonly disclose such incidents, but the interesting aspect is that they have rarely associated these incidents with their present-day tendency to prejudice.

Prejudice also works as a defence when we are not quite secure in certain situations. The man who has not been to the university is often insecure in his dealings with graduates. As an unconscious protective reaction he feels against these people. Such a person may not hire a man simply because of his university background. It is usual for such a decision to be unconsciously rationalized so that some more plausible, but actually false, reason is given for the decision.

Prejudices concerning wealth and social position are common. The individual finds it hard to get along with such people, and in this way his general efficiency is impaired. For instance, at present I have a very good and relatively successful architect as a patient. He has come up the hard way and is prejudiced against people of wealth or social position. This has made him both envious and hostile. When such people approach him as clients, he becomes anxious and hostile so that he simply does not function effectively.

Prejudice is related to suspicion and jealousy. Suspicion of course is a protective state of mind. It is a kind of automatic guard against being too trusting, and so being in danger of exploitation by others. In this way a moderately suspicious attitude may well be prudent and helpful in business. But over suspiciousness is crippling as it impairs our relations with other people. Attitudes of suspicion towards whole groups of people, racial, social economic or sub-cultural are based on unconscious prejudice, and hinder our progress in life as our relationships with these people are so emotionally coloured that our judgement is clouded.

Jealousy, like suspicion, is a kind of crude protective mechanism. It spurs us into action to keep our mate. This is a biologically useful purpose; but if jealousy becomes too active it can be ruinous. It spreads out from the mating of man and woman, and extends into our relationships with those at work.

Close, exclusive friendships provoke prejudice in others. A patient discussing problems at work said to me, 'I can't stand so and so; he is always with that other man.' It is very unlikely that the person in question was even aware that his friendship was in any way giving offence to others. Yet it was, and this type of reaction occurs quite easily.

Any close friendship which develops exclusive qualities is potentially dangerous and often destructive; and within the firm such a friendship will sow the seeds of prejudice, suspicion and jealousy. The reasons for this are twofold, practical and psychological. The practical reason is that others in the firm are in fact excluded from easy contact with the two people in question. This results from the exclusive quality of their friendship. The other reason why such exclusive friendships disturb others is the latent homosexual element in these relationships. In most cases there is no physical contact, and the two individuals are not aware that their friendship is latently homosexual. The same applies to the others who work with them, but although they are not aware of the homosexual element, it still unconsciously makes them feel aggressive.

We can transcend prejudice by examining our attidudes. We should all do this. If things do not go well between us and some other person, let us examine our attitude. Is there something about his manner or his background that makes us prejudiced against him. We will find very often that this is the case. This may not only apply to our dealings with individuals, but may also apply to different branches of our work. We say to ourselves that we are not so good at this particular aspect of things. We feel that we are not so gifted in the area. This may be so. But it is also a possibility that our less successful performance in this area is due to some unconscious prejudice rather than any lack of innate ability.

Problems of isolation

The young man often thinks of success in terms of money, leisure, entertaining and hosts of friends. This immature dream is seldom fulfilled. More often, the further we go on the way up, the more we tend to become isolated.

Wealth and position tend to isolate an individual from his fellows. In our leisure, we are usually more at ease with people like ourselves. If we go away for a holiday with others, we usually go with friends who are roughly of our own status. This makes things easier in a material way about arranging money matters, and it also makes things easier in conversation. There are fewer psychological barriers. The man of increasing wealth and position finds it harder to find such companions. Many of his old friends of school days and early life seem so limited in their interests that their company, which he once enjoyed, now seems a bore. There are plenty who would take their places. But it is clear that they benefit from his friendship in a material way; and he recognizes them as hangers on. The dream of success with parties and hosts of friends has somehow melted into the reality of isolation and loneliness.

Top executive status isolates one from others in the firm. I can hear you say to yourself, 'But I take steps to stop this. I am just the same to everyone.' This of course is a delusion. It is just wishful thinking. We are what we are. This is inescapable. The boss cracks a joke with the office boy. But they are not on an equal footing. In this it is the boss who is deluded rather than the office boy.

I know that some American firms try to establish the principle. 'We are all equal here. It is only that we do different jobs.' These glib slogans deceive no-one. There may be some superficial comraderie. But the boss is the boss, and his psychological isolation is just as complete as ever.

The executive of course has contact with his subordinates. But this does not break his isolation. It is a guarded contact. From the very circumstances of the situation, the subordinates have to be 'yes men'. We hear a lot of executives who say, 'I won't tolerate "yes men". I encourage my young men to be forthright and disagree with me.' Yes. Yes. But the young man knows very well when it is wise to disagree, and when it is wise to hold his peace. There still remains a lack of real candour. This is on both sides. The executive cannot be fully candid with the young man. His isolation is greater than he suspects. The lack of candour with which he is surrounded impairs his perception of real situations, and he tends to lose touch with basic facts of the business.

We need the banter and criticism of friends to keep our feet on the ground. As the executive proceeds on the way up he becomes more isolated, and almost exempt from the chastening influence of the criticism of friends. In my own experience the most conspicuous examples of this process have occurred in the elevation of barristers to the bench. There is plenty of give and take at the bar, and barristers delight in scoring off one another in friendly and witty criticism. But when a man becomes a judge, he is suddenly denied all this. I can think of two instances in which there has been quite a change of personality. It would be kind to attribute the change to their increased responsibilities on the bench, but I believe that lack of criticism from friends is the more important factor. In the same way, in war time the C.O. of a regiment suffers from a similar isolation which may have its effect on his personality.

When there is no criticism we come to think that all our ideas are right. This soon extends beyond the area in which we are genuinely expert. We have all seen this in the top executive who suddenly speaks as if he were an expert in fields far removed from his area of competence. As there is no criticism, he believes

[82]

that he is right; and he gradually comes to develop the habit of expressing himself as if he had some kind of God-given authority. We have all seen examples of this.

Isolation leads to suspicion. The lack of criticism seems unnatural. He unconsciously feels that there is something phoney going on. 'They don't say anything to my face; they must talk about me behind my back.' This type of reaction may lead to the close-lipped suspiciousness which we sometimes see in the top executive. This is most likely to occur in a man who is introverted, and who is not really secure in himself.

What can we do to prevent the bad effects of isolation? There are two things we can do. In the first place, we can strive to prevent ourselves becoming too isolated. This means a conscious effort to maintain contact with friends who accept us as an equal, and who do not defer to us on account of our position. The second way to combat the deletions effects of isolation is through being aware of the problem as you are now from reading about it.

Growing older

Some grow old well; and some grow old badly. Just look around you, and you will see how true this is. Of one man they say, 'He's great. We shall all miss him when he retires.' Of another, 'He's a b . . . . The sooner he goes, the better for everyone.' These comments are more than just a reflection of a man's popularity. In a way they are an assessment of his success or failure in growing older. It is probable that the first man did not have these endearing qualities twenty years ago. They are something that he has gained on the way up as his personality has matured. It is probable that the second man has not been a b . . . all his life. It is just that on the way up he has not grown old well, and now they can think of nothing good to say about him. You and I, how will we fare in this? Some judgements we may escape or defer, but this one is inevitable, and it is part of the way up.

And in this respect there is a further sobering thought.

Respect for age is at a low ebb. This is the era of youth. Wisdom is sought from the mouths of the young, from the students rather than the professors who teach them. This does not make growing old any easier. We must face it. For you and me there will be a stiff standard demanded.

What do we aim for in growing older? There are many things. We aim for peace of mind and ease of body. We like to see our family, our children and our children's children. We want wisdom, and we want understanding. And we are practical people, who live in a world of material reality. We want some kind of financial security. And it is not too much to say that we want friends and respect. Perhaps beyond all these things we seek some spiritual understanding and philosophical acceptance of life and death.

'Just the ideas of the establishment', says the young man. But don't forget that the ideas of the establishment are founded on generations of experience.

What can help us grow older well? We must be relatively free of tension and anxiety. If our struggle on the way up has conditioned us to a pattern of habitual nervous tension, we are not growing old well. I have seen people as patients who have spoken along these lines. 'I know I am tense now. I am working flat out. I must make this next promotion. It will be better than, and I shall relax.' This is widespread delusion. The young man is only conditioning himself to a pattern of life of chronic anxiety. He will not grow old well. Yes. He needs to make this next promotion. And if he is really on the way up he must make it, but at the same time he must learn to work with reasonable ease in himself. Then growing older should bring still greater ease of mind.

Grow older; grow wiser. This does not come automatically to everyone. It is essentially a matter of learning by experience. Yet it eludes many of us. The events of life, and all our day to day encounters in business are in this way experience, and must not just brush over us. Somehow the lesson of these daily incidents, the meaning of it all, needs to be integrated into our personality so that we gain by it. In learning by experience in this way, the bad incidents, the failures, the humiliations and all the things that go wrong are as good as the good experiences. We talk of learning by our mistakes. But do we? I once published a book describing a particular technique of psychiatry; to emphasize the point that we learn most from our mistakes I quoted only cases that had gone wrong. If we can integrate our experiences of life, we profit by them. This is the basis of wisdom, and we grow old well.

Grow older, and grow in understanding. But how does it come to us? How do we do it? It must surely be a matter of using our experience of life to full advantage. Around us at our business there are things, material things, machines, filing cabinets, typewriters; there are also the people who work these things. The perception of their feelings is a part of our life experience. We learn to know how they feel. This is empathy. And we grow older with understanding.

Grow older, but keep the mind open to change. There is change all around us. New buildings, new machines, new processes, new was of doing things, new patterns of thought, new standards of behaviour. This is life. And on the way up we have been in it to the full. But growing older brings two problems with the process of change. As we grow older our joints are likely to get stiff. We stiffen in the mind too. As with the joints it is a physiological process. In the case of our mind it is due to reduced blood supply to the nerve cells of our brain. But, as with our joints, we can do a good deal about not getting too stiff in the mind. The second aspect of the problem is that any change requires mental adjustment, and so is likely to increase our level of nervous tension. In order to combat this, we may unconsciously develop the habit of avoiding change. This is just another unconscious defence. But to grow older well, we must keep with the changes of our times. We don't have to know all the technical aspects of the changes. But we must keep with it, so that we know what the changes are about, their meaning and their significance. And of course the easy and natural way of doing this is to maintain contact with younger people. Their conversation discloses the changing ways of looking at things, changing patterns of thought.

[85]

But we must do more than this. Besides keeping up with the things around us, we must ourselves retain our capacity to change and to adjust to change. The rapidity of the changes of the present era will make growing older so much the more difficult. There are greater adjustments to be made, and more is expected of those growing older. We must keep ourselves flexible. This comes of doing new things ourselves. The pleasure and security of the old way must not deter us from the continued experience of new things.

We must watch our physical health. We should exercise. We should occasionally exercise to the point of being physically tired, but as we grow older, never to the point of exhaustion. We can let ourselves get out of breath, but not to the extent of being distressed.

We need games and leisure and fun. Exercise which combines leisure and fun will help us to grow old better than will a dull routine of physical exercises.

Many executives eat, drink and smoke too much; if your happiness depends on this, you are living second class. I know that everyone cannot live first class; but if you are on the way up you will find that second class only goes half way.

The medical evidence of the harmful effect of excess weight, excess alcohol and excess smoking is irrefutable. But they say, 'A short life and a gay one. That is for me.' Others put it, 'Life would not be worth living without these simple pleasures'. This is what you hear in the second class.

What makes people grow old badly? Rigidity is an important factor. Much of it develops out of the psychological defence against anxiety by avoiding change and simply doing things by routine pattern. This can be avoided in the early stages of the way up; but by the time we are growing older the pattern of rigidity can become fixed, and change is then very difficult.

Irritability is a common feature of those who grow old badly. This is a symptom of chronic nervous tension established in the pattern of anxiety in earlier years. An unpleasant suspiciousness may also mar the process of growing older. It comes of insecurity which itself is the product of underlying anxiety. The

[86]

individual is insecure. He feels that younger men are waiting to oust him from his job. He is suspicious of them. When they talk together he feels they may be discussing some way of making things difficult for him. So he becomes narrow and petty, and sometimes vindictive. His suspicion makes him hold on to all that he has, and he is frightened to hand over to others even small and unimportant jobs in the firm.

The pain and discomfort of the bodily changes of ageing have their effect. But we can deal with the bodily changes at two levels. First, there is a lot we can do with the sensible use of diet, exercise, rest and leisure. Secondly, we learn to adjust to minor degrees of bodily discomfort without it distressing us. In achieving this, our inner calm is most important. When we are calm our bodily discomfort no longer makes us irritable and distresses us. Anxiety and nervous tension always make our minor aches and pains so much the worse.

We must avoid over-compensation as we grow older. This is common. The senior executive, consciously and unconsciously, becomes aware that he cannot do so much. So he drives himself harder and harder. He is unconsciously driven to prove it to himself that he is still the same man. He is as good as ever he was. So he embarks on a train of activity to prove this. He does more at the office. He drinks more and he plays harder. But any perceptive colleague in the office will notice a strange incongruity about it all. It is not so much that he does more at the office, but rather that he has to let everyone know about it. He not only starts playing harder and drinking harder than he has for ten years; but he is inappropriately flamboyant about it. It may even go further. He may have an affair. And he lets people know about it. All this is only a silly and pathetic way of bolstering up his morale, when he feels himself growing a little older.

As we grow older, we must develop some inner philosophy, or it will all have been in vain. I said I was writing a practical book. So I am. An inner philosophy is just as much a part of practical living as it is to be free of nervous tension or depression.

But what do we mean by it? The man who over compensates at the threat of growing older is lacking in an inner philosophy.

But this is a negative description. What are the positive signs? Perhaps it is a balance between striving and acceptance. And the balance may not be the same for each of us.

3

Coping with others

Coping with anxious people

This is the age of anxiety. Civilized man has lost the knack of keeping his nervous system running smoothly. Many of us keep our bodies fit by exercise and the application of the common sense rules of health. But there are very few among us who would not be better and more productive people if we were more relaxed. It takes animals, including man, some time to adapt to gross changes of environment. We have not completely made this adjustment to the new stresses of civilized urban life. Our bodies have adjusted fairly well because there is not much required of them; and our brains have adapted well because we can use them to advantage in this new way of living. But the management of our emotions has lagged far behind, as this way of life does not allow us free expression of our emotions. We have not learned to let ourselves relax as we work in these new conditions, and the result is that nearly all of us have an unduly high level of anxiety.

Nervous tension is the dominant psychological factor of our time. We want to get the best out of our staff. This means that we inevitably have to cope with many anxious people.

Anxious people tend to make us anxious too. This is one of the problems of the young psychiatrist. He is likely to catch the jitters from his patient. Even if this does not show openly, it makes him tense inside, and the interview does not go as well as it should. The same thing happens every day in any large firm. There is a failure of communication. Things don't go as well as they should, and the smooth running of the organization is impaired.

I expect most of us are aware of this phenomenon in our important interviews at top level. Because of the importance of these discussions, we are inclined to make mental post-mortems of the incident to see where it went wrong. On these occasions we can often recollect that one of the others was very tense and this somehow put us off, so that we failed to handle the situation quite as well as we would have hoped. It is easy to see this psychological process at work on these important occasions, but the same thing happens in hundreds of minor interviews and discussions without us being aware of it. Just as with measles, we can catch the anxiety of a person very inferior to us in the organization. Some workman comes to us with some genuine complaint. He is very nervous. If we are not careful we can take on some of his anxiety. We just feel a little uncomfortable. But this is sufficient to impair our functioning, so that we do not deal with the situation quite as well as we should.

Don't tell the anxious person to relax. He is well aware of his nervous tension. He is doing his best to relax. But he can't. If you refer to it, you only make him more anxious. This is all so obvious that you would expect people to follow such a simple rule. But they don't. Even people who should know better make the same mistake. Go to any hospital and you will hear doctors irritably telling patients to relax.

Communicate your own relaxation to the anxious person. This is something quite different. In the first place you must be relaxed and at ease in yourself, and sufficiently so that the other person's anxiety does not stimulate anxiety in you. Then you must communicate this ease of mind to the other person.

Please don't say to yourself, 'I'm not a psychiatrist. I am a business executive. I have not got time for all this.' If you were to say this, I would answer, 'If you are really on the way up, you must have time.' It is these subtleties, these intangibles, which distinguish the man who is really on the way up from the others. And strange as it may seem, once you get into the way of this kind of approach, it takes very little time indeed and in the big picture time is saved through your functioning more effectively.

Words are no good in helping an anxious person to feel at ease. It

is no use explaining that there is nothing to worry about. Even if this is true it does not work, and of course in nearly every case it is not true. There is something to worry about. Anxiety is an emotional state and is not allayed by logical explanations except in extremely simple cases which are in fact quite rare. It is even more complex than just letting the anxious person see that we are relaxed. He must see it. But there is more to it than that. He must feel it. Somehow he comes to experience our relaxation. We must bring him to do this. It's not too difficult. And once you can do it you will find that it works. His words are staccato. You talk slowly and the words are drawled. His face is tensed up with anxiety; your inner ease smooths out the muscles of your face. His eyes are wide and popping and he searches your face; your eyelids are so relaxed that they flop closed for a moment. Please do not think that I am exaggerating. This type of reaction happens with intuitive people every day. Perhaps you have not trained yourself to be sufficiently perceptive to observe it.

But our relaxation is not indifference to the plight of the other person. We are concerned for him, but still completely at ease in ourself. He senses this from the comments we make. An 'umm' or an 'ah', not spoken, but breathed the right way at the right time may have more meaning to an anxious person than ten minutes of logical explanation in words.

I must emphasize just once again that such an approach does not waste time. It is just the way of doing it. It is the way of getting the best from anxious people.

People with problems like our own are likely to make us anxious. For this reason we often find it hard to cope with such people. This is rather strange. One might think that similar problems would produce an affinity of feeling. But it usually does not work like this. Knowledge of the other person's problem, stirs up our own worry, and makes us tense.

A junior comes to us. He is having trouble with his immediate superior. We try to tell him to coast along with his superior and get on with him as best he can. This very simple situation is likely to make us anxious, if it so happens that we ourself are having difficulties with our own superior. As a result of this it may well happen that we do not handle the interview as well as we should.

Avoid the unconscious tendency to provoke further anxiety in anxious people. When the other person is anxious, and we ourselves are at ease, we have power over the other person. It is as if we were big and strong, and he were small and weak.

We have assertive propensities within us; some more than others, and men more than women. This is part of our biological heritage. This tendency sometimes comes to the fore when an individual finds himself in a position of power. This is the psychological background of the traditional arrogance of the petty civil servant who finds himself in a position of authority. The executive does not abuse his power directly in this way because he is better educated and more sophisticated. He has an understanding of the situation when it is as simple as this. But we do not see it quite so clearly in the case of our power over an anxious equal. Our assertive tendency may unconsciously exploit the situation. We find it is easy to make him more anxious, and so increase our power over him still more. It is just a kind of senseless bullying. Yet, if you will look about, I am sure that you will find examples of this going on around you.

Coping with hostile people

Hostility provokes hostility. This is our biological heritage. It is the law of the jungle. In primitive times it has helped us to survive by preparing us to meet a hostile adversary. But a hostile reaction in ourselves is usually not the best way of coping with a hostile business competitor, and it is certainly not the way to deal with someone in our own firm who comes to us with hostility in his speech and manner. So we must learn to transcend our primitive biological heritage, and remain calm in the face of expressions of hostility. In doing this we must in fact not be hostile for the other person senses hostility even when there is no overt display of it.

This is one of the earliest lessons in psychiatry. One might wonder why a patient would be hostile to his doctor. This is often a part of the treatment. The patient is hostile with someone else and transfers it on to the doctor. We experience the full blast of this hostility and the patient learns by the experience. An essential point is that the psychiatrist does not react to the patient's hostility. He remains calm, and is thus able to manage the situation. Similar circumstances arise in the office every week. If we remain calm, we can handle it all right.

Insecurity and frustration breed hostility. Insecure people feel threatened when others in similar circumstances would not feel this way; and the experience of feeling threatened evokes a hostile reaction as a defence. If we see that an individual is insecure by nature, we should do what we can to counter this by giving him all the security we can in his work. This means a stable job, no sudden and unexpected demands from him, and as far as possible some emotional support in the way of companionship and friendliness.

Frustration is a common cause of hostility that can be largely prevented. This reaction is seen in an exaggerated form in the army. Foolish orders, unproductive tasks, orders given and then rescinded. These things happen in the firm only in less dramatic form than in the army. Employees are frustrated and soon become hostile. Don't rationalize, and say to yourself, 'They are paid for the day; they don't care what they do.' This is wrong. Even the most casual employee underneath his offhand attitude has some psychological need to be doing something useful. If this is not satisfied, he is frustrated and tends to become hostile. You may ask how I know this. The answer is simple. I have often asked a patient why he has given up his job when the wages and conditions of work were so good. 'One says do this, another says do that; and half the time there is nothing to do; if I stayed there I would go silly.' Remember, boredom brings as much discontent and hostility as overwork.

Be relaxed when faced with a hostile person. This is the key to success in these circumstances. As soon as we perceive that the other person is hostile, irrespective of whether anything aggressive has been said or not, we should consciously take ourselves in hand. As we talk with him we let ourselves experience the feeling of relaxation of both the body and the mind.

With a little practice it is not hard to do this. And we say to ourselves whatever happens we will not react aggressively to the other's hostility. If the circumstances should require a display of authority on our part, we do it with fairness, clarity and logic, without our judgement being clouded by an aggressive reaction to the other's hostility.

If we remain relaxed, the other's hostility peters out. This happens every day in psychiatry, and the same principles hold for events in the office. We let the other blow off. We don't say anything to bring us into more direct collision. This would only feed his aggression, and he would be more hostile than ever, with the result that it would be so much the harder for ourselves not to fight back.

I can see you asking yourself, 'But why shouldn't I fight back. I need not tolerate his hostility. I can give as good as I take.' Yes. I understand how you feel. But once you fight back, the situation is virtually out of hand, and a sensible resolution of the difference is so much the more unlikely.

It is better to say 'umm' and 'ah' rather than to confront the hostile person logically. It does not matter what we say at a logical level, the hostile person will argue with us, and as he does so he will become more hostile. But if we just say 'Umm' and 'Ah', we show him that we are listening, but it gives him nothing to fight about. This can be done very easily and naturally so that the other person does not realize what we are doing. He soon calms down; his hostility peters out, and so does the pressure of his ideas which were previously driven on by the force of his aggression. We are now in a position to deal with the situation quietly and sensibly, and now, after blowing off his hostility like this, the other can accept a direct approach from us in a way that would have previously been impossible.

When hostility is expressed as chronic irritation, should we have a confrontation? The situation which we have just discussed was an acute one. The person was openly hostile and we managed the situation by a passive approach. But sometimes it is quite different, and the hostility is shown in a kind of chronic irritation. If we use the passive approach, the chronic irritation just continues.

It may be that you sense this hostility in some subordinate. Nothing is said. But you sense it, and you know it is there. It is most likely that he has some grievance. What do you do? You can call him into your office and ask him what the trouble is. If you do this, he may just look at you blandly and say, 'What trouble?' You are then forced into the position of explaining that you sense some hostility about him. This is hard to do, and if the other person maintains that there is nothing wrong, the situation is only aggravated. On the other hand, he may take your lead and blow off his hostility and then you can handle it in the passive way just described.

An indirect approach is usually better. You suspect he has some grievance, and feels hostile to you. He may feel that some other employee has been promoted over him, or that you in some way favour the other man. These things may be true, and consequently difficult to handle in direct confrontation. In such circumstances nothing is lost by the indirect approach. This is essentially emotional and non-logical. It is merely a matter of communicating to the chronically hostile person that you have nothing against him. This is done indirectly. Never attempt to do it directly in words, or an impossible situation will develop. Instead of avoiding him on account of his hostility, have a few words with him. It can be just about the weather, an enquiry about his family, anything; a slightly favoured job or some task which is rather sought, communicates the same idea.

Think before you regard such an approach as just pandering to a difficult employee. I would rather consider it as a civilized way of resolving a problem in human relationships.

Some superior people consciously use indirect means to help others with their hostility. These people are really superior because their action transcends both the biological urge to meet hostility with hostility, and the commonly accepted civilized attitude of leaving the hostile person to fry in his own juice.

I can explain more clearly what I mean by an example. A man in his middle forties consulted me. At first he was rather vague about the purpose of his visit. However, he eventually disclosed that he was really seeking help about his wife. Some years ago, during an operation, she had suffered a cardiac arrest. This had resulted in some brain damage which had caused a change of personality into a difficult and hostile woman. The husband was a very perceptive person and he realized that if he felt irritable or upset by his wife's hostility, it made her worse although he said or did nothing to communicate the way he felt. I helped him to cope with his own unexpressed hostility and things improved. This man is living life at a higher level than most of us will attain; but it still may be possible for many of us to use just a little of this approach in our everyday dealing with hostile people.

Coping with depressed people

The individual may not realize that he is psychologically depressed. This raises a problem. It is often quite hard to recognize psychological depression. In fact it is probably one of the most commonly missed diagnoses in the whole of medicine. This happens when there is little or no subjective feeling of depression or sadness. In these circumstances the most common sign is simply that the person is not getting on with things as well as he should. Everything seems more difficult than it used to be. It is hard to get started. He may be slower at doing things. There are a lot of causes for symptoms like these. Laziness is one of them, and in these circumstances this comes to the employer's mind quite easily. Strangely enough, the depressed person himself often blames himself for being lazy.

Don't try to jolly up the depressed person. Don't say, 'Come on, pull up your sox, snap out of it.' The unfortunate man is trying to do this, but can't. So if you approach him like this you may only make things worse.

Don't go up to him and start laughing and cracking jokes in an attempt to cheer him up. This would make a normal person happy so that he would join in the fun and laugh with you. But the person with nervous depression is different. He is not quite normal, and in his present condition this sort of thing only irritates him.

And the logical approach is no good either. It does not help to explain to him that there is nothing to worry about. If you show him that everything is all right, you do not convince him, and he argues with you that it may all go wrong tomorrow. In these circumstances he often adds, 'I know it will go wrong because I have not done my work properly.' This is part of the depressed person's way of looking at things, and as a result the logical approach simply has no effect on him.

Let the depressed person share some of his worries with you. It only takes a few moments, and it may be a great help to him. It is a matter of your keeping quiet and letting him talk. Show that you are attentive and concerned for him. You do this by your manner, not by what you say. Help him to keep talking by an 'Umm' or an 'Ah' when he seems doubtful about continuing. It can all be done in a few minutes, and although the time with him is short, there is no question of him feeling that you want to get rid of him. This is communicated by your leisurely manner. Here we can learn again from psychiatry. If there is only a short time available to help a depressed person, do not try to cover a number of topics. If you do this, he is aware that you are in a hurry and he feels rejected. The shorter the time available the more leisurely we must be, then this feeling of rejection does not arise.

Let the depressed person feel that you like him. This is easily the most effective way of helping him. At first thought, it may seem rather odd; but you accomplish it by what you do and not by what you say. In these circumstances it is the communication by acts which counts. By spending a little time with him, you let him know that someone likes him. This has an infinitely greater therapeutic effect on the depressed person than no end of logical explanation.

Avoid the temptation to keep reassuring him. If you do this the depressed person starts to argue with you, and the friendly feeling which you want to convey to him is lost.

Don't let anyone downgrade his job while he is depressed. The depressed person has difficulty in coping, so he comes asking for a lower grade job. He says his present job does not suit him; it is too difficult; he is not up to it. By all means give him a lighter job while he is not well, but don't permanently downgrade him while he is depressed. What he tells you in this state is coloured by his depressive pessimism and in fact is not true.

I do want to emphasize this point to you. I have seen some dozens of successful men who have started on the way up. They have suffered a minor depressive phase and have temporarily lost their previous robust optimism. I can remember several whose first words to me were, 'I resigned my job last week, and thought I would take the opportunity to come and see you'. They were all well and as capable as ever again in two or three weeks, but the job had gone for ever.

If a man resigns his job for no apparent reason, talk with him to see if he is depressed. If you have doubts, get him to defer the matter, and ask for a doctor's opinion. One of the problems is that the depressed person is often unaware that he is depressed or that he is sick at all, and such people are very resistant to the advice of friends who suggest seeing a doctor. Make him defer his resignation, otherwise you may lose a good man, and he may lose a job which he cannot easily replace.

How do we deal with a depressed colleague? Sometimes the picture is slightly different, and the depressed person shows an obstinate determination to manage things himself. He often says, 'Leave me alone, I'm all right.' But you can sense that he is not all right. So what do you do? Even if you can get him to admit that he is not functioning as well as he should, he will probably say, 'But I can get over this myself, thanks'.

There is an important principle involved here. The executive with nervous depression should somehow be relieved of his responsibilities about decision making. This is essential as his distorted pessimistic judgement will lead to missed opportunities, and the acceptance of prices below their proper value. If he is seriously depressed he should be given leave of absence under medical care. If he is not so bad, he should still be sent on a holiday so as to avoid the bad effect of his depressive pessimism on the staff. In arranging this one can usually rely on the depressed person's full recovery.

[98]

4

Communication

How we communicate with others

Successful communication with people is a necessity on the way up. The strange thing about it is that most people just take it for granted. They seem to think that we can all speak, therefore we can all communicate. But it is not as simple as that. One man will convince us while another in the same circumstances will not. This is not a matter of mere chance; it is a matter of skill in communicating. In the final analysis your skill in communicating with people and coping with them will determine the smooth running of the firm, whether it be big or small.

It is not sufficient to know what you want to say and say it. This is only spouting words, this is not communicating. True. Many people communicate well who have never studied the subject. These are gifted people who have intuitively hit upon the psychological mechanisms involved in communication, and use them quite naturally and unconsciously. But less gifted people like ourselves can gain a great deal by consciously studying the psychological processes involved. Then in a little while they become second nature to us, and we use them quite naturally without thinking about it.

You may well ask for my authority to write on such a subject. As you know, I am a psychiatrist, and communicating meaningfully with one's patients is the main skill of psychiatry. I have made rather a study of this. In fact I have written a book and a number of scientific papers on the subject.* The same principles of communication apply whether it is in medicine or business.

*THE MEDICAL INTERVIEW, Charles C. Thomas, USA 1957
RAPPORT WITH THE PATIENT, The Lancet, September 1954
COMMUNICATION WITH THE PATIENT, The Lancet, March 1960
WE TALK WITH THE PATIENT, Consultant, March 1962

In fact, what I am about to do, is to apply the principles of a psychiatric interview to a business setting.

But there are some things which we must remember. Calling someone into your office, and giving him an order is not an interview in the psychological sense, nor is it simply a matter of being tactful when you tell another what to do. A psychological interview works on elements of the other person's mind so as to bring about changes in his manner of thinking and feeling. This is the approach to the problem which I hope to bring to you.

Real communication involves the other person in full understanding. This is something much more than merely hearing and comprehending the words that are spoken to him. Real understanding involves more than the intellectual appreciation of the meaning of the ideas which are expressed. Ideas are not just isolated entities, and to convey full understanding they need to have some kind of emotional tone attached to them. This adds to the fullness of the understanding and the completeness of the communication. This must be our aim. We have our ideas; and we must communicate them so that other people understand fully and are convinced.

Do not say to yourself, 'But we are talking about business, and this is quite different from psychiatry'. No, you are wrong. The business interview follows the same psychological principles as the psychiatric interview.

The successful communication of cold business facts involves some emotion. Without this emotional component the facts are in the nature of mental abstractons. The other person may fully comprehend all that we are saying to him. But without this other quality, it does not really concern him. There is no active interest. Without emotional involvement the facts remain isolated entities in the mind of the individual. He does not feel any need to do anything about the ideas which we have conveyed to him. But when we involve him emotionally, he becomes interested and the idea takes on a fuller dimension of meaning. He is no longer toying with it as a mental exercise. He is involved. And the idea takes on the quality of being good or bad. It is only then that it has significance to the other person in a way that the pure idea in itself cannot have.

You may say to yourself, 'What if I communicate by writing a letter; then there is no emotion.' But there is if you write well. You set it out so that the reader comes along with you, as it were. This is the type of emotional accompaniment which is essential to full communication.

The emotional accompaniment may be communicated by our relationship with the other person. If we know the other person, or if circumstances allow a personal approach, we can use this in our communication. We engender in the other person a feeling that he likes us. He feels that he is for us; and the feeling soon extends to the idea which we are communicating. This is a matter of first forming rapport with the other person before you attempt to make the important communication with him. This is a sound psychological principle, and like most sound psychological principles we find that it is applied intuitively in our ordinary life. Thus there is the common practice of the business lunch. Over good food and a bottle of wine we first get to know the person. Then the emotional state between us is such that he will come to accept our communication in a way that has full meaning.

Sometimes we can use our own emotional feeling to involve the other person. It is more difficult when circumstances are such that a personal relationship is not possible. We then have to communicate some emotion with the idea itself. But this has to be done indirectly or it is not accepted by the other person. For instance, we cannot communicate emotion by saying, 'This idea of mine is very good, you will like it.' This would only make him suspicious. So we have to communicate the emotion indirectly. There are many ways of doing this. A very effective way is simply to speak of the idea with enthusiasm by the way you say the words. This is an expression of your own emotion. The other person unconsciously picks it up, and experiences your emotion. He then has some feeling for the idea as well as an intellectual appreciation of its meaning, and the result is a communication with full understanding.

The opposite situation arises when someone reads a statement with monotonous voice and deadpan expression. There is no emotional accompaniment, and the chance of the communication producing any action is very much less. If in fact such a communication does produce some action, it is probable that the idea of the communication was already known to the other person and already had some emotional significance to him.

Sometimes we can present the idea unemotionally, but in a way that evokes emotion in the other person. This can be used successfully when we have not had the opportunity to establish a relationship with the other person; and when circumstances are such that it would be improper to express our own enthusiasm for the idea. This comes most easily when the idea we are communicating has some latent emotional significance to the other person. If we suspect this, we can play on it in the way in which we present the idea. A simple example of this psychological mechanism would arise if we were to discuss some minor improvement in running the business with some senior person in the firm. The successful running of the business is a subject of latent emotional significance. So we offer the idea in a way which will bring the latent emotion of the other person into the open; and in so doing we bring the statement of an idea into the realm of a full communication.

Sometimes we can link the idea we wish to communicate with some subject of emotional significance to the other person. If the other person is keen about success, it may not be too difficult to link our idea with being successful. Then the other person's emotion concerning success spreads to the idea we are communicating. Or money may be a suitable subject. Don't forget that money is not only a cold fact of business, but it is also an emotional topic in the minds of those who run the business. With other people it may be possible to link your idea with some more humanistic concept. If the other person is someone particularly interested in doing good, it may be quite a simple matter to associate your idea with this aim; then the other person's emotion about doing good comes to include the idea of your communication.

There are different levels of communication. To get the full meaning across we need to use more than one channel, as it were.

Our expression, our gestures, our attitudes, our behaviour, and the actual way we say the words all add to the meaning of what is said. By this means ideas expressed in the words that we use become emphasized and clarified so that a meaningful communication is possible. These matters apply to any communication, but we shall see how they become increasingly important when we are talking with someone who is opposed to us, and who does not want to accept the ideas which we are expressing.

The cold facts of business are expressed by the logical use of words. It is essential that the facts are expressed accurately. So we must always be clear and precise in our logical use of words. Simple words and short sentences express the logical meaning more clearly. Concrete nouns rather than abstract phrases are more easily understood. In business long words and complex sentences are an affectation. They are used as a kind of 'one-up-manship', and are something to be avoided in the logical expression of facts. Complex ideas can still be expressed in simple words with a minimim of technical jargon. This is the art of the use of words. But we must always remember that full communication requires much more than the logical expression of the facts.

We tend to over-value logic. Of course, as a psychiatrist I see more of this than you do. It is no use telling a person not to be afraid of going in a lift if he feels that way. Logical communication has no effect on a phobia. This is psychiatry; but in business the same principle applies, and we tend to over-value the importance of logic. The reason, of course, is simple enough. It is our ability of logical thought which has allowed us to master our environment in the wonderful way that we have. This leads us to forget that the mind has other ways of functioning besides the logical one. If these other emotional aspects of the mind are denied, the logical facts are left in a vacuum, and are not translated into action.

The logical use of words commits us; but if we are not sure of the other person we may not wish to commit ourselves. This is an ordinary situation in negotiation between two people at any level of employment. We need to sound out the other person

H [103]

before we can commit ourselves. This is a necessary part of our interaction with the other person before we know enough of him for an unequivocal logical statement. The person who is skilled only in logical communication is at a disadvantage in this phase of any negotiation.

Sometimes we can communicate more effectively by the implied rather than the logical meaning of words. In this way we can test out the other person before committing ourselves by logical communication.

A simple example of communication by the implied meaning of words is the common way of opening a conversation. 'It has been a nice day today.' The logical meaning is a comment about the weather; the implied meaning is something quite different. It is simply a greeting and an offer of friendship. 'I want to be friendly.' In this case the advantage of communicating the offer of friendship by the implied meaning of words rather than their logical meaning is one of prudence. Because the offer of friendship has not been stated as such it cannot be openly rejected. We do not leave ourselves open to being snubbed. In this way, by the implied meaning of the words, we can test the other person, and find out how he feels without committing ourselves.

Other conventional phrases such as, 'How are you?', carry an obvious implied meaning. There is no real inquiry about the individual's health, and the implied meaning is simply, 'I greet you; I want to be friendly'.

We can introduce an idea by the implied meaning of words, and the other person can take it up or leave it as he wishes. A simple example will let you know what I mean. If there is some problem which we know to be concerning the other person, we might say, 'How are things?' This implies the same idea as would be expressed logically, 'How are you getting on with the problem that we both know about?' If we communicate the idea logically, we force the other person either to discuss the problem or to reject our enquiry in a way that will come between us. In most circumstances this is poor negotiation; so we express the idea indirectly by the implied use of words, and give the other person the chance of avoiding the subject and still retain a good relationship with us. He can do this by simply saying, 'Things

[104]

are all right; I am fine.' We get the message that he is not ready to discuss the problem, and we move to another topic. This type of communication is most important in dealing with tense and anxious people in psychiatry. You can see that the principle has equal application in the ordinary matters of business communication.

We can test the other person by introducing ideas peripheral to our main topic. We probe, and find out how the other person feels about things close to the central idea which we want to communicate. By the implied meaning of words we can offer ideas which he may accept or reject as he sees fit. If he accepts the peripheral idea, it probably means that we can go on and offer the central idea. If, on the other hand, he rejects the idea which we have offered indirectly in this way, there is no loss of face on our part, no head-on collision; and both of us come to understand how the other feels about things. This type of interchange is a prelude to any sensible and productive negotiation, and is most effectively carried out by communicating by the implied use of words.

The implied meaning of words can communicate an idea very subtly. In commerce and industry there is an emphasis on 'the cold hard facts of business'. When the young executive is talking with others, he may well fall into the way of thinking only of the cold facts; whereas many of the ideas concerned in running a business are not cold facts at all, but are really ideas of considerable subtlety which need an equal subtlety of communication. It is this type of communication which is best made by the implied rather than the logical meaning of words.

Let me give you a simple example of what I mean. Suppose you are discussing various members of staff with a view to appointing one of them to some new job. There will be factual considerations which you communicate logically, but there are also intangible impressions which are less than fact, but at the same time may be most important. Some-one might say, 'If you were to ask him, he would tell you that he could do the job all right'. The implied meaning of course is that he is over confident. Without using this form of communication, we cannot exchange our ideas in this type of discussion with full competence.

By the implied meaning of words, we can say those things which should not be said. They should not be said because they might give offence, but at the same time effective management demands that they must be communicated.

Let us examine the ethics of this. I have seen many young people as patients who have been suffering from anxiety. They very often say to me that they must see someone and 'get things straight with him'. They feel that by resolving the uncertainty they will relieve their anxiety. It so happens that such a confrontation would have a disastrous result in inter-personal relations. So I suggest that the patient should get the message across indirectly rather than directly. However, the young patient has sometimes argued that this would be dishonest. He feels that to be honest one must be direct. This of course is a perversion of honesty. The real honesty is to get the message across, and at the same time be able to maintain good inter-personal relations. To achieve this we convey the message by the meaning that lies between the words rather than the logical meaning of the words themselves.

The emphasis, the pause, the accompanying expression, and the way the words are spoken all contribute to the implied meaning. This is obvious. But how often do we neglect this simple principle. The business memo may record the words that were said, but because it omits these other aspects of the communication, it may carry quite a wrong meaning. Perhaps more important is the recording of the minutes of a meeting. It may be that each word is taken down by a stenographer, but when it is read out at the next meeting the words have missed the subtlety of the original communication. If we are at the meeting, and what we say is being recorded verbatim, we should aim to rely on the logical rather than the implied meaning. Even if it is a less adequate means of communication, in these circumstances it is less open to subsequent distortion.

Sometimes a grunt or a sigh, or an 'Um' or an 'Ah' can communicate what words cannot say. This is known as unverbalized phonation. These sounds which we make are full of meaning. They communicate an idea just as clearly as any logically constructed sentence of correct syntax. They are primitive means of communication, and are used to communicate rather basic, primitive ideas. The actual meaning of what these sounds communicate depends both on our knowledge of what the other person is thinking, and the emotional relationship between the two of us at the time, as well as on the tone of voice in which the non-verbal communication is made. In this way productive communication takes place easily and smoothly. We say 'Um', and the other person knows that we understand what he is saying, and that we want him to continue. And we communicate the idea without any interruption of the other person's flow of speech.

In another setting there may be a slight pause. From the ideas that have just been expressed, we know what is the subject of thought in the other person's mind. We say 'Um'. He accepts this as an invitation and expresses the ideas. Whereas if we were to tell him by the logical use of words to express what he is thinking, his flow of thought would be interrupted and he would be put on guard.

In still other circumstances we say 'Umm', and the other person knows that we are in agreement with him. But if we say it with a slightly firmer intonation he gets the message that we are doubtful or in disagreement.

A grunt can clearly communicate agreement without formally committing oneself. Again, this is not duplicity. It is the type of sophisticated interchange of ideas which are often a necessary preliminary to any successful negotiation. It is a part of the 'feelers' that one has to make. In these circumstances the affirmatory grunt lets the other person know how we stand without any real commitment on our part. He is then free to continue and express further ideas in the knowledge that we agree with him as far as he has gone.

A grunt can clearly communicate disagreement without the problems of formal confrontation. This again gives the other person the cue as to how we feel. In negotiation head-on collisions are to be avoided as they both inhibit the flow of ideas and destroy the emotional relationship between the two parties. A disagreeing grunt can inform the other person that we do not accept what he says in a way that allows him to modify what he is saying so that the two of us are not brought into head-on collision. Communication in this fashion allows the free flow of ideas, back and forth, so that some useful agreement finally results.

Unverbalized phonation is the best means of communicating one's feelings in a time of crisis. If there is very good news for the individual, or very bad news, and he tells us about it; we can only communicate our own feeling to him most effectively by unverbalized phonation. In these circumstances the unverbalized phonation is given its full meaning by the expression on our face. In a similar way we can communicate delight, anger, sympathy or disappointment when we are given news of some business matter. These are basic feelings, and in these circumstances the primitive quality in unverbalized phonation adds to its effectiveness as a means of communication.

Pauses and silence can often communicate meaning which cannot be expressed in words. Don't just think, 'Lovers communicate in silence, not businessmen'. Silence also has a place in the business interview. A relaxed pause in the conversation between two people can often be used as a communication of friendliness. We are only relaxed when we are with friends. So by being relaxed a person says, 'I am relaxed; you can relax; we are friends in this discussion'. In appropriate circumstances the minor pause can drift into a period of silence, and the meaning of the communication is more profound. In this way silence says what words cannot say.

The meaning of a pause or silence is determined by the idea which has just been discussed, as well as the emotional relationship between the two persons. The pause can thus give weight to the idea which has just been logically expressed.

This of course is a common trick of rhetoric to emphasize an idea. It gives gravity, and allows the idea to sink in, as it were. On other occasions the pause is an invitation to the other person to ponder the idea which we have just communicated. It is made in a way to give him time to think about it. We have seen that a pause or silence may be a communication of friendliness. But if the discussion has been going badly, and if the logical disagreement has aroused aggressive feelings, then a pause or silence can be used as an unequivocal expression of hostility.

Silence can be used to increase the other person's level of anxiety. If the other person is too comfortable, too much at ease, he may unconsciously feel so secure that he does not tell us the things that he should tell us. He feels so secure that he lacks psychological motivation to discuss these matters. In such circumstances it is necessary to increase the other person's level of anxiety. The person who is a little uneasy is often more likely to tell us the things that he should. A long pause often achieves this very effectively.

In our culture silence often produces anxiety. If there is a sudden lapse of conversation at a dinner party, the momentary silence causes anxiety in those present. In fact many people talk, not for any real communication of ideas, but merely to avoid the anxiety of silence. This situation can be observed at any cocktail party. We evoke the same mechanism in the business discussion when we deliberately become silent in order to make the other person anxious.

A skilful interviewer learns to tolerate silence without anxiety. This is a necessary basic skill for anyone who negotiates with others at any level of business. We use our own emotional state to influence the other person. This is one of the elementary skills of psychiatry, and the same principle applies to two people talking together in any circumstances. We achieve the tolerance of silence by being relaxed and at ease in ourselves, and by an understanding of the psychological mechanisms which are operating as we talk with the other person.

Silence can be used to force the other person to talk. This is an aggressive use of silence. It is used much more than it should be in psychoanalysis. In an interview which has been well conducted it should not be necessary to fall back on such a manoeuvre. As silence of this nature is aggressive, it necessarily provokes hostility in the other person. Nevertheless, under some circumstances a person can simply be forced to speak by our remaining silent. In this it is the other person's mounting anxiety which forces him to speak. We ourselves remain completely relaxed, and if we want to put further pressure on the other person to reinforce the effect of the silence, we let our eyes look at him steady and in a completely relaxed fashion.

The absence of a normal pause can be used to avoid discussion of an idea. This technique is used in two rather different sets of circumstances. Sometimes we want to expose a person to an idea in the hope that he will accept it uncritically by the process of suggestion. In the process we aim to communicate the idea, but at the same time prevent the other person examining it at a logical level. So we express the idea in a rather inconsequential way, and then very quickly, with no pause at all, the next phrase contains some other very important and quite different idea. In this way discussion or critical evaluation of the idea is avoided. We can use such a procedure when we know that the other person is unreasonably opposed to the idea which we are communicating.

The other way in which we use an absence of normal pause is to communicate in an authoritative way that this is not at present a subject for discussion. This mechanism differs from the one just described in that it is a conscious process. The other person gets the message, 'He does not want to discuss this'. Whereas in the former case, it is a process in which the other person is exposed to the idea and then this attention is immediately diverted to the second idea so that he is hardly aware of what is going on.

Facial expression is an important means of communication. When we first meet the other person, our facial expression makes a communication which influences the way in which our subsequent discussion is carried out. The logical content of what the other person first says will be materially influenced according to whether our expression is open, friendly, guarded, hostile or poker-faced.

Our expression, of course, alters the meaning of the words that are spoken. We are familiar with the idea of two levels of communication going on simultaneously. There is the logical

[110]

meaning of the words, but our facial expression may give those same words an extra-verbal meaning. A very simple example of this mechanism occurs when someone is formally reprimanded for some technical offence, but the person giving the reprimand communicates by his expression that the other person is not to take the reprimand too seriously. There is thus a simultaneous communication of two separate ideas.

This same principle may be used in a business discussion. For example we may have to put forward some idea, and at the same time we can communicate what we think of it by our expression.

Facial expression communicates ideas without the individual being aware as to what is going on. This is why the study of the expression of other people, and the easy control of our own is so important in psychiatry, and it is equally important to anyone who aims to negotiate successfully in business.

We must be practical about this. Many people, perhaps most people, tend to feel that any serious study of facial expression is beneath them. Better for us to look at it this way. Skill in communication is essential to the way up. Facial expression is a part of effective communication. Let us find out as much about it as we can.

We must avoid letting our face express ideas which we do not wish to communicate. This is obvious, and the most common way in which we fail in this respect is in the unconscious expression of hostility. Our face expresses it without our knowledge. When this happens the other person is provoked to act aggressively, and the discussion deteriorates. It is also very easy for the inexperienced individual to let the other person know that he is worried about certain things by the unconscious expression of anxiety in his face. This of course places him at a disadvantage in any negotiation. If our face expresses excitement or eagerness when negotiations are about to be finalized, it might provoke the other person to demand a higher price.

A 'poker-faced' expression is unconsciously sensed as unfriendly, and puts the other person on guard. An awareness of the danger of disclosing their feelings by their expression has stimulated many young executives to cultivate a kind of 'poker-faced' expression. This may be effective enough for a game of poker, but it is inappropriate in business discussions. It tells the other that this person is on guard. He is holding himself in check. He is not open with us. Therefore, we had better be careful in our dealings with him.

The far more effective way of avoiding unintentional disclosure of our feelings by our facial expression is simply the cultivation of ease and relaxation. If in fact we are really relaxed, we do not feel either anxious or hostile. These emotions do not arise within us and there is no likelihood of inadvertent unconscious communications by our expression.

The expression on the other person's face may tell us important things which he did not want to communicate. It is a matter of training ourselves to be observant of quite minute details, and at the same time appearing quite casual about it. We must on no account give the other person the impression that we are observing him too closely. If this were to happen, he would immediately be on guard, and our chances of bringing him to our way of thinking would be so much the less.

We particularly watch for the signs of anxiety, and hostility. Changes in the facial expressions are more important than the expression itself. If we are going well, and he is developing a friendly feeling towards us, the lines of the face become less marked, and there is less tension in the muscles around the mouth and eyes. But if something happens that makes him hostile or anxious, the lines become more marked, the muscles are more tense so that the jaw may be pushed forward, the upper lip pulled back to show the teeth and the upper lid of the eyes is more fully retracted and the pupils dilated.

Watch for change of expression with change of topic. We not only observe the changes of emotion from the unconscious changes of expression, but we can tell exactly what brings about these changes by noting the way they are associated with different subjects of discussion.

To do this we have to learn to do several things at the same time. We have to maintain a logical discussion at a factual level, and at the same time make various extra-verbal communications.

At the same time we control our emotional relationship with the other person, and still at the same time we watch for those unintentional communications of expression and connect them with the ideas in his mind. While all this is happening we must be calm and at ease and perceptive of all that is going on. This may seem a lot, but with a little practice you will find that it comes quite easily. Practice these things in all the inconsequential discussion of everyday life, and then the procedure will come easily to you on important occasions of business.

You can read the other person's expressions more easily if you make him a little anxious. If he is really at ease he may not make these emotional responses to different topics of discussion. So we increase the level of his anxiety by use of the methods we have discussed. This has the effect of sharpening up his emotional responses, and we have a correspondingly better chance of reading these unintentional communications.

Ideas are also communicated by gesture. Persons of hysteric personality habitually use this method of expressing themselves in their everyday life. A sweep of the hands and a shrug of the shoulders adds further meaning and emphasis to what is said in words.

When we are talking we are often not fully aware of what gestures we are making. So it is wise to pay attention and see that we learn to use our gestures appropriately. The person who talks without gestures appears to us as lifeless and quite unconvincing. On the other hand the person who relies too much on his gestures appears theatrical, and is also quite unconvincing. Our gestures need to be natural and easy, and to carry the quality of sincerity.

The way a person sits in his chair may tell us quite a lot about him. The anxious person sits on the edge of his chair. As a person comes to feel hostile, he leans forward a little. The position of the hands gives many cues. A person commonly sits with his arms resting on the sides of the chair and his hands projecting over the edge. If he is really relaxed, the wrists are flexed and the hands flop down. But very often the wrists remain straight and the hand is held projecting forward. This indicates nervous tension. A change in the attitude of the hand is quite important. With hostile feelings the fingers tend to close up from the semi-flexed position of natural relaxation. This reaction, which is quite easily observed, is interesting in that it would seem to represent an unconscious move to make a fist in preparation for fight.

A person's behaviour clearly communicates his degree of confidence about the matter in hand. This is valuable information for us, and we can often use it as a guide in how to start the discussion.

The person's degree of confidence or lack of confidence is communicated by the way he walks, the way he speaks, the way he sits down and by his posture while seated. Any hesitancy, stiffness or awkwardness is usually a result of anxiety and reflects a lack of confidence about the matter in hand.

We must distinguish behaviour which is aimed to mislead us. The person who lacks confidence about the matter in hand will probably try to cover it up by assuming a confident manner. We recognize this because there is an incongruity about it. It lacks the spontaneous quality of real confidence. There may be clear signs of tension in his face which are inconsistent with his outwardly confident manner. The assumed confident manner has stiffness about it which is absent in real confidence. This results from the underlying anxiety. Nervous tension produces muscle tension, and the limbs do not move quite so freely. His arms don't swing as they do with a confident person, and the stride of the gait is stiff and short instead of being free and easy.

An appearance of extreme relaxation may cover up a high degree of nervous tension. I have noticed that the facade of extreme relaxation is a common psychological defence among young executives. When they come to see me they flop down in the chair, the outward picture of complete ease. Then they say, 'Can you help me with my nervous tension?' And when I come to examine them, I find that under this facade they are very anxious indeed.

In a business interview or discussion of any kind it is important to estimate the level of the other person's anxiety so that we can make an appropriate approach to him. These people who use a facade of relaxation to cover up their anxiety are recognized by the extreme quality of their relaxation. The individual seems aware of his relaxation in a way that a truly relaxed person does not. Another diagnostic point is that this relaxed facade breaks down if you ask the person to do something. In a medical setting this is easily achieved by some simple examination such as listening to the heart to taking the blood pressure, and then the individual's full anxiety is quite unmasked. In a business setting a similar end can be achieved by asking him to write down something or better still to read out something. This will clearly show whether or not he is trying to disguise his anxiety by his posture of extreme relaxation.

Some of the things we do have a symbolic meaning and communicate at a deeper level. It is ordinary politeness to offer a cigarette. But this is more than just being polite. It is giving something. In this way it is a symbolic offer of friendship, and so has an effect in the emotional relationship between the two people. Of course the offer of the cigarette must be made at an appropriate time. If the moment is inappropriate the offer will make the other person nervous. In the same way, if you take the other person's hat and coat, you symbolically establish a kind of host-guest relationship which will be reflected in subtle undertones in the discussion.

If you interview the other person across a desk, you impose a symbolic barrier. This separates you, not only physically, but also status wise and emotionally. It will activate past memories when he was interviewed by the headmaster or bank manager. This may be what you want, if you seek to use your authority over the other person. But the very use of authority may detract from the interview by inhibiting the other person so that he does not volunteer things that might be useful to you.

To keep the other person waiting angers him, shows your superiority and also discloses yourself as discourteous. In this way we see that a single act may have a number of different emotional consequences. In fact this goes for most of our behaviour. For the purpose of the discussion it may be necessary to show our superiority over the other person. This is a very commonly used way of achieving it, so much so that it rather smacks of the amateur.

The way our office is furnished acts as a communication. It shows all who come to us the image we have of ourselves. This image may be quite near to what we really are, or it might be something quite different, the person that we would like to be.

Do we present ourselves as important by having a pretentious office? This may impress some. Others with more perception may feel that the person with a pretentious office is basically insecure in himself. This is why those who have achieved too rapid success feel they need a pretentious office. They have gained material success, but they have not made the way up in the full sense.

Do we present ourselves as a homely person by having an informal comfortable office. Then those who come to see us are put at ease. But such an office does not help us to be authoritative. Some men, who find home a rather bleak place on account of domestic conflict, react by trying to make their place of work as homely as possible. A photograph of wife and children on the desk is a communication of unmistakable meaning to female visitors.

Do we have an office of bare essentials with everything geared for efficiency? In such we present ourselves as an image of masterful efficiency. In doing so we also disclose ourselves as cold, and rather lacking in the human touch.

Communication with another person takes place at both conscious and unconscious levels. At a conscious level there is the communication by two distinct channels, the logical meaning of the words and the extraverbal, implied meaning of the words. As we talk we consciously evaluate these separate communications and in our reply we consciously use both methods.

We have considered the importance of non-verbal phonation as expressing meaning in our ordinary business discussions. These are the 'Umms' and 'Ahs' the sighs and the grunts that are a part of normal communication. An important factor in successful negotiation is to remember that the individual is aware of the giving and receiving of some of this non-verbal phonation, but is quite unaware of giving and receiving other parts of it. The successful negotiator learns to bring as much as possible of this communication into his consciousness so that he can use it purposefully to help bring the other person to accept his ideas.

At another level there are communications which are for the most part quite unconscious. But these still have an important effect on any discussion. There are two distinct groups of such communications. In one there is the unconscious communcation of hostility and anxiety about the logical ideas expressed. This in turn is unconsciously perceived by the other person. The second group of unconscious communications concerns the emotional relationship, the rapport, between the two individuals. Both these groups of unconscious communication are made primarily by expression, gesture, posture and behaviour. The psychiatrist learns to bring this normally unconscious communication into his awareness. Some skilful negotiators learn to do this intuitively. But others who wish to negotiate to the maximum of their ability can learn to use these usually unconscious communications just as psychiatrists do.

We receive communications without being aware of them, but they still influence us. I wish to emphasize this as it is such an important principle, and those not familiar with the ordinary events of psychiatry may have difficulty in appreciating its full significance. A good example of the way in which we can be unconsciously influenced is in subliminal advertising. In it a message is flashed on a moving picture film so quickly that viewers are not consciously aware that anything has happened. Yet it was proved beyond doubt that such messages influence people's behaviour. Because of the obvious dangers of political misuse, subliminal advertising is prohibited in most countries. But it demonstrates very clearly that people can be influenced without being aware as to what is going on. We can use similar principles in ordinary business discussions to help bring difficult people to tell us what they should and to accept our way of looking at a problem.

How do we make communications for unconscious reception? This is not as difficult as it might seem. The psychiatrist does it

[117]

regularly both to bring people to give up irrational beliefs and to lead them into better patterns of behaviour. There are a number of different approaches using different channels of communication.

I have mentioned the way in which we can use logical communication to express the idea in a simple phrase, and then very quickly, without any pause at all, we express some other idea which is very important to the other person. This is again expressed in a short staccato phrase. The idea is then immediately followed up and elaborated. In these circumstances the other person is hardly aware that he has been exposed to the first idea. The similarity to the principle of subliminal advertising is obvious.

Another simple way of making communications for unconscious reception is to communicate by our expression, gesture, posture and behaviour while we are engaging the other person in logical communication. This is used continuously in psychiatry. An example in a business situation arises when we interview someone who is hostile to us and on guard against us, and we want to bring him to our way of thinking on some matter. Because he is hostile and on guard he will not accept our logical communications. So we engage him in logical communication on some other matter. While he is occupied in this we communicate friendliness by our expression, gestures, posture and behaviour. He is not aware of this because he is preoccupied with our logical communication. But he is influenced, and unwittingly becomes more friendly towards us. As a result he is not so much on guard, and is now much more likely to accept our proposition.

For full communication one must use all the channels available. This means a knowledge of all these mechanisms and experience in their use. Without this one is not equipped to use his full potential in any business discussion or negotiation. Some gifted people sense these things and come to use them in intuitive fashion. Others need to study, understand and practice these psychological principles; then as they become more familiar with their use, they find that they are using them quite naturally and without conscious effort. This is what happens to the young psychiatrist as he becomes experienced as a result of his training.

Anxiety is the most common cause of failure of communication.
Again, this is the everyday experience of the young psychiatrist.
Anxiety inhibits our mental functioning because we have to
occupy some attention in controlling our anxiety. This makes it
difficult to manage effectively all the different things that are
going on at the same time. Communication is impaired, and we
do not acquit ourselves as well as we should.

**In communicating with anxious people we must first establish
rapport and then they will understand us better.** In fact we should
establish rapport for any interview or discussion; but if the
other person is anxious, rapport is all the more important. It
reduces the other person's level of anxiety so that his ability to
understand us is not inhibited. He can communicate more
effectively with us. Otherwise we do not know what is really in
the other person's mind and negotiation is so much the more
difficult.

**In communicating with obsessive persons we should be precise,
accurate and detailed.** Communication of generalities tends to
confuse the obsessive because this is contrary to his habitual
pattern of precise thinking. As a result he gets muddled, and
the quality of our discussion deteriorates. In a similar way, the
obsessive is ill at ease with vague ideas. He does not handle
these well. So we make it easier for him by expressing ourselves
in accurate and detailed fashion. On the other hand, if the
circumstances of the discussion demand it, we can introduce
vague and generalized ideas to increase the level of the obsessive's
anxiety.

**If the other person is an hysteric, we must remember that he is
probably exaggerating to try to convince us.** This is part of the
hysteric defence. Basically, he is rather insecure, so he exag-
gerates to bolster up his lack of security. In this way he thinks
that he will convince us, as he feels more at ease in himself.
This is just another example of the way in which the individual's
anxiety determines his pattern of approach to things.
**Don't forget that communication is a two way affair, so we make
it easy for the other person to express himself.** This is a matter of

avoiding hostility and of reducing the other person's anxiety by establishing a friendly and trusting relationship. We respect the other person's emotional state. If he is nervous, we do not hurry him. We give him time, both by speaking slowly and naturally, and also by introducing some rather unimportant topic so as to give him the chance to collect his thoughts. The other person either consciously or unconsciously realizes what we are doing, and reacts by feeling friendly towards us, and at the same time he comes to express himself more easily because of his reduced level of anxiety.

Rapport in business communication

In medicine, rapport is the emotional relationship between patient and doctor, when the patient trusts him and feels that he can help him. When the patient feels like this he will disclose his innermost feelings without reserve. The psychiatrist uses this to help the patient to a better state of mind. It is the basic element in the psychological treatment of nervous illness. Without rapport we can do little to influence another person in the way that he thinks, feels and behaves. This psychological mechanism which is so important in the medical interview is equally important in the business interview.

In business, rapport is the emotional state between two persons who are friendly and trust one another. This is the background of all successful communication. When we have rapport we are at ease so that we communicate clearly in a way that we cannot if we are not at ease. In the same way, when we have rapport we perceive the other person's communications clearly and with full understanding. When we have rapport, we can lead the other person to tell us what he should, and we can bring him to accept our ideas in a way that is not possible without rapport.

Don't react by saying to yourself that this is all too involved. 'I am a business man. I am busy. I have no time to make phoney friendships with everyone whom I interview.' Just let me explain. It is not quite like this. With a skilful interviewer, rapport is not a laborious process. It comes very quickly, three or four minutes in most cases. Nor is there anything phoney about it. Rapport is a very natural human relationship. And remember this. It does not matter how great your authority, the other person will not volunteer that vitally important extra information unless you have rapport with him.

The first task of the interview is to establish rapport. It used to be taught in psychiatry that the first task of the doctor is to make a diagnosis. If we start off immediately to make the enquiries to settle the diagnosis, the friendly feeling of trust of the patient eludes us. If we do not gain it at the start, it will probably mean that we never gain it. So making the correct diagnosis is pointless, as without rapport it is unlikely that any psychological treatment will be successful.

Now, let us apply these principles to a business interview. If we immediately enquire of the other person the purpose of his visit, we are like the unskilled doctor who immediately sets about finding the diagnosis. If we immediately try to clarify the purpose of the other person's visit, we remain strangers to each other. Then it does not matter how well we have clarified the logic of what we have to do, our discussion will never fulfill its full potentiality for the simple reason that there is no rapport, and as a result the two discussants are psychologically held apart.

How do we form rapport? Rapport is an emotional state, and it is determined by emotional rather than logical means. It is very important to remember this. The doctor's higher qualifications and professional knowledge do not help in the formation of rapport. Neither does the businessman's knowledge of his subject. Rapport is an emotional state between the two individuals, and is determined only by psychological reactions which concern the emotions.

It is no use telling someone, 'You can trust me'. This is an attempt to establish an emotional relationship by logical means. It simply does not work. In fact, it has the opposite effect. By talking logically about trust you alert the other person. His suspicions are aroused. He immediately thinks, 'Why this talk about trust?' And instead of a relationship of friendly trust, there develops an attitude of suspicious alertness. A similar state of affairs develops in response to any other logical approach to an emotional state. One of our problems in studying this is that we are well accustomed to analysing our logical responses, but we are very much less experienced in analysing our emotional reactions.

We offer friendliness; and this brings the other person to be friendly towards us. This is an act of primitive simplicity, and like many such acts we do it instinctively. We do it without thinking about it, just because it seems the natural thing to do. This is all part of our intuitive perception of the psychological needs of the situation. You may well ask, 'If this is something that happens naturally, why bother to write about it'. The reason for my wanting to describe it is simple. True, this is a reaction which takes place naturally, but we are very inclined to examine things, and if we don't see a logical reason, we are likely to discard them. We think, 'Time is money; don't let us waste it, let us get down to business straight away'. This is the danger. If we follow this principle which might seem logical enough on the surface of it, we omit these little offers of friendliness, we never form real rapport, and things just do not go as well as they might have.

A few moments spent in natural courtesies is not time wasted. It allows us to offer friendship as a first move towards establishing rapport between the two of us. The comment about the weather or the news topic of the moment is nothing but an offer of friendship. If the young executive tries to be so efficient in saving time that he omits these natural courtesies, he loses something which he cannot make up subsequently in any logical communication.

If we appear to be in a hurry, the idea of friendliness simply evaporates. When in fact time is short, we must always remember to make these first few minutes appear utterly leisurely. We can make up for lost time in the logical part of the interview, never in the emotional part of establishing rapport.

We offer friendship by letting the other person know that we are interested in him as a person. The half a minute spent in enquiring about his family or about some project in which he is personally involved, will let him know that we are interested in his welfare. I would like to to make an important point here which is relevant to us all. Please do not interpret what I write as a series of slick moves which we can make to take advantage of the other person. No. That is not my purpose at all. I rather aim to describe natural psychological reactions which bring fulfillment to both parties. In other words, we concern ourselves about the other person, not to exploit him, but because we feel a concern for the human being with whom we are dealing. Then there is genuine two-way rapport between the two of us, and the interview can achieve its full potential for both parties.

We can offer friendliness by acceptable symbolic acts. These are little things which we do intuitively. If a child wants to be friendly, he gives you something, perhaps one of his play things. The offer of a cigarette is a symbolic act of friendliness, the meaning of which far exceeds any factual analysis of the situation, and it unconsciously brings the two people into a closer emotional relationship.

We take his coat, we pull up his chair. Don't think that these are just trivial acts of no consequence which everyone does without thinking of it. They are of consequence because they have the unconscious significance of symbolic acts of friendliness. For this communication to be fully effective it needs to be done naturally and instinctively, and it needs to be accepted without thought by the other person. Then these acts, like all forms of symbolic communication, appeal directly to something deep in the mind without any conscious evaluation at all.

If we want the other person to trust us, we must be open with him. This is obvious; yet people fall down on this elementary principle. In bringing the otherperson to trust us, is it as well to remember that he does not expect unlimited openness. It is rather like other matters of everyday life. We have a good friend. We are open with him and he trusts us. This is a part of our friendship, our rapport together. But our openness together is not complete. For instance, we do not disclose to each other the details of our intimate life, as this would be inappropriate. So it is in business. We are open with the other person so that he trusts us, but at the same time the openness is not unlimited as this would be inappropriate to the occasion. And in being

[123]

open with the other person, we must not only be open in our mind, but we must communicate this openness otherwise the effect of it is lost.

A very practical way of communicating openness arises when we realise that there is something to our disadvantage which the other person does not as yet know about, but which is pretty certain to come out in our discussion. In these circumstances it is much better to get in first and openly disclose the matter. We then at least use the situation to our advantage in our emotional relationship with the other person. A medical example of this process occurs when the doctor has made a wrong diagnosis or wrong assessment of the patient. This will soon become obvious to the patient and relatives. The sooner the doctor explains the situation openly, the better for himself.

Any guarded statements indicate distrust, and prevent rapport. In most cases it is better not to make any statement at all rather than make a guarded one. This generalisation applies particularly to the beginning of an interview or discussion. At this stage of proceedings, a guarded statement immediately alerts the other person and makes him suspicious. There is no raport; communication is difficult and incomplete; and successful negotiation becomes more remote.

On the other hand, at the end of the discussion things are different. We then often have to summarise our conclusions in some kind of acceptable fashion. It may well be that we then have to make a guarded statement, but at this stage it does not have quite the same bad effect, as the question of rapport will have been settled.

We show the other person that we trust him; then he comes to trust us. Again, I am not advocating a slick way to exploit other people. As with a medical interview, a really successful business interview must be based on trust. Many people are suspicious and guarded; we must bring them to discard their suspicion, and trust us in the way that they should.

To do this we show the other person that we trust him. Perceptive people, who are mature and well adjusted in themselves, do this quite naturally. It just comes to them intuitively as the natural way of talking with someone under these circumstances. Watch a friend who is a good negotiator, and you will see this type of reaction happening all the time.

We can offer personal trust in various ways. To let the other person know that we have failed in some minor respect or that we are worried or concerned about some incident is an offer of personal trust. A person without psychological knowledge who does this intuitively may well regard it just as a means of breaking the ice.

Remember that this voluntary communication of concern is not an expression of anxiety or insecurity. It really has the opposite effect. It communicates the idea that we are so natural and open, and so at ease in ourselves that we volunteer these things which other people might well wish not to disclose.

There is another important point. We offer personal trust by letting the other person know that we are worried about something. But we always do this with some incidental item, never ever with the central item, as this of course would place ourselves at a material disadvantage. It is at the start of the discussion when we are aiming to establish rapport that we make such a comment, and at this stage the other person does not know that we do not consider this particular item important. But we must remember that in this it is not the factual situation which is important. It is the symbolism of what we do which is significant in the effect on the other person. We have voluntarily disclosed our weakness to him. As children we have done this with our mother, and later with the one whom we love, this is why it helps in the formation of rapport.

We can also offer factual trust. This really means that we disclose some weakness in our proposition without the other person finding it out for himself. I have already mentioned the matter of getting in first by disclosing some weakness which the other person would be sure to find out. But I now refer to some weakness which is unlikely to come to the other person's knowledge. Provided that this is really only a detail, the voluntary disclosure of this weakness may well so increase rapport that the main proposition is accepted much more easily. A disturbed patient may be reluctant to accept my advice to go into hospital for treatment. If I tell him that hospital may not be very comfortable, but it will be only for a short time, he is more likely to accept my advice than if I were to tell him that he will be looked after very well. The communication of my weakness that the hospital may not be very comfortable, encourages rapport and he trusts me. The thought may come to you, 'But this would not be the right approach for me'. If in fact some such thought has come to you, it means that you are assessing the situation logically. The decision that the sick person makes to go into hospital is not logically determined, it is based on trust.

We must not be anxious, as anxiety destroys rapport. We have discussed the effect of anxiety on a number of different aspects of communication. Its effect on rapport is very great indeed. We cannot put our trust in a person who is anxious himself. Under some circumstances we can accept the advice of an anxious person because advice is a logical matter; but we are biologically conditioned against emotional trust in anyone who displays anxiety. This goes very deep. The child with an anxious mother never has the same degree of rapport as the child with a calm mother. We only really trust someone whom we feel can help us. The anxious person in unconsciously communicating his anxiety informs us that he himself is unable to cope with life effectively. So we have become biologically conditioned against putting our trust in such a person.

We must be free from aggression, as the other person would sense this, and his hostility would destroy rapport. This is another basic biological proposition. We only trust someone who is friendlily disposed towards us, who is for us, who is on our side. To trust people who are against us would be biological suicide. So as a protective mechanism we have become conditioned to trust only those who are favourably disposed towards us. If we unconsciously sense aggression in the other person, this automatic protective mechanism prevents us putting our trust in him; and in place of trust our hostility is stimulated, and this of course puts an end to rapport.

[126]

Emotions and communication

Any significant communication involves our emotions to some extent. An idea without any emotion attached to it tends to become an abstraction. We have no feeling for it. It does not seem to concern us. Somehow there does not seem to be any interest in it for us; and there is no motivation in us to do anything about it.

I do not mean that the emotion concerning an idea need be so strong that we feel firmly for the idea or opposed to it. We may not be conscious of it at all. But unless the idea has an emotional tinge, it is really meaningless to us. This is something very important. Unless the cold facts of business engender some kind of feeling in the individual, he simply does not act on them.

In controlling our emotions we may inhibit our thinking. This of course occurs in the other extreme, when we have too much emotion concerning the idea. This happens when we have to put forward some pet theory, or give an explanation of some project which we ourselves have developed. In these circumstances, the whole idea involves us in a good deal of emotion. At the same time as we discuss the matter, we have to exercise some control over the way we feel. The exercise of this control of our emotions tends to inhibit our thinking. We become aware of this, and then anxiety adds to our difficulties. The answer, as with so many of these problems, lies in the way that we train ourselves to be relaxed in an easy effortless fashion.

If we consciously have to control our anxiety, we cannot pay full attention to what the other person is saying. This is a very common experience. Patients often say to me, 'I don't know what has gone wrong with me; quite often I can't understand what people are saying; I think I must be going insane'. Perhaps you have not experienced the feeling as acutely as this; but I believe that most people when they have been very tense at some time, have found it hard to follow what is said to them. Students prior to exams often have this difficulty. An interesting feature is that people frequently do not realise that it is simply a matter of inhibition by anxiety, and if they would allow themselves to relax a little all would be well again.

If we allow ourselves to become hostile, we express ourselves aggressively, and provoke resistance in the other person. This is something we want to avoid if the other person is to communicate freely with us. The danger is that this happens very easily without our being aware of what is going on. It can be provoked by very simple and quite irrational events. For instance, if the other person's visit has interrupted something we were doing, we may feel hostile about it. It is quite likely that we would deny this hostile feeling because we can see that it is irrational. This is a kind of psychological defence preventing knowledge of things that are distasteful to us. But the hostile feeling is still there; and it will have its effect on our attitude to the other person without our being aware of it. The other person picks it up from involuntary communications by our expression and behaviour; and although he may not be clearly conscious of it, he is put on guard and becomes resistant to what we say. Again, the answer to such problems lies in our emotional adjustment so that we are relaxed and at ease and are not easily put out.

If we become aggressive, the other person's attention is occupied with our aggression and not with what we say. Even if we say it clearly and loudly, as we often do when we are aggressive, it simply does not sink in. If he is asked about it afterwards, it is quite likely that he will give an accurate account of our being aggressive and of the way in which this was expressed in our face and gestures, but at the same time he will be quite vague about the logical content of our communication.

Watch for signs of hostility in the other person. This is a matter of the greatest importance. If we are aware of the other's hostility, and remain detached from it, we can do much to control the situation. But if we allow his hostility to provoke our own aggression, we lose this opportunity. So like the psychiatrist, we watch the non-verbal lines of communication for signs of hostility. If we see them, we relax so that we do not make inappropriate emotional responses prompted by our own aggression.

What do we do if the other person is becoming hostile. This is a fundamental question of psychiatry which applies equally to the business interview. First we do not let his hostility arouse our own aggression, and we do this by being relaxed in ourselves.

In most cases we want to reduce the other's hostility. We do this by both logical and emotional approaches. We switch the logical content of our discussion into some area in which he does not feel hostile. This switch of topic must not be too abrupt or the other will notice it and will respond with more hostility. Such a change of subject can often be made by picking up some phrase which the other has said and using it as a transition to a new topic.

We also deal with the other's hostility by an emotional approach. At first when he is hostile, we withdraw a little, We do this in a neutral fashion. It is not a hostile withdrawal, nor is it a retreat in the face of hostility. We can communicate this quite clearly by our expression and gesture. This temporary emotional withdrawal allows a pause for a moment, and gives the other's hostility a chance to settle. We then move closer again emotionally. We are very relaxed. He unconsciously perceives the relaxation and openness and reacts with the feeling that there is no need for aggression, and his hostility subsides. Of course, in some cases, but these would only be a few, we use the person's hostility against him.

When a person is angry he may say more than he intended. This fact is often exploited by barristers during cross examination in the law courts. Similarly, in a business interview we can make the other person angry in the hope that he will then tell us the things that he should tell us. This of course is rather a last resort to be used when other measures have failed. Its most suitable application is in cases when the other person is openly unco-operative. It is not difficult to do. It is merely a matter of needling the other person's hostility by repeated references to some topic which makes him feel hostile. The danger is that once the other person is really angry, we do not have the same control of the interview, and things are likely to be expressed which were better not said.

We must train ourselves to be continually aware of the other person's level of anxiety. This is another basic principle of psychiatry which is applicable to any kind of interview or discussion. It is merely a question of learning to read the other person's non-verbal communications. You may say to me, 'But in a business interview of high pressure negotiation, I cannot stop to work out if the other person is anxious or not'. No. Of course not. You must be like the psychiatrist and become habitually aware of the other person's level of anxiety. This in fact is necessary if one is to get the best out of business discussions and negotiations. The point I wish to emphasize is that it is something that comes quite naturally and effortlessly. It is rather in the same way as a fashion conscious woman automatically becomes aware of the details as to how other women dress. The psychiatrist and the competent negotiator are automatically aware of other people's level of anxiety.

Watch for changes in his level of nervous tension with changes in the topic of discussion. This is the way the psychiatrist comes to discover the patient's areas of conflict. If a person is putting up some proposition to us, and we observe that his level of anxiety is greater when he discusses some particular aspect of it, we can be sure that the weakness of the scheme is in this area.

In such circumstances do not expect any gross manifestation of anxiety. The signs of variation in level of anxiety to which I refer are quite subtle, and you are likely to miss them unless you take the trouble to train yourself to observe them. It is just the slight change in expression, the slight change in the position and the slight change in the tone of voice. Although these signs may be minimal, they are unmistakable, and they are just as reliable in their meaning as if the message had been spelled out in monosyllables.

When the other person is more anxious he may agree to things which he should have agreed to any way. I am not suggesting that we should terrorize people into agreeing with us. But a certain level of anxiety provides psychological motivation in the way of a desire to get things done or to get the task finished. Some people, who are difficult by nature and who lack the anxiety to provide this type of psychological motivation, may not agree with us out of sheer perversity. We can often bring such people to agree with us in the way that they should by simply increasing their level of anxiety.

[130]

If necessary we can increase the other person's level of anxiety by continually returning to a topic that worries him. This is a very obvious method. It is used by barristers in cross examination to make the witness nervous in the hope that he will inadvertently disclose information which he would prefer not to disclose. The same principle can be used against difficult people in a business setting.

We can also increase his anxiety by making him feel unsure of himself by changes in our attitude and emotional tone. We can be friendly as is natural. But if the other person is unco-operative we can quickly switch to being hostile. This switch to being hostile needs to be made suddenly and unexpectedly. There will be a reaction in the other person, and then we can quickly return to our former friendliness. The other person is left up in the air, as it were. He is less sure of himself and his level of anxiety is increased.

We can make quick changes of attitude in all kinds of ways. We can accept everything he says without question, then we can change and query all that he says.

We can engender feelings of uncertainty by quick and unpredictable changes of mood. We are easy, relaxed and happy. Then we are tense and intense; then our mood changes again perhaps to one of abstraction or disinterest. Of course the changes must be communicated naturally and effortlessly. This is a common part of psychiatry, when the psychiatrist allows his mood to change according to the momentary needs of the interview situation.

We may bring the other person to tell us what he should by playing on his innate sense of guilt. Again, this is a common manoeuvre in psychiatry. The patient may feel that the matter which is worrying him is too awful to mention to anyone at all. Yet to help him it is necessary to know what the matter is. As we all feel guilty about one thing or another, it is easy enough to hit on some minor incident about which the patient feels guilty. When we play on the sense of guilt, he will soon disclose the matter which he had previously felt was too terrible to speak about. We are then in a position to help him.

We can use this principle in business. There is something

[131]

that the other person has not done very well or very successfully. Underneath he feels guilty about this. If he becomes difficult with us, we can keep referring to this incident and so mobilize his guilt feelings.

If the other person is too frightened to tell us what he should non-verbal reassurance is effective. Parents use this with frightened children who have done something wrong. Psychiatrists use it with apprehensive patients. We reassure the other person non-verbally by communicating that we are both concerned for him but at the same time completely relaxed and at ease. The communication must contain both elements. If we only communicate our concern, he feels that we are too anxious, and he feels more frightened than ever. If we only communicate our relaxation, he interprets it as indifference or insensitivity to his plight, and so is made worse. But if we can combine these two attitudes, concern for him and ease in ourselves, he is reassured, and can communicate more easily.

A woman in business is still a woman. Let us not forget this. For the logical component of the communicaton sex makes little difference. But we have seen that the full meaning of a communication is greatly affected by the simultaneous communication of emotional undercurrents. A woman both sends and receives these emotional undercurrents of communication differently from a man.

Communication with a woman in business involves different emotional responses. Although this is obvious, I do not think that business executives take it sufficiently into account. For instance, we have discussed at some length the problem of hostility and the way in which it provokes aggression. But the normal mature woman is by nature less aggressive than a normal mature man. So her responses in the interview are of necessity slightly different.

Again, a normal mature woman is more tolerant of authority than is a normal mature man of the same cultural group. So a woman will often accept an authoritative attitude which would provoke a man into an aggressive response.

If things are not going well in an interview, a man's usual

defence is an aggressive reaction, whereas a woman's defence may be the development of an unconsciously seductive attitude. This communicaton really means, 'You can see I am a woman, so be nice to me'. The woman evokes the defensive attitude without consciously realising what she is doing, because it is a natural form of psychological defence for her. At the same time the man is unconsciously influenced by her attitude. The degree to which he is influenced may be quite obvious to an observer. But the man will still deny that he was influenced in this way. This sequence of reactions is common in psychiatry. The woman patient unconsciously uses her feminity to try to stop the male psychiatrist asking the question which will hurt her, at the same time the young psychiatrist finds it hard to realize that he is being manoeuvred in this way.

Some simple mechanics of a business interview

When we talk with someone, a number of different psychological processes takes place at the same time. I cannot emphasize this too strongly. The success of a business interview depends very much on the way in which we perceive these psychological undercurrents and make appropriate responses to them. These psychological undercurrents comprise two rather different groups of reactions. There are the extra-verbal and non-verbal channels of communication which are continually modifying the meaning of the logically spoken words. Then there is also the constant fluctuation of the emotional relationship between the two people. This in turn adds to the completeness of our understanding of the logical communication; and also provides much of our psychological motivation both to communicate and to understand the other's communications.

Preoccupation with the factual logic of what is said may cloud the communication and hamper negotiations. This is a difficult area. The factual logical exchange is all important. It must be clearly expressed and clearly perceived and evaluated. On the other hand, any over preoccupation with the essential logical communication to the exclusion of these other psychological undercurrents means that the full significance of the logical communication is lost. I think we all know young men, who are full of facts and who know all the right answers and who do all the right things, but who somehow do not achieve very much. Having seen some such men as patients, I think that many of them cone into this category. Their preoccupation with facts has excluded a full comprehension of the psychological undercurrents which give the facts full and significant meaning.

What is the real reason for the other person wishing to talk with us? This is something that we should always ask ourselves. We must not be content with an acceptance of things on their face value. Another example from psychiatry will explain what I mean. It is very common for patients to make an appointment to see me for help with their headaches. When I see the patient he tells me about his headaches and the circumstances in which they arise. This is all quite genuine. He suffers from headaches. But I soon get the impression that there is something else to it. He has not really come about his headaches at all. It is something quite different, something deeper and much more important. He comes for treatment of his headaches while he is testing me out to see if I can be trusted with the greater problems. This is a very common experience in psychiatry, and of course the same manoeuvre is common practice in successful business negotiation.

There is usually an ostensible reason, and also a deeper reason for any discussion. An associate calls in on you just to have a chat. He has not seen you for a while, and it is good to have a talk with an old friend. This is the ostensible reason for his visit; but as likely as not there is some other unexpressed reason. It may be that he just wants to see how you stand on some particular issue.

Your superior calls you into his office and questions you about the work you are doing. This is legitimate; he must keep himself informed. But the main purpose of the interview may be to see if you ar a fit person for some other job.

Remember, we will still have to live with the other person, so we don't want to make him hostile. This is important to the smooth running of our business. The man on the way up develops the knack of being able to interview a person, and obtaining what he wants from him even if at first he is reluctant to give it; but at the same time he is able to conclude the interview in a friendly atmosphere. As a result the other person remains a co-operative member of the organization. This becomes possible largely through use of the passive techniques of interviewing and negotiation.

This principle applies very dearly when a senior has occasion to reprimand a junior over some shortcoming of his work or behaviour. It is obvious that the reprimand must be communicated in such a way that a junior will not offend in this way again. At the same time it must be done in such a way as not to alienate the junior. The reprimand communicated effectively improves the junior's performance at his job without introducing any ill-feelings. In this respect remember that introverts, because of their sensitivity, are easily hurt and humiliated, so should be reprimanded with caution. Whereas the robust extravert can accept reprimand 'straight from the shoulder'.

It is usually best to start an interview from a passive attitude. We are friendly, but not over friendly, nor are we remote. We are certainly not hostile; we are just neutral in a way that can be best described as a passive attitude. The advantage of this is that we can then move into a more defined attitude according to circumstances as the interview develops. If we declare our attitude at the start of the interview we deny ourselves these easy manoeuvres. Furthermore, at the start of the interview we may not be aware of the deeper motive for the meeting, so we might easily come to adopt an attitude which we later come to regret.

From an initial passive attitude we can become authoritative if necessary. I know that some people hold the view that if you have authority, it should be used from the start and then it is less likely to be questioned. But we have seen that the display of authority in itself produces hostility in the other person so that he is unlikely to volunteer communications that would be helpful to us. Better to start from a passive attitude, neither authoritative or subservient. Then if the occasion should arise we can evoke our status and conduct the discussion from a

K

[135]

position of authority. But if we were to start with an authoritative attitude the damage has already been done in arousing the other person's hostility.

A few minutes talk on inconsequential matters allows us to assess the other person. The few moments conversation on the weather or the events of the day is not time wasted. As with so many of these basic principles, this is very well demonstrated in psychiatry. A patient cannot come in, sit down, and immediately divulge the problem which is deep in his mind. We must know a person before we can trust him with important things. From the biological point of view this is something which we have evolved because of its obvious protective value to us. So it is with the business interview. We need a few minutes to assess the other person, and equally important, we must give him the chance to assess ourselves. Without this he will not feel at ease to talk freely with us.

If the other person delays in coming to the crux of the matter, ask yourself why. It is often easy to sense this situation. It happens with patients. When it does, I can usually see that the patient is wondering whether or not I shall be sympathetic and understanding in the problem that is worrying him. Similarly in a business interview, the ostensible purpose may appear to have been fulfilled, but the other person keeps the interview going. It would seem that he has learned something about us, for good or bad, which makes him uncertain as to how to proceed. A very simple example occurs when a junior arranges a meeting with his senior for ostensibly legitimate reasons, and hopes to use the occasion to ask for some favour. If the discussion of the ostensible reason does not go too well, he naturally hesitates to come to the main purpose of the interview.

In an interview there is an unexpressed struggle for superiority. This is something very real. If you closely observe people in discussion, you will see just how true this is. It would seem that deep down within ourselves we interpret the situation as a contest. It is a symbolic fight, and from the biological point of view we can see it is an outlet for the self assertive elements of our personality. This is the psychological background. Then on top of this there is the practical reality of the situation that the interview is more likely to be a success in the material sense if we establish superiority. This is a further example of the way in which aspects of our behaviour are determined at more than one level.

Sometimes we can assume authority, and so put ourselves in a superior role. We all tend to re-enact patterns of behaviour which we have learned in childhood. As children we accepted the authority of our father or father substitute. Now in adult life we very easily fall back on this former pattern of adjustment. So when someone presents himself with authority we are very likely to accept it unthinkingly, and to fall into an inferior role without any critical examination of what we are doing.

This is one way of establishing superiority in an interview. In most cases it is not a very good way, as it involves the disadvantages of the early use of authority.

By indirectly talking down to the other person, we can put ourselves in a superior position. This is a rather trite manoeuvre; but it is effective, and has a place in discussions with difficult people.

This is effective because of the tendency of people to act out roles which are offered to them. You can see this in a group of people in social discussion. One person will somehow fall into the role of being the wise man, and another the humorist, and so on. If we offer the other person the inferior role in our interview, he will accept it much more readily than one would expect. Another psychological mechanism also comes into play. By assuming a superior attitude we communicate by non-verbal means that the other person is inferior. In these circumstances the idea that he is inferior acts as a suggestion, and tends to be accepted into his mind without critical evaluation.

We can often establish a mastery by remaining silent and at ease. This is a much more mature approach. In using it remember the two distinct components, the silence and the ease. Our non-verbal communications make it clear that this is not a hostile silence. This must be quite definite, otherwise we would provoke aggressive responses in the other person. What we are aiming to do is to lead the other person to accept an inferior role, and to accept it passively so that his aggression is not aroused in the process. That is why it is so important that we communicate our ease. If he is anxious, as he probably is, we now gain our superiority by simple biological processes. He is anxious; he sees that we are at ease; he feels that we are the better person.

If the other person is anxious, we can impose our superiority in a way that would not otherwise be possible. The anxious person is basically apprehensive and ill at ease. Because of this he feels insecure and lacks confidence. The mere fact of letting him see our own natural ease and confidence is often eough to establish ourselves in the superior role. So the accurate assessment of the other person's level of anxiety is very important. In this respect do not be misled by the young executive who uses an over relaxed and over confident manner to cover up his inner anxiety.

There is also an unconscious struggle for initiative. This is slightly different from the struggle for superiority. We may establish our superiority, yet we may still not retain the initiative. It really amounts to a complex psychological relationship between the two people so that one of them is able to determine the exact topic of discussion and the way in which it is to be discussed.

If we maintain the initiative, the other person is unable to surprise us. This of course is a great advantage in negotiation at any level.

In studying this, it is well to keep in mind that the business interview, talk or negotiation is in fact a contest. It is not something which is like a contest; it is a contest, only it is rather disguised, and is carried on within the framework of conventional rules which both parties tacitly accept. When we realize this, it makes it easier to understand the nature of initiative in a business situation.

When two men are boxing, for a few moments one will hold the intiative while the other is on the defensive. The boxer with the initiative virtually dictates the moves the other boxer has to make to defend himself. Then there is a change, and the initiative somehow goes to the other man. Even in such a physical contest as boxing, these changes of initiative are often determined by psychological rather than physical factors. This is shown by the way in which a man who is taking physical punishment can in fact often grasp the initiative and become the aggressor. Similar psychological mechanisms operate in the contest of negotiation. As with boxing, the surprise comes when we allow the other person to wrest the initiative from us.

We can maintain initiative by authority. This is simple. We ask a question, and immediately an answer is given we ask another question. We simply do this until we obtain the information we want. This is a poor technique because it denies us the possibility of further exploring the topics of our questions. Our use of authority prevents the other person being led out so that he will volunteer information.

A different use of authority to maintain initiative occurs when the person in authority uses it to make statements to the other person in such a way as to prevent the other person discussing or criticising the statements.

A skilful interviewer can maintain the initiative quite passively. This is a much more skilful, sophisticated and productive way of handling the situation. This is really a matter of the skilful interviewer controlling the situation by the psychological interaction of his own personality with that of the other person. So the control is still there, but it is a subtle control, and quite distinct from authoritarian control. There is no need to ask questions quickly so that the other person cannot break in to dialogue. It is just that the other person knows not to, although there is no logical reason at all why he should not. This situation is difficult to describe because I am limited to the logical use of words to describe something which does not follow the apparent rules of logic; but anyone who has had experience in interviewing will be familiar with the situation to which I refer.

This is probably a regressive phenomenen. The strength of one person's personality, or in other words its better integration, can establish him in the role of father figure or leader so that the other person falls into the role of child or follower, and is thus inhibited from taking the initiative.

It may be an advantage to force the other person to take the initiative when he does not want it. Again, the analogy with boxing is obvious. When we take the initiative we are more exposed and our defence is not so complete. This makes us vulnerable if our opponent is in a position to fight back.

If we are in a position of power, either through knowledge of facts of which the other person is uncertain, or through the type of psychological superiority to which I have just referred, we can often make the other person expose his weakness by forcing him to take the initiative.

To force the other person to take the initiative we do not use words. If we question him or command him in the hope of manoeuvring him into the initiative, we fail, because in so doing we are in fact retaining it ourselves. Instead we allow a silence to develop. I have already discussed the way in which silence has a different meaning according to circumstances. This is not a hostile silence, nor is it a silence of disinterest. We make it clear by our expression and gesture that it is an enquiring silence, and the meaning is unmistakable, 'what do you say?'

'How should we react when someone tries to force the initiative on us when we do not want it?' As in nearly all these situations our protection lies in our own relaxation and ease of mind. If in fact we are at ease, we can cope with the situation in one of two ways. We can simply ignore the silence and communicate indirectly that we are quite relaxed about it. In this way we turn the other person's manoeuvre against him. It is now likely that the failure of his manoeuvre will increase his anxiety, and superiority in the interview comes to ourselves.

The other way to parry the move to force us into the initiative is to be sufficiently relaxed to reply to the silence with conversation on some quite unimportant but related topic. This of course frustrates the other person and superiority passes to us.

In an interview people use various unconscious defence mechanisms. This is natural and just what we should expect. In discussing the different types of personality we noted that each type had evolved characteristic patterns of reaction for coping with nervous tension. Thus the introvert typically withdraws while the obsessive attempts to control his anxiety by trying to have everything right. These psychological defences become part of the individual's habitual pattern of behaviour. People use similar habitual patterns of reaction to help cope with the anxiety of an interview situation. To get the best out of interviewing and negotiation, we need to have an understanding of these reactions.

A confident manner may cover up weakness. Some people evolve a superficially confident manner to disguise their inner insecurity and anxiety. The biological reason for this is simple enough. They feel that if they disclose their weakness other people will take advantage of them. This is a sound rule for life in the jungle, and it is equally sound for present-day business life in the contests of interviewing and negotiation.

Is his confidence real or is it just a facade? This is a question we must answer because it affects our approach to the interview. If the other person is consciously assuming a bold front for the interview to cover up his anxiety, there will be no difficulty recognizing what is going on. It does not matter how confident the words may be, the tell-tale signs of anxiety will show through in the tightness of his face, his uneasy gestures, the stiffness of his movements and the quality of his voice.

However, if the confident manner is the individual's habitual cover up for his insecurity in all the minor problems of living, then it will be better integrated into his personality and more difficult for us to recognize in our interview. In these circumstances our cue is a certain incongruity about him. He seems more confident than he should be. This makes us suspicious. When we look, we can see the minor signs of anxiety. We can prove the point by subjecting him to minor stresses, such as quick changes of topic, quick changes in our attitude and making him get up from his chair to look at something. The really confident person is quite unaware of any stress caused by these manoeuvres; but the anxious person with a facade of confidence feels the stress and reacts with anxiety which we can easily recognize.

An attitude of humility may stop the other person being too tough. Many people use this type of defence to life's problems in general, and it is common psychological reaction in an interview situation. We must remember that these defensive attitudes are not consciously adopted for the occasion but are part of the individual's habitual adjustment to life. This defence by humility involves sound psychological principles. We only get really tough with someone when our aggression is fully mobilized. We have seen that aggression is increased by signs of hostility in the other person, and it is reduced by his passivity. So a defensive attitude of humility does in fact have the effect of preventing the other person being too tough. This defence is used by men, but is more commonly used by women because it fits in better with the passive feminine personality of the mature woman.

Sometimes a person will introduce an indirectly seductive attitude. A woman may get into the way of communicating the idea, 'I am only a poor frail woman, surely you will not do anything to hurt me'. Many women use this attitude in their habitual adjustment to life. They are usually quite unaware of it, and in an interview it is common for a man to be equally unaware of the degree to which her attitude has affected his approach to her.

However, defence by a seductive attitude is also used by men against men. This is used by sophisticated homosexuals when it is obvious enough. But it is also used by some men who are quite unaware of any homosexual traits in themselves. Their attitude communicates the message, 'I will make you like me; then you will not do anything that would hurt me'. The psychological basis of this defence is that all normal people have homosexual traits in their personality of greater or lesser degree. These are normally disguised or sublimated so that the individual has no knowledge of them. This defence by a seductive attitude is an unconscious approach to the disguised homosexual component of the other person's personality. An interesting aspect of this psychological reaction is that some men get taken in by it while a few react very violently against it. In these latter it is probable that the homosexual component of their personality is more marked or nearer a conscious level, so that they react with a kind of instinctive loathing towards such people, which in turn is an unconscious defence against homosexual seduction.

An aggressive attitude is a poor defence, but a very common one. The idea that offence is the best defence does not pay off in most business interviews and negotiations. This is a simple primitive biological defence which we have inherited from our remote ancestors in the jungle. It has obvious merit in the fight or perish conditions of the jungle, but cannot be well adapted to the sophisticated conditions of business life.

A social, superficial or cocktail party attitude may be used to try to avoid discussion of some deeper topic. This defence is commonly used by psychiatric patients of either sex. The patient introduces a social element into a professional interview. By this means he communicates the idea, 'I would like to talk about these nervous symptoms, but keep off my extramarital sex life'. By introducing the social element he aims to avoid discussion of matters which would be inappropriate in a social context.

People make use of similar defensive manoeuvres in a business setting. If a junior is able to introduce a social element into the interview, he may be able to prevent his senior using his authority against him because such would be inappropriate in a social setting.

Sometimes people avoid a problem by discussing it as if it did not belong to them. In fact it is their problem. But when we come to discuss it with them, they stand outside of the problem and talk about it as if they were a spectator. They analyse all the pros and cons with us at an intellectual level, but they are not involved. They look upon the matter as something that has happened, not that they have caused it to happen. As a result they show an alarming lack of responsibility for the situation which always tends to anger the other person.

In psychiatry this type of defence is known as dissociation. In it the person's feelings are dissociated from his thoughts, so that he can think about the bad thing he has done without it worrying him.

There are different ways of asking a question. And it is very important that we use the appropriate way for the particular occasion. We can put the question aggressively if the other person is being difficult and we want to beat him down. On the other hand, if we have a good relationship with him, we put the question in a friendly fashion. At the beginning of an interview, when the attitudes of the two people have not clarified, it is wise to frame the question in a more passive style.

A direct question is most effective when the other person is rather anxious. Because of his anxiety he is not able to parry the direct question in the way that he would if he were normally at ease. The direct question poses a sudden problem which has to be faced immediately and without warning. Anxiety makes it difficult to deal with this situation so, as likely as not, he answers the question in unguarded fashion which is just what we want.

An indirect question is useful when the other person is thinking of the relevant subject. In a discussion there are little pauses. In these little pauses we know pretty well what the other person is thinking about. By putting the question obliquely, we can often bring him to give unguarded expression of the thoughts which were in his mind. The simple question. 'What do you think?' may have this effect if it is asked in a very relaxed way.

A more extreme example of the same principle occurs which the other person is quietly pondering some matter, and we bring him to disclose what is uppermost in his mind by a simple interrogatory grunt.

If the other person puts an indirect question to us, we may be able to use it against him to gain the initiative. We do this by making him be explicit. We can do this because the meaning of an indirect question is not stated logically. The other person then has to explain what he means. As the meaning of an indirect question is purposely vague, he is immediately placed at a disadvantage. It is then easy to follow up our advantage by making his indirect question appear rather silly. The nature of an indirect question lends itself to this treatment, and the other person can do little about it, as he has been caught out, as it were, in trying to take advantage of us.

We can help the other person in an interview, or make it difficult for him without being openly antagonistic. An interview or discussion is essentially a two way situation. If we just sit politely and make no response, the other person soon finds that the situation is becoming difficult. I emphasize that we should maintain an air of politeness. Our polite unresponsiveness soon frustrates the other person. This gives us the initiative, and we can then move into a more active role in the discussion.

In a business interview there are usually two motives, to negotiate successfully for the firm, and to acquit oneself well personally. As long as the young executive identifies himself closely with the firm this fact presents no difficulty. But he should always remember that this double motivation is a fact of reality. The skilful young negotiator may be blind to the situation that the firm is not doing as well in the negotiations as he is.

Try to arrange an important interview on the home ground. Don't be misled into thinking, 'I can discuss the matter just as well anyhow'. The fact is, you can't. The home ground gives a great advantage in the way of an intangible feeling of security. As a result of this you think more easily and more clearly, and so function more effectively. Similarly with the other person. He is in strange surroundings; he is just ever so little uneasy, his anxiety is a little higher, and he starts the interview at a slight, but quite factual, disadvantage.

This principle is demonstrated very clearly in psychiatry. If I see the patient in his own home where he feels relatively secure and at ease, he is reluctant to discuss problems which are disturbing to him; but if I interview him in my professional rooms, he is less secure, more anxious and much better motivated to disclose his deeper worries.

Can you trust the other fellow?

This of course is something vital in any communication or negotiation. All of us develop intuitive hunches which help to guide us in determining whether or not the other person is telling the truth. But there are some quite clear-cut psychiatric rules which may be helpful.

You can trust an obsessive. We would expect this from our knowledge of his personality. He defends himself against anxiety by trying to have things just right. He unconsciously feels that if he can get things right there will be nothing to worry about. Any degree of dishonesty is the opposite of having things just right. So he avoids it to the extent of being scrupulously honest.

Although many obsessives are religiously minded people; it is interesting to note that the extreme honesty of the obsessive is not really a matter of religion, morality or ethics. Honesty to the obsessive is essentially a pattern of behaviour which induces less nervous tension. If the obsessive person does in fact do some minor act of dishonesty, it is quite likely that he will be so distressed by nervous tension that he will go to all manner of means to put right his dishonest act even though it was a matter of little consequence.

You can trust the very insecure person. But the insecure person's honesty comes from quite a different motivation from that of the obsessive. Because he is insecure he is fearful. He is too afraid of the possible consequence of dishonesty to take any risks. The insecure person is easily recognized as such by his high level of anxiety and by the way that he seems threatened by any minor changes. We realize that he does in fact feel threatened because we observe the signs of increased anxiety when he is confronted with changes such as new work, or new people to deal with, either as subordinates or superiors.

You can usually trust the well adjusted person. He is secure in himself, and because he is secure, he has no real psychological motivation to be dishonest. We recognize such a person by his openness in his dealings with others and by his general lack of anxiety. We intuitively respond to these traits in his personality with feeling, 'I know I can trust so and so'.

Church-going people are not necessarily trustworthy. This is a fact that is frequently brought home to the psychiatrist. People frequently go to church for the very simple reason that they are disturbed by inner feelings of guilt. And the cause of their guilt is very often their dishonesty in matters of greater or lesser degree. In saying this I am not in any way detracting from the honesty of those who attend church from genuine religious motivation.

The psychopath is dishonest by nature. He has a defective conscience, and as a result he does dishonest things without any feeling of guilt or anxiety. If he is caught and punished, he does not profit by the experience and mend his ways as do normal people. As he has this defect of conscience he repeats his dishonesty. The psychopath is recognized by his past history of dishonesty, by his absence of anxiety and his cold lack of concern for others.

Don't trust paranoid persons. They are the suspicious people who often add up two and two and make five. Because of this disorder of their mind they have a distorted idea of what is really going on. They may feel that certain people are against them when in fact they are not. They produce inconsequential evidence to support their mistaken beliefs. We recognize these people by their suspicious attitudes, their evasiveness and their tendency to make innuendos against certain groups of people. Persons whom we consider to have a chip on their shoulder often come into this category.

We must be careful about trusting the paranoid person not because he is likely to be dishonest in the way of deliberately misleading us, but rather because he is likely to mislead us as a result of his mistaken beliefs about other people.

We have an in-built lie detector. This is something quite important. But like many things which we don't understand, we are rather chary of using it. Our automatic lie detector just gives us the feeling that we should not trust this person. Then we say to ourselves, 'Why not?' There does not seem to be any logical reason, so we dismiss the message from our automatic lie-detector. This of course is an example of the way in which our logical faculties overrule the intuitive mechanisms of the mind.

From simple biological considerations we would expect to have evolved some way of knowing when people are telling the truth. Such a mechanism is of importance to our survival; and we would expect that it would be evolved by the process of natural selection. This is what has actually happened; but we find it hard to accept these apparently unreasoned promptings of our inner mind.

Our in-built lie-detector probably works by our mind registering observations which do not enter our consciousness. Unless he is a psychopath, when a person tells a lie he suffers some inner emotional reacton. This inner emotional reaction produces physiological responses in the body. These may be quite small, but they can still be observed. Thus the common lie detector which is used in the American courts works by the fact that the palms of the hands become slightly more moist when the subject tells a lie, and this is registered by an increase of electrical conductivity.

But there are many other minor physiological changes as well. These include slight changes in the blood supply of the face; there are also variations in pulse rate and the rate of breathing; and there are changes in the size of the pupils. In fact they are the usual signs of anxiety showing in minor degree. It is probably that these changes are observed, but not registered in consciousness; and as a result of this we are left with the apparently irrational feeling that the other person may not be telling the truth.

We can train ourselves to recognize falsehood in others by closely observing minor physiological changes in them. This follows standard practice in psychiatry in which we recognize topics which are of emotional significance to the patient by observing minor signs of anxiety. The same principles apply in assessing the truth or falsehood of what the othe person says in an ordinary business discussion. It is merely a matter of training oneself to be observant, and at the same time not letting the other person know that you are watching him.

It is hard to control the quality of our voice by act of will. The untruth produces some degree of emotional response, and this increases tension in the muscles of the larynx which in turn produces the tell-tale change in the tone of voice.

The person who is not telling the truth may be evasive on the subject or unnecessarily dogmatic. As with Hamlet, 'The lady doth protest too much, me thinks'. It is a matter for us to train ourselves to be continually on the watch for these variations. They often appear at times when they are quite unexpected. They are usually more easily detected if we start with a friendly discussion of unimportant matters. The other person then relaxes, we can then switch the subject abruptly to the important area, and it is easier to observe any changes from his previously relaxed state.

Communicating with groups

An ability to communicate with groups is a necessity for those on the way up. It is apparent in almost every aspect of business life. We see it in the committee meetings that we all have to attend, the lectures we have to give, the board meetings, in fact an ability to communicate with groups is an integral part of business and professonal life. The man who does not learn to communicate effectively with groups gets so far and no further, and his progress on the way up has come to an end. The last patient I saw before coming home tonight was an old university friend whom I had not seen for more than thirty years. In spite of being rather tense and anxious, he had done very well. He has just been offered further promotion. 'I would have to chair the meetings, there are only half a dozen there, but I couldn't do it. In these situations my face twitches, and my voice sounds strange. I couldn't do it.'

Lack of confidence is a common problem with the young executive. We have seen that most of the problems on the way up are a question of anxiety manifesting itself in different patterns. Our feeling of natural confidence is intimately related to our general level of anxiety. The more tense we are, our task seems so much the greater, and our lack of confidence is so much the worse. On the other hand, if we are really calm, the feeling of ease is with us, and we experience the feeling of natural confidence. So the young executive who is threatened with lack of confidence at the prospect of speaking to a group, must first establish a working degree of inner calm. This is best achieved by practising the relaxing mental exercises which we have already discussed.

You must learn to speak without notes. If you are young and on the way up, there are certain things which you simply must

[149]

learn to do. They require a certain amount of self-discipline, but let it be the easy relaxed type of self-discipline rather than a matter of screwing up your courage and forcing yourself to do it. You must learn to stand on your feet and express your views to a group of people without the use of notes. There is no alternative. This is simply something that you must learn to do. Many young men panic at the prospect, but it is not difficult. The key to the situation is learning to be relaxed in oneself. If you are tense, the anxiety inhibits the free flow of thought, and you face the embarrassment of being lost for words. But if you are at ease the flow of thought comes just as naturally as if you were talking with a friend. You then need only remember four or five headings for the different aspects of the subject which you intend to discuss.

Don't learn a lecture parrot fashion. If it is a matter of a set lecture, do not write it all out and try to learn it parrot fashion. This is hopeless. It is obviously hopeless because this approach will necessarily increase your anxiety, spontaneity is lost, people in the audience sense your tension and so feel uncomfortable themselves, and of course there is always the chance that you will miss your cue and get stuck. It is far better to make your four or five headings, and jot down sub-headings and useful phrases. In preparing the lecture go over this in your mind. If you like, have a rehearsal, and without any notes speak aloud all of what you propose to say. Speaking it aloud in a natural and unhurried way is a real help. The headings and the significant phrases stick in the mind more easily. If you can persuade some member of the family to act as an audience so much the better. Some years ago I used to stand on a wall in my garden and deliver any important lecture to my large labrador dog. In fact I think 'Sandy' heard more psychiatry than any dog in the town. I would strongly advise any young executive to practice his public speaking in some such way. But no notes, please.

Insufficient preparation is a pitfall for older executives. This is true, so if you are in the older group, face up to it. 'I can do it off the cuff. I have chaired this meeting scores of times. I can sense what is coming.' The younger men also sense what is coming. They sense that you are on the way out.

There are two reasons why senior executives fail in this way. There is the false confidence of familiarity. We are liable to think, 'We have done it before, and it has gone all right. It will go all right this time.' But we forget that our previous success was based on sound preparation. The other point is a more difficult one, but it is equally real. The senior executive is not as young as he was. Early signs of the ageing process are manifested in different ways. Some people become more introspective and more conscious of their short-comings; but more commonly an insidious lack of self criticism creeps over the ageing person without his awareness of what is happening. He leaves the meeting feeling. 'That went all right. I never have trouble chairing these meetings.' But the younger men may think differently.

If it is a matter of giving a lecture on some familiar subject, the senior executive is liable to overlook the rapidity with which things change, not only in technical knowledge, but also in our accepted attitudes towards things. The lecture that was really first class two years ago, today may only bring the hollow ring of polite applause.

We must establish rapport with the group. I think that all business men accept the importance of forming a good relationship with the other person when communicating in an individual interview. But this basic principle is often neglected when communicating to groups. Too often the executive reads a statement or reads a lecture, and feels that he has made an adequate communication. He feels, 'These are the facts, and I have given them the facts'. If you are on the way up, this is not good enough. The emotional tone of the individual influences his reception of the facts. If there is something in your manner, style or approach that in some way offends those at the meeting, they are unconsciously hostile, and tend to reject the facts which you are presenting. Please remember that this does in fact take place below the level of consciousness. The speaker is not aware that he is giving offence, and the members of the audience are not aware that they are being influenced by their own unconscious hostility.

L   [151]

Without being aware of it, the speaker can easily evoke this kind of reaction by being over confident, or by talking down to his audience. On the other hand, an attempt to be humble or polite may be interpreted by the audience as ingratiation or obsequiousness. In a similar way, any failure of clear speech and syntax such as the repetition of 'Eh' will irritate the audience, they tend to be hostile, and the facts, however good they are, will be less readily accepted.

So we must establish a friendly relationship with the members of the audience. It does not matter how technical the subject, the principle applies in every case. This is why I have emphasized the importance of speaking without notes. If we read what we wish to communicate, no matter how well it is written, we simply cannot establish the same natural and friendly relationship with the audience which we do when we just talk to them. I can sense that some of you are doubtful of this, saying to yourselves, 'Yes, this is all very well; but in my work I have to be accurate and talk in figures'. Quite so, but if you want your audience to accept your figures and evalute them in the way that you wish, then you must spend some time at the start without notes, speaking in generalities and relating yourself to the audience in easy and natural fashion. Then, when you have the audience with you, you can read a short statement of the figures. But when you do this, pause at appropriate places and look up, and perhaps make some comment, 'This seems quite good'. 'We have problems here.' 'You follow what I mean.' Little intrusions of this nature serve to keep the emotional tone of the audience with you, so that the facts are more readily assimilated.

Communicate your own ease to the group. If the members of the audience are at ease, they are likely to go along with us; whereas if they are edgy, they are likely to turn critically against us. So we use the simple biological mechanism that is rooted in each individual of the audience. He has a built-in tendency to take on the emotional tone of others near him. We have learned over countless generations that it is prudent to be afraid when others are afraid, and we alert ourselves to the dangers which the others have perceived. Likewise we have learned to relax when the others are calm and at ease. They see no danger, therefore we can also be off-guard. This is the psychological mechanism which we use at the meeting. When we get up to speak, we let the others see how relaxed we are, and they without knowing it take on a greater relaxation themselves.

Identify yourself with the group. This is one of the simplest ways of bringing the group to be on your side. Again it uses a very simple biological principle. We have a natural tendency to identify. We have developed this because it is a biological advantage for the child to identify with the parents, and so grow up like them. This tendency to identify lingers on into adult life. At the meeting we use this psychological reaction by first identifying ourselves with the group. As we talk there is no, 'I do this; you do that'. It is always expressed as, 'This is what we must do'. We thus identify with the group. But because of this in-built tendency to identification, the individual members soon come to identify with us. Then, of course, they are with us, and accept what we say.

Emotional involvement unites the group with you. This is a different matter from the way in which the group takes on your emotional ease which we have just discussed. This follows another psychological principle that a shared emotional experience unites people together. I expect that this has its biological origin as a protective mechanism. For instance, if a group of people is attached, its individual members tend to become united, and so can better ward off the attack. In this way the tendency to become united has a biological survival value for the individual members of the group. We can see this principle in action with many minority groups at the present day. Passengers in a delayed aeroplane share an emotional experience and tend to unite into a group. But sharing a good experience has a similar effect. Following a good play or concert, members of the audience are inclined to smile at each other or exchange a few words as they leave the theatre. A kind of union together results from the shared emotional experience. We can sometimes use this principle at our meeting. We do this by bringing the others to experience some emotion which we share with them. Our success together, our failure and how we must do better, the inspiring qualities of our project, the wonder as to where it will all lead, our shared pride with some member who has had some unusual success, or our mutual sorrow over some friend who has suffered, these matters may all seem trivial; yet they all involve some emotion, and if we can refer to some such event, and bring the others to experience some emotion with us, they will tend to become united with us and accept what we say.

Sometimes you can win over a potentially hostile group by seeking advice. This uses the psychological principle that aggression in one person sparks off hostility in another, but passivity allows hostility to peter out. Thus, if we sense that the group is hostile, we must avoid being in any way aggressive, or we will unite the group to vent its hostility against us. Instead we must be passive. The practical difficulty is to find a suitable way to communicate our passivity. If we are running the meeting we have to do something, and it is hard to communicate passivity in the usual ways. An attitude of seeking advice allows the hostility of the group to settle down. This gives us a chance to gain rapport, and then when we have rapport we can go on with what we have to say with much less danger of arousing the group's hostility.

There is nothing like a laugh. This is the emotional experience that we would all wish to share with our audience. We laugh with friends. If the audience laughs with us we are right. But we must remember that a great number of attempts to produce a laugh actually fall flat. And if this happens things are worse instead of better. I think this often happens when the speaker is not sufficiently sensitive to the mood of his audience. The mistake comes when the speaker has prepared what he is going to say in too much detail, so that he becomes too rigid and cannot change the mode of his presentation to suit the mood of the group which he is addressing. This is always likely to happen with anyone who is foolish enough to include a joke in the paper which he reads to his audience.

There is another point in using laughter as a shared emotional experience. We laugh at something. It is not uncommon for the potentially hostile audience to laugh at the speaker rather than the joke. This type of hostile laughter at the speaker is ruinous. But there is another way of laughing at a speaker. This is a friendly benevolent laugh at the speaker in which the audience accepts him and goes with him. This can sometimes be successfully induced by the speaker starting off by telling some joke against himself.

If we are tense, the others sense it, and are on guard ready to become hostile. I cannot emphasize this too strongly. It is the old biological reaction again. They sense our tension. If we are tense there must be some danger about. They are alerted. Aggression is ready to be mobilized, and in the meeting will be expressed as hostile questioning. This is what we must avoid at all costs; and our own inner ease and calm is the answer to the problem. Remember, if we are in fact in a difficult situation at the meeting, it is all the more reason why we must present ourselves easy and relaxed. But it is more than presenting ourselves this way, we must in fact be easy and relaxed or the audience will surely sense our inner tension and react to it.

If there is a difficult problem, bring it up yourself rather than have it ventilated by a hostile questioner. This is simply a matter of prudence. To gloss over the difficult problem leaves the speaker hopelessly vulnerable. It only needs one individual to pick on it, and the whole audience is united against the speaker.

There are different ways of bringing up the difficult problem. It can be introduced in such a way as to indicate that the fault lies with some third party for whom we could not be responsible. I doubt if this approach is ever really convincing. A slight variation is to emphasize some abnormal circumstances which we could not be expected to foresee. I believe that it is usually better to make a simple statement of the facts in a way that leads the others to identify with the various steps taken. 'We did this, then we did that.' The guilty third party or the abnormal circumstances can easily be brought in during the discussion when this type of argument is likely to lend more weight.

Sometimes we can score off a hostile questioner, and turn it against him. The hostile questioner is himself vulnerable. This is so for two reasons. His very hostility makes him vulnerable so that under his hostile emotion he may put his case badly. There is also a second psychological factor which makes him vulnerable. The speaker of the meeting, even if he has made mistakes, still has the advantage of the prestige and authority inherent in being the speaker. The questioner, on the other hand, is only one of the people. The situation is psychologically analogous to the father and the questioning child. The skilful speaker, in virtue of his innate prestige as speaker, can often play on these unconscious psychological undercurrents in such a way that he is politely treating the questioner as a child. The questioner loses status, and the group tends to dissociate itself from him. In doing this, it must be done subtly and in a way that is acceptable to the group. Thus any overt attempt to belittle the hostile questioner should be avoided, as this is likely to make the group side with the questioner as others do not like to see fellow members treated harshly.

The skilful speaker can use the hostile questioner's emotion against him. This is done indirectly by first making the audience aware of it. If this can somehow be done with a smile, the group will very easily come to side with the speaker against the hostile questioner. This comes about through the hostile emotion of the questioner. He is directing his hostility against the speaker. But we have seen that hostility in one person arouses hostility in others. So the group in general experiences some rise in aggressive feeling. This is momentarily directed against the speaker. But if the speaker remains easy and passive, this aggression in the other members of the group can quickly switch on to the hostile questioner himself.

Sometimes this process can be accelerated by the speaker interpreting the hostile questioner's emotion to the other members of the group. This is rather like a psychiatric interpretation in analytical group therapy. The speaker may comment, 'The questioner is disturbed because of such and such'. This tends to put the speaker in rapport with the other members of the group against the hostile questioner.

Sometimes we can side with a hostile questioner against some third party. This is just another way of manipulating the questioner's aggression. We quickly side with him. We talk of the guilty third party. We do this by expressing our aggression and hostility against the third party. The questioner's hostility is thus deflected on to the third party and away from ourselves. The other members of the group, who have had their aggression kindled by the emotion of the hostile questioner, follow these emotional responses but at a lower level of intensity. The result is a general feeling of hostility against the third party, with us in rapport with both the hostile questioner and the rest of the group so that we can proceed further with what we were about to say.

If a hostile questioner is right, we may be able to disarm him by quietly agreeing with him. 'What you say is right.' 'I feel like this myself.' 'Of course we must remedy this.' 'I am most grateful.' 'Is there any suggestion you would care to make?' Such phrases disarm the hostile questioner, as on the surface he now has nothing to be hostile about. If he still persists with hostile questioning, it is likely that the rest of the group will unite against him in favour of the speaker.

The manoeuvre of inviting suggestions from the hostile questioner must be used with caution and with a clear assessment of the questioner's personality. Many hostile questioners are purely destructive. If we are sure that he falls into this category, we are safe, as it is unlikely that he can give any sensible suggestions, and the group turns against him in favour of the speaker. But sometimes a hostile questioner is an aggressive rather paranoid person full of ideas of his own. If such a person is given the chance, he will tend to take over the meeting to the speaker's disadvantage.

A skilful speaker can sometimes divert a hostile questioner by bringing up something which catches the attention of the group. The manoeuvre works this way. The hostile questioner asks his question. The speaker says a few sentences which indicate that he is replying to the question. But just before he comes to the point, he suddenly switches to some topic that is of vital interest to the group. He discusses this important topic with intensity and emotion so as to involve the group. By this means the hostile questioner and his difficult question are forgotten in the general interest of the new topic. The success of such a manoeuvre depends on the speaker's ability to make an easy change of subject from the question to the new topic, and also on the importance of the new topic so that it can quickly absorb the interest of the group.

A skilful speaker may be able to fob off a hostile questioner with a platitude. He thinks his question has been answered when in fact it has not. Many politicians are experts at this. The questioner expresses his question in concrete terms. The speaker answers by expressing his platitude in abstract terms. The questioner is not quite sure whether this answers his question or not. While he is pondering it for a moment, the general discussion moves on to some other topic, and the questioner loses his chance to pursue his question.

In answering a hostile questioner, always consider the effect of your reply on the rest of the group. We do not want to score off the hostile questioner to such an extent that it either angers the rest of the group or makes them feel sorry for him. This can happen when the hostile questioner is either stupid or not well informed. We are then in a position to assert ourselves and annihilate him completely It is tempting to do this. We feel that we would gain in stature and have undisputed control of the group. But displays of power always induce some degree of psychological counter-reaction in the other. Displays of power frighten us, so we have a hostile feeling against the person who displays such power. We want to avoid this type of reaction in the other members of the group. So we use our power sparingly; and we do it in such a way that the group is aware that we have the power to annihilate the hostile questioner, but at the same time we refrain from using it fully. In this way a hostile reaction against power is avoided, and our rapport with the group is increased.

A group can be stirred up hysterically. In business and industry we see this most commonly in mass meetings of employees. So it is just as well that you, an executive on the way up, should know something of the psychological reactions involved.

These mass reactions result from the mobilization of some emotion which is normally latent within each individual member of the group. Aggression is the most common emotion to become activated in this way. We are all endowed to greater or lesser degree with aggressive impulses. This is a part of our biological heritage giving us the drive to fight and defend ourselves, and so survive. Under normal circumstances of civilized living these aggressive impulses are inhibited, and so kept under control. However, under certain circumstances the psychological forces inhibiting this aggression can be loosened, the aggression can be stirred up and ventilated in open action.

The cold logic of reason is an important inhibiting force. So the speaker who would stir up the group discards reason and involves the group in an emotional response. He does this by letting himself experience the emotion. He experiences the emotion and communicates it. Thus a speaker with a ready capacity to hate, can more easily stir up the group, because he genuinely experiences the emotion of the members of the group and they come to experience it with him. Group reactions now operate. There is the natural protective reaction of the individuals of the group to act in cohesion. So individuals, who would not normally express their aggression in this way, now come to ventilate it with the others. The mass hysterical reaction thus gets under way, and the members of the group may say and do things quite contrary to their normal personality.

Sometimes we can use the individual's unconscious tendency to accept group attitudes. This is a constructive way of using the group reaction which we have just discussed. If two or three individuals persist in a different attitude and so hold up some project, we may be able to bring them to our way of thinking by simply involving them in a group experience. The unconscious tendency to identify with the group may be sufficient to change their attitude. They, of course, will not see it this way. They will rationalize, and give some acceptable reason for their change of attitude.

In this reaction there is no question of the group discussing its attitude with the dissident individuals They feel they belong to the group. When they feel this, they come to identify with the group, and they take on the attitudes of the group. This reaction can obviously work in a way that is destructive to the individual. We see this in the common case of the youngster who keeps bad company. He associates with a group whose members have low moral and ethical standards, he comes to identify with the group and unconsciously comes to accept its attitudes.

Your performance at the meeting will be better with adequate psychological and physiological preparation. This is obvious. Yet so many people neglect the simple facts of life. You are going to speak without notes, so you need to have the ideas easily ordered in your mind. There is plenty of evidence to show that the best time to do this preparation is two or three days in advance. This allows the ideas to become organized in the brain. Don't say 'If I prepare it three days in advance I will have forgotten it when the time comes'. This is not so. When you stand on your feet the ideas will just come naturally. Furthermore, by preparing the subject some time in advance you allow an anxiety which may be associated with the thought of addressing the meeting to settle down. On the day of the meeting quietly go over the headings just to refresh your mind. Do not under any circumstances prepare your speech just prior to the meeting. If you do this your level of anxiety will be high, and you will not acquit yourself as well as you should.

There are some basic physiological rules. Don't go to the meeting tired. No athlete goes to the contest tired, but business men do this every day. If you have to fly to another city for the meeting, leave yourself adequate time to settle down from the flight. This applies particularly to my fellow countrymen. I have seen a number of businessmen as patients, who have told me that they did not do as well for themselves as they should have at meetings in New York and London. It is a long flight from Australia. They had allowed themselves a few hours rest, but this had been disturbed by visits from friends and last minute business conferences. It should not need a psychiatrist to point out why they had not done well at their meetings. Anyone flying from Australia to a meeting in Europe or America should allow himself at least twenty-four hours complete rest before seeing friends or attending preliminary conferences. Let me give you a personal hint. I believe the only way you can do this is to arrive twenty-four hours in advance of schedule. Then no one knows where you are, and you can have the rest that your body needs.

There is another very simple physiological problem about meetings. It is often the custom, particularly among doctors, to entertain the speaker to dinner just before the meeting. In these circumstances, if you are going to speak without notes, you simply cannot afford to have much to drink.

There is another personal tip that I myself have found very useful. Just before the meeting there is a dinner or lunch, or at least a good deal of high pressure conversation. I find it hard to step straight out of this atmosphere into giving a serious lecture. So just before the meeting starts I slip away from my well meaning hosts for ten minutes, and just let myself be quiet. A few moments stroll down the street allows the mind to clear, and the sequence of ideas for the talk comes easily.

Communication by correspondence

All the psychological principles of a personal interview apply to negotiation by correspondence. When we write a letter we communicate the essential facts by the logical meaning of the words. But there is also the meaning between the lines. This is the extraverbal communication. By this means we give the other person leads or hints that he can take up if he so desires.

We construct our letter so that the reader becomes interested in our communication, as without his emotional involvement the bare facts of the proposition have little real meaning.

We also use our letter to establish a friendly feeling with the reader. This is the rapport of the personal interview; and although our present communication is by correspondence, it helps in just the same way to bring the reader to accept our ideas.

In a letter we use both verbal and extra-verbal communication. When we read a business letter we comprehend certain facts which are expressed by the logical meaning of the words. But a well written letter also evokes in us some kind of emotional response. We vaguely feel, 'That's a nice letter', or 'That's a nasty letter'. And this happens quite irrespective of whether or not the logical content of the letter was good news or bad. This feeling is conveyed to us, not by the logical meaning of the words, but by their implied meaning, the extra-verbal meaning, or as we sometimes describe it, the meaning between the lines.

In negotiation it is necessary to make 'feelers' to test out the other person's attitude on certain matters. We do this by using the implied meaning of the words rather than their logical meaning. By this kind of extra-verbal communication we allow the other person to put a variety of interpretations on our communication. This both tests him out, and gives him room to manoeuvre, as it were. By this means we introduce a flexibility into the discussion which would be quite lost if we were to pin the other person down with a question communicated by the logical use of words.

In the same way we construct our letters using extra-verbal communication to give the reader hints. As the idea is not expressed in so many words, the reader is given the option of taking the hint or not, without the loss of face by either side.

We can use the same means to communicate an indirect rebuke to the other person. As the rebuke is not specifically expressed by the logical meaning of the words, he is not given grounds to be offended, and although the meaning is clear, we have not given him anything sufficiently tangible to complain about.

We can gain rapport through correspondence just as we can in a personal interview. This idea is very important. We accept logical ideas more readily from someone if we have a friendly feeling towards them. I know that people, whose mental outlook is restricted by an over emphasis on logic often find it hard to accept this proposition. But it is true; and its psychological roots are deep within us from the time we accepted ideas from our parents whom we loved, or in times past when we accepted ideas from tribal leaders whom we respected.

So we must use our letter to gain rapport, then our reader is so much the more likely to accept the proposition which we are offering him in the logical content of our communication.

We can communicate friendliness and trust in a letter. This follows the same rules as in a personal interview. We express ourselves openly in the letter just as we do in conversation. The reader perceives that we are open with him and he comes to trust us.

We can introduce personal touches just as we might if we were talking with the reader. Just a few words, a phrase or sentence can add the personal touch, and the reader feels that he likes us although he may never have seen us. As in conversation, the personal touch must just be a touch; that is something light; it must never be belaboured or the whole point of it is lost. In appropriate circumstances, a few words penned in our own hand at the foot of the page may communicate friendliness.

Just as we do when we are talking with the other peson we can offer trust in a letter by voluntarily disclosing certain weaknesses. I have explained that this has significant psychological meaning because in ordinary circumstances we only disclose any weakness to someone who we really trust.

We mentioned that there are certain barriers against the formation of rapport in an interview. The same applies in a letter. A very formal letter lacks the friendly quality and so reduces rapport. Some business correspondence is so formal that it is stilted, and all the advantages of forming rapport are quite lost. A letter that is unnecessarily guarded tends to make the reader suspicious, and rapport becomes impossible. Errors in dealing with local customs may spoil rapport. I am thinking particularly of correspondence with foreign countries. For instance Americans come to call each other by first names very much sooner than do the English. In correspondence Americans like to use their first name, the initial of their second name and then the surname, while Englishmen and Australians usually omit the initial. American doctors like their letters addressed M.D. while their English and Australian counterparts like their letters addressed as Dr. unless the person is a surgeon when Mr. is preferred. In Spain and South America most men like the formality of all their names on the envelope. There are endless such examples. But a failure to appreciate these niceties in correspondence reduces rapport.

The way a letter is set out is part of the communication. It has meaning just as the way that our office is set out has meaning.

The blatantly headed notepaper has the same significance as the flamboyantly furnished office. It impresses the unsophisticated and leaves the others wondering why the writer is so insecure that he tries to bolster himself up in this way. The style in which a letter is set out discloses the writer's general level of competence. Don't say to yourself, 'This has nothing to do with the writer's competence; the typist sets out the letter'. You forget that competent executives see to it that they have competent secretaries.

A letter must not be too long, and it must not be too short. It must be appropriate to the occasion. Just because we are discussing these matters at some length, please do not think that the psychological approach requires the use of long letters. Quite to the contrary, letters should be as short as possible provided they do not offend by being so short as to be curt or discourteous. The psychological principles which we have been discussing are implemented by the wording of the letter not by its length. A long letter is often a cover-up. The writer feels guilty about something and this provokes him to try to explain things away or to exonerate himself. If a doctor is ill at ease about the way he has managed a patient, he unconsciously writes a much longer letter when referring the patient to a specialist.

In your letters leave the other person room to manoeuvre. I mentioned this because we tend to express ourselves much more definitely in our letters than we do in a personal interview. When we have the other person actually with us, we have rapport, and the friendly feeling that goes with it tends to stop us nailing the other person down too closely. There is also the other point. We feel that we can expedite a decision by being definite in our correspondence. Let us rather be clear, but not definite in any way that prevents the other person offering counter-suggestions or coming up with new ideas.

Symbols and images are a form of communication

A symbol is something which represents an idea. It may be something very simple or it may be something of the utmost complexity. The written word is the symbol for the idea it expresses. The red traffic light expresses an idea. A flag or a cross may communicate quite complex ideas. Ordinary every-day articles may come to symbolize some idea connected with the use of the articles. A dress can symbolize the idea of woman or femininity. A man's formal suit may express ideas beyond man and masculinity, and come to communicate the idea of formality. In this way we are continually using the language of symbolism.

Symbols are important as they communicate ideas without us realizing what is happening. The man on the way up learns to use symbols effectively. The Rolls Royce radiator is a universally accepted symbol of quality. Has your product got a good name with people? Do people think of it as associated with an appropriate attribute, quality, durability, attractiveness, elegance or some other desirable quality? When this happens, symbolism becomes an effective means of promotion.

The firm itself should aim to acquire an image which has the effect of symbolic communication. Can you associate the firm with ideas of reliabilty, skill, promptness or enterprise?

Can you present your product so that it becomes unconsciously associated with some universally desirable human quality? This is the way to use symbolism in advertising. The product may be always shown in association with a picture of a pretty girl. The picture of the girl symbolizes desirability. This idea is communicated unconsciously through the language of symbolism. The idea of desirability thus becomes associated with your product. A picture of an attractive man works similarly; so do images which communicate ideas of home and the family circle.

The shape of the package or the crest or emblem may have symbolic significance. This usually relates to disguised sexual symbolism. Sex symbols, the elongated shape for the male and the hollow female counterpart have an unconscious attraction for us if they are presented in appropriate form. This is a communication; and it leads us to be attracted to the article which is

[165]

adorned in this way whether it is a motor car with such a symbol on the radiator or a bottle of perfume moulded in the appropriate shape.

5

W omen on the way up

The executive's wife

You have your problems on the way up, but there are also problems for your wife. We don't live in isolation, and what we do affects others, and the effect is greatest on those closest to us. How does your wife feel about your struggle on the way up? Does she see it the way you do? Does it come between you? Does it leave her sexually unsatisfied? Is she left to manage the children without your help? Does she feel that she plays a second fiddle to your career? Have you drifted apart into two different worlds? Or does she identify with you so that your success is success for her as well?

These are questions that every man on the way up must answer. And if he cannot answer them in a way that is satisfactory to himself, he is really not on the way up. And it is all a sad delusion.

A man may be a first class executive, but not so good as a husband. In fact many of the qualities found in the top executive are not the attributes of a good husband. The executive is often cold and detached whereas your wife looks for someone warm and loving. The executive may get into the habit of keeping an emotional distance from those around him, but at home she wants you close with her. In viewing the big picture of events, top management often comes to disregard the feelings of the individual, and the executive may become less perceptive of the individual's wants and needs. The intense competition of commerce and industry may engender a ruthlessness which can win the fight in business only to lose on the home front. In other words, some of those qualities of mind which work for success in business may in themselves reduce one's chances of success in marriage.

Which comes first, your career or your marriage? Many a man on the way up comes face to face with this question. We hear many answers, or perhaps they are only half answers. 'It is a question of degree.' 'My wife must come along with me.' 'After all I work for her too.' Then there are others who immediately say, 'My marriage of course', but then add as an after-thought, 'But it mustn't interfere with my work'. In other words, it is a matter on which many of us are quite confused, and because we are confused about it, we unconsciously avoid the subject.

Let us consider some of the facts of life. The man whose whole life is preoccupied with wife and family does not go far on the way up in the material sense. Furthermore, in this idealized way of living, he falls short of the full life, because it is not enriched by the striving forward which is such a part of our higher aspirations. On the other hand, the man who puts work first at all costs, may well achieve success only to find it sterile in his grasp. But of course, these things should never be evaluated like this. We must transcend these simple dichotomies. We live life. Marriage and profession are integral parts of life. If one is distorted, the other suffers. If we are really on the way up, it is our life in its fullness that counts.

Your wife may not have the same general competence as you have. She may find it hard to keep with you on the way up. As a result her anxiety is increased, and she unconsciously defends herself against this inner tension. She is ill-equipped to deal with the social aspects which are part of it. It is all so different from her earlier life, and she lacks the background of earlier experience on which the others depend for their feelings of security. Your own inner competence has given you the feel of it. You have adjusted to the change, and are secure enough in it. But it is different with her. She is not quite like yourself in this respect. Adjustment to the social changes is difficult. Sometimes she feels gauche, awkward, ill at ease. She is more tense than she used to be. It shows in her increasing irritability. And to save herself the stress of it, she withdraws more and more from social activity.

'He has his success; I have the house and the children.' This may be rationalized, 'We have a different sense of values'.

[168]

Some wives defend themselves against anxiety by isolating themselves from their husbands activity. Very often it is simply the reaction of the wife, who is a little less competent than her husband, and who finds it hard to keep with him on the way up. She allays her anxiety by isolating herself in the home, and gaining her emotional satisfaction with her children. The husband is left to enjoy his success single handed. I have spoken with patients in this situation. The successful husband has usually been disappointed and bitter, feeling that his wife does this purposely to spite him. But this is not really so. It is rather a matter of the wife having unconsciously evolved a pattern of living which reduces her nervous tension. The answer in most cases, of course, is that with a little understanding and support, the husband could bring her along with him.

Sometimes the wife may belittle her husband's success. There are many reasons for this unhappy reaction. But one, which is often overlooked, is simply that the way of life which goes with her husband's success makes her tense. She unconsciously falls into the way of bolstering up her own ego by belittling her husband's success. This reaction is a clumsy unconscious way of relieving her anxiety; but it irritates the husband, and as a result of these conflicts her anxiety is further increased. So a vicious circle mechanism is established. With more support from her husband, she is less anxious and the need to belittle him ceases.

Some wives identify with their husbands. When he has had a success, it is, 'We have had a success'. His success is her success; his joy in it is her joy. This is life at a higher level. People who have never experienced this, sometimes fail to realize the genuiness and the depth of this kind of identification. They see it that the success is her husband's, and when the wife talks of 'we' they feel that she does so to please her husband. In real identification this is not so, and the one's joy in the other's success is just as deeply felt as if it were her own.

A further effect of the wife's identification is that the husband's motivation to strive for success is greatly enhanced. In this way the identifying wife unconsciously helps him on the way up.

Many a wife talks of 'Our success and his failures'. Sometimes the identification is not so complete. It is much easier to identify with success than failure. But with true identification there is no wavering with failure. 'Bad luck that we missed out on that.' Identification in failure reduces anxiety, reduces guilt, and so helps them both on the way up, for it is not his way up but theirs.

Keep your wife in the picture so that she can identify with you more easily. Love is the basic ingredient for the type of identification which we are considering. Without some element of love this cannot be achieved. One person can often identify in general terms without knowing very much of the other. But for the identification to be complete, and meaningful, the wife needs to know as much as she can about her husband, his aims and aspriations, his fears and his failures. Husbands have often told me, 'I never talk to her about business. I don't want to worry her. There is no point in us both worrying.' This may sound commendable. But it is usually said by men who want to deny to themselves the emotional gulf between them.

If your wife is in the picture about your day to day activity, real identification comes much more easily, and is also much more complete. I am not suggesting that you harass your wife with all your anxieties. Rather it is a matter of just letting her know how things are going. If this has not been your way of life, don't just disregard what I am saying. The psychological power of identification is very great. We cannot consciously evoke it; but we can set the circumstances of our life so that it can spontaneously develop, and we reap the benefits, both psychological and material.

Social changes may bring insecurity. You are on the way up. Your success brings social changes. Your wife goes along with you. But she may find adjustment to these social changes more difficult than you do. This can make her insecure and spoil it all.

It may be that you are more gifted than she is, so she finds the going more difficult than you do. This is the common situation of patients with this background who have consulted me. The husband needs to understand this and give more support.

There is another factor in the wife's greater insecurity in adjusting to changed circumstances of life. It is you who is the success, and this gives you a degree of confidence that does not come to your wife. Furthermore, you already know many of the men from professional contact with them. Your wife may not have the feminine counterpart of this. So she operates rather in a vacuum, and if she is a little insecure by nature, it is all so much the more difficult for her.

Patients often discuss these difficulties. There is a change to a circle of friends who are more sophisticated and with a wider cultural interest. In all this the wife is at a disadvantage. She is ill at ease; anxiety is high; and the feeling of panic is not far off. When I have spoken with women in these circumstances they have nearly all shown a tendency to manage this anxiety by trying to assume a sophistication which in fact they did not have. This is a poor defence. As it is only a facade, the underlying insecurity remains and is in fact perpetuated. It is much better to present yourself to new friends as you are. Remember it is only your insecurity that would prevent you doing this. If you can present yourself as you are, your psychological adjustment is on firm foundations. Then cultivate the wider interests of your new friends.

And with success there are other social problems which can cause anxiety. There are glimpses of old friends who did not make the way up, and have been left behind. Sometimes their lack of wider interest makes them seem a bore, at other times an embarrassment. Then there are the others, the hangers on. In the new milieu it may be hard to distinguish the grain from the straw, the genuine from the fake, and those who would befriend you may not have your interests at heart.

You work hard, and this makes demands on your wife. You bring home work at night. There is little choice. You pretty well have to. But how does it affect your wife? Does she identify with you and feel that, 'We must get this done tonight'. Or is there a smouldering resentment about it all. More often it is not expressed in words, but she feels, 'I expected more from marriage than this'.

And you work hard and you work late. You are tired when you get to bed, too tired for anything. How does this affect her? And the children, how much have you seen of them in the last few months? We get caught up in things too easily and often

without realizing what is happening. It is well to stop and think
for a while, and assess what is going on. Then perhaps we can
make a few changes before it is all too late. She has a right to a
full life too.

The overseas trip has its hazards. I am an Australian, and perhaps
overseas trips are more the pattern with us than with others.
Every young executive has to make overseas trips This is part
of his education and basic experience. And there are hazards. I
know this to be true as I have helped to sort things out on a
number of occasions. There is one inescapable conclusion. It is
simply this. Many young executives behave incredibly foolishly
on overseas trips. The real foolishness is that their behaviour is
out of character. At home they stick to the rules, and conform
to a pattern of behaviour which is demanded by the firm and
their professional group. A few hours in a plane and all restraints
are suddenly lifted. He experiences the freedom of anonymity.
'Nobody knows.' 'I do what I like.' 'Why not?' 'It hurts nobody.'
'It is all so easy, so convenient with the girls there at hand.'

The problem arises because this behaviour is out of character
for that particular person. If this is a part of your ordinary way
of life there is no problem. But with those who have subsequently been so disturbed as to see me professionally, it has
been out of character. Sometimes it has just been a matter of the
individual's conscience, it keeps plagueing his mind. Guilt
feelings and anxiety develop. Concentration falls off. Work is
impaired; and he feels the need to talk it over with someone.
Others have told their wives about it. There has been a domestic
scene, and the matter has been getting out of hand.

Sometimes the foolishness has been even greater. Many young
men have homosexual phantasies. This is often stimulated by
the current vogue of homosexuality as a topic of interest in
plays, films and general conversation. 'Why not?' He is anony-
mous. 'Just once for the experience. It can't do any harm.' But it
can do harm, very great psychological harm. This, together with
drug taking, is one of the fields of human experience in which
experimentation is really dangerous.

**You may audit the firm's accounts, but not your wife's house-
keeping.** She was like many others whom I have seen; 'I can't

stand it. He gets on my nerves. It's not that I am extravagant. He wants to know where every penny goes.' It is easy to bring one's business training into the home where it does not belong. I have seen it in other spheres, the professional soldier who tries to impose a barrack-room discipline on his wife and family.

Be the boss at work but the partner at home. This would seem obvious enough. We are all likely to get into patterns of behaviour, but it is not always wise to bring the pattern from work home with us. Of course the situation is different in different households. Some women with well developed passive and dependent traits in their personality like their husband to be boss in everything. However, if you are inclined to be bossy at home, remember that this does not apply to all women, and those with a more self assertive personality cannot easily tolerate a husband who brings home with him the bossy attitudes from work.

Some women expect too much. The woman who is more intelligent than her husband, who has had a professional training herself, or who has a father who has been very successful, not uncommonly looks for a higher standard of success than her husband is able to attain. 'Don't just ask the boss for a rise, make him give it to you.' It has been the subject for humorous cartoons for years. Yet it is with us every day. Women who react in this way usually have the self-assertive side of their personality well developed. In psychiatry we call them masculine-aggressive women, as this tendency to assertion is akin to the aggressiveness of the normal male. It is not uncommon for such women to marry rather passive and dependent men whom they dominate. Then they expect too much of their husbands. They are not on the way up fast enough. On the other hand, such women bring with them tension, anxiety, conflicts and domestic disharmony wherever they go; but on the other hand, and this is the bright spot, they can get very great help from psychiatric treatment.

What can the executive's wife do to help?

'I am his wife not his psychiatrist.' Sometimes they have said this to me, when I have been about to explain how they could help. There is bitterness in this. The executive is tense from stress; he works late and neglects her; and she is bitter. Granted, it is he that needs the help. But very often in his tense irritability he refuses to seek it, and it is the wife who sees me. At first she does not understand that if she plays psychiatrist just a little, she will soon have a much better time as wife.

Of course the mature woman is an intuitive psychiatrist, and does all the things I mention here quite spontaneously and without even thinking about them. It is her natural feminine response to the situation. But there are others, less mature, who can be helped in this direction. I know this to be true because I have seen the results.

A wife can increase her husband's efficiency. She can also destroy it. You have great power. This comes from your ability to either increase or lower your executive husband's level of nervous tension. I often ask patients, 'What is the best time of day for you'. Men frequently answer, 'Getting home to my wife'. Others tell me that going home is the worst part of the day. 'She is tense and on edge, just when I can't take it after the stress of the day.' How do you, the two of you, stand in this? Of course you, the wife, have your stresses during the day too. You also have a right to feel tired. I know this. But try to transcend it.

Let him talk about the things in his mind even if you can't fully understand. You relax. Sit with him a little while. Have a drink together if you like, or just sit by the fire. But you must be relaxed; this is essential. He is tensed up. All the problems of the day are still streaming through his mind. He is anxious to give them expression. He wants to ventilate these thoughts that are pressing on his mind to someone who is sympathetic and understanding. It only works if you yourself are relaxed. 'How about so and so.' And he is off, telling you all about it, telling you all that you don't understand. But you understand this greater thing, that it is helping him to unwind, helping him to relax, helping him to be a better man. You don't understand what he is talking about, but you don't ask him to explain. That would spoil it. You just say, 'Umm'. And you understand more deeply than he knows.

Identify yourself with his efforts. You are behind him in what he does. When he has made the difficult decision, you back it. His anxiety is less. He is less tense, and consequently better able to carry out the decision. Don't think you just have to say 'Yes' to every thing. No, that is not it. Discuss, and present your own point of view when you can. But let him feel that you are with him in it.

At the opposite scale of things the terrible situation can arise when the wife remains uncommitted. She does not support him, but she does not oppose him. She is just a spectator. Then if things don't turn out too well, she may not say it openly, but she communicates the meaning clearly enough, 'It was your idea'.

Woman maketh the man. I have seen this so often. I have now been practicing psychiatry long enough to have seen youngsters grow up into adult life. Some of these young men have been struggling along, then with marriage it has all changed.

When things go well, you have pride in it. This is real, something that you experienced deep within you. No need to say much in words. He knows how you feel, and you know that he knows. And he is better for it, this that you experience with him.

Support him when things go badly. We need our friends in adversity, and we need their support. Move a little closer to him. Your unexpressed understanding takes the edge off his tension. He is better able to cope, and better able to face the problems the next day.

Cuddle him. A cuddle can help him on the way up. This is not a romantic phantasy, but a practical fact of life. While he is tensed up he can no longer function effectively. He can't relax. He can't do it himself. He needs your help. And because you are an intuitive woman you understand. It is all natural, and it happens without you consciously thinking about it.

The executive's sex life is often one of extremes. I base this statement on experience with patients. In one extreme there is

[175]

gross sexual neglect of the wife. Women in this position have come to me seeking advice. There would seem to be two causative factors. Psychologically speaking we have within us a primitive driving force known as the 'libido'. In ordinary circumstances much of this finds expression in direct sexual outlet. However, some men unconsciously transform this primitive libido into non-sexual channels, and it becomes part of their drive to do things. This process is known as sublimation. The successful young executive, conspicious for his drive, may in fact have sublimated so much of his libido that his sex drive is quite lacking. This may be augmented by another factor. It is simply that the young executive who is pressing along on the way up works so hard that his sex drive and performance is reduced by simple fatigue.

How do you react to this? He does not make love to you in the way that you feel that he should. What do you conclude from this? 'Perhaps he has another girl.' Don't jump to this conclusion too quickly. Try to get him more rest; and he needs leisure away from the business. A holiday might do the trick. But in the meantime this is something which you must understand and tolerate.

The other extreme in the sex life of executives is just the reverse. Such a man is unusually highly sexed. This may be associated with his drive which has brought him success as an executive. We have discussed the way in which the drive to do things is derived from our primitive aggressive urges. Men with a lot of latent aggression may sublimate much of it into their drive, but some of the aggressive urge may also be transformed into sex drive. This transformation may not be quite complete, so that love-play and intercourse have an aggressive quality about them, and lack the tenderness of more mature sexuality. So young men of this type on the way up seek frequent sex and they act aggressively in it. Can you understand? Can you try to go along and help? It may not always be easy.

It is unfair that he transfers his irritability on to you. You sense that you are the whipping boy; and this is true enough. Things are tough at work. The boss is on his back. He would like to answer back, but he can't. His job is at stake. So he bottles it up. He comes home, still seething inside. You make one slip, and you get it all. You get all the aggression that he feels for the man at the office suddenly unleashed on yourself for no reason at all. It is unjust. Your own aggression is roused. You are going to fight back. But don't. Please don't. The reason is this. He has all this aggression mobilized within him from the conflict at work. If you show your own aggression it will quickly unleash still further aggression from him. However, unreasonable it may seem, don't seek justice. Seek to cope with the situation. And you do this passively. He will quieten down in a little while, and things will be better. And the chances are that later in the evening he will thank you for your understanding. He will probably do this indirectly rather than in words because it is difficult for a man to express himself in a situation like this as it conflicts with his masculinity.

The executive's wife may have to be half father as well as mother. He does not spend as much time with the children as other men. This is rather a blow to you. Visions of the family circle and romps with the children have materialized into cold reality, 'Dad is working tonight, just go to bed quietly'. Disappointed? Yes of course you are.

What is the answer? As in many things there is no good answer. Bring him to compromise with you. This will help, but of course it can never be complete. This is his life, it is part of the way up. It is your life too by identificaton. Can you understand? Logic doesn't help. It is only the deep understanding that transcends logic which saves us.

Keep in with his business friends. Don't reject them. This is a common cause of misunderstandings. It is easy to say what you feel. 'They are not like us.' But help him with them.

There is also another angle. We cannot consciously bring ourselves to identify with someone else. But by doing something together we can provide a background on which identification can more easily occur. Seeing his business friends at least brings you together, and of course it also helps in a material fashion on the way up.

His secretary is younger than you are. And in actual fact he spends more of his waking life with her than he does with you. They have a pretty good understanding together, the two of them. Maybe he talks over his business problems with her. Perhaps he discloses his own worries and seeks her advice. If this is so, good. It is good for him and good for you, because this is such a help to a man. This is his technical business life, and she can talk and advise on this in a way you cannot. And it should not in any way threaten you. Remember that you are different, and live in a different world. It is really only your own inner sense of insecurity that can threaten you in this situation. If this should make you jealous, then you are in fact threatened because the jealousy in you will tend to turn him from you.

What should I do when I see he has had a bad day just as soon as he comes through the door? There are certain moments when our relationship with other people is more vulnerable than usual. This is one of them. It is a matter which frequently comes up in discussion with anxious patients. 'I knew immediately he came in that he was on edge; but what could I do?' Then she adds in self defence, 'After all I had a bad day too'. It is all so true. First of all there are several things which we must avoid doing.

Don't let his tension trigger off your own aggression. This is of fundamental importance. Yet judging from people who discuss these things with me, it must happen hundreds of times in almost every home.

The sequence follows this pattern. He has been frustrated at work; but he has to contain his frustration as he cannot blow off at his senior. As a result of it he comes home tense. You perceive his tension. You may be consciously aware of this, or it may be quite unconscious. In either case your level of anxiety is increased. You may or may not be aware that this makes you feel uncomfortable. In response to this situation you become aggressive to what has made you feel uncomfortable. But as you show your aggression to him in his tense and frustrated state of mind, he replies with his own aggression. And so it is on.

These initial exchanges of aggression are of course veiled. You may merely say, 'What's gone wrong?' On the face of it, this is innocent enough; but with the way you say it, and his own increased sensitivity on account of his tension, it can be felt as a hostile welcome. So might the simple remark, 'Well I've had a tough day too'. Any unconscious expression of aggression on your part is likely to evoke his hostility, and you are then almost certain to reply with some further aggression. There are a few quick exchanges; then one of you consciously realizes what is happening and makes himself keep quiet, and the incident simmers down. But damage has been done, and we should be able to avoid this type of situation.

Don't let his tension increase your anxiety and so make you fuss. You see him tense. You love him. You are immediately worried on his account. So you anxiously ask, 'Are you all right, dear?'

Your anxiety at his tension only makes him more tense. In addition it makes him feel guilty. He loves you. He sees that he has somehow upset you, and this stimulates his feeling of guilt. Then the same sequence starts again. He does not like feeling guilty, and he becomes hostile to you who have quite innocently made him feel guilty.

So when he comes in like this, relax for a moment and control your anxiety until things settle down. Remember that your anxiety is most commonly communicated by fussing as expressed by doing things for him that are not quite necessary and are more than the situation demands. Please don't think that all this that I say is unnecessary, or that it is unjust.

Don't seek justice. Seek a happy human life. The means of attaining a happy human life may involve you in something less than justice. But it is the end that counts.

This situation, when he comes in the door unconsciously tense, requires a kind of giving on your part. It is an emotional giving, and it comes at a time when it might seem umjust that any giving on your part should be required.

My answer to your attitude is this. It is giving when giving is really needed that counts. I have seen a number of women who, out of their intuitive wisdom, have managed their lives along this pattern with very great rewards. I see others, who seek only what is fair and just, and they have failed miserably.

Don't ask a lot of questions. You see something has upset him. So you ask questions to find out what it is. This would seem rational enough. If I were to ask you why you question him, I think you would say, 'To find out what is wrong, so that I can help him'. Very good. But I think that this is probably a rationalisation, and that you really ask the questions because the situation has made you anxious, and asking the questions reduces your anxiety.

Whatever the reason for your asking him the questions, your probing has a bad effect on him. Questioning always makes a tense person more tense. So let him sit down first, and have a rest for a few minutes and perhaps a drink and then he will be able to tell you the trouble easily and naturally.

So long as you don't let your anxiety get out of hand, your intuitive responses will guide you. What I am saying is, 'Be natural'. But you can't be natural if you are tense and anxious and het up at seeing him like this. So once again, the management of our own anxiety is the key to the situation.

To be natural means that you are calm; and this is not just a question of making your face appear calm, it means that you are in fact calm inside. You are calm, but you are also concerned for him because you love him. This is different from anxiety which is the opposite to calm and does not exist with it. Your concern is communicated naturally and affectionately by your manner and by what you do. And this bad moment, when he comes in the door all tensed up, passes and all is well again.

How will you stand up to his retirement? 'This will be fine. I have been looking forward to it for years.' Of course! You will see more of him, whereas in the past his work has so often come between you. There will be time to do things together again.

Be warned. I know from talking with patients that it does not always turn out like this. Many men who have had an active life, suddenly become anxious on retirement. This comes about because they feel that their world has suddenly fallen apart and they are left with a feeling of emptiness. You may recollect a similar feeling when the last of your children came to leave home. If he should experience anxiety in this way, he will unconsciously turn to you for emotional support. This may come quite unexpectedly, as it is out of character with his decisive personality as a business executive. Instead of taking you for a trip in the way you had imagined, you may find that the increase in his anxiety makes him want to stay at home. Instead of a gallant escort, you find him just restless about the house, not knowing how to fill in his time, not wanting you to leave him but not being very communicative when you are there. These are the common signs of a man having initial difficulty in adjusting to retirement. He will come through this all right; but while he is making the transition he very urgently needs your understanding and support.

There is a further point to this. If he is now at retiring age, there has probably been some falling off of his sexual power over the last few years. If such a man experiences retirement anxiety like this, it is quite likely that his sexual power will cease altogether. He feels this as a further step towards his final disintegration. Again, your understanding and support is vital to him. As he adjusts to his new life in retirement, and his anxiety settles down, there is a good chance of a return of potency.

The woman executive

A woman is not the same as a man. We hear people say, 'In the office we don't think of a woman as a woman. They are just members of staff, like anyone else.' But a woman is not the same as a man, and say what you like, their reactions are always slightly different. They need not in any way be overtly sexual; they need not in any way be complicated, but their reactions are different and that is equally important, we react differently to them. Why is it that we want to deny this, and try to convince ourselves that in the office a woman is the same as a man? This attitude is an unconscious psychological defence to make things easier for us by taking the sexuality out of our relationships. In this respect it serves a useful psychological function. But at the same time it tends to blind us to the advantages and disadvantages that a woman executive has in relation to a man.

Be a woman executive; don't try to be a man executive. I think it is here that many women executives make a mistake. They are venturing into new territory, into the area which was previously the world of men. It is new; it is uncertain. There are few guide posts as to patterns of behaviour. For this reason the woman executive is likely to have a high level of anxiety. So she unconsciously moulds herself into patterns of behaviour to reduce her tension. In this life, the more like a man she is, the easier it is; and she copes more easily because her anxiety is at a lower level.

This reaction of aiming to be like a man fulfills its unconscious psychological purpose in reducing anxiety, but at the same time makes things more difficult in other ways. She is thrown into direct competition with men on their own ground, where she will always be at a disadvantage. This is not what you want. Don't aim so much to compete with the men, but rather to compliment the functions of the men. Be a woman executive, and bring to the organization those particular assets of your personality which are lacking in a man.

Some women unconsciously want to be men. This is not an uncommon psychological reaction. Research in psychoanalysis and hypnosis has shown that it sometimes has its origin very early in life with the little girl being bathed with her brother and being jealous of him because he seems to have more than she has. This idea becomes repressed so that the girl no longer remembers having felt that way; but the vague idea that she would like to be a boy may persist. Then in adult life she may act out the idea by doing what a man does. She becomes an executive. But all the time she wants to be a man executive, not a woman executive, and for this reason her chances of success are less.

Other factors may contribute to the little girl's basic psychological desire to be a boy. The parents may have wanted a boy. Even if they never say anything about their disappointment to the girl, they may still unconsciously communicate it to her by their actions. For instance, they may dress the little girl in rather boyish clothes, give her toys that are usually given to a boy, and even give her the name of a boy. So she grows up wanting to be a man, and she competes against the others rather as a man than as a woman.

What can a woman offer to business that a man can't? Is it just that business is expanding and there are not enough men to fill all the jobs? You want a career and you fill one of these positions. I am sure that this happens. But if you are an executive woman on the way up, you want more than this. In fact you want the opposite of this situation. You must aim for a position in which being a woman gives you certain advantages over a man. Some of these positions are very obvious. A woman is usually much better at typing and shorthand than a man. But there are other more complex and more subtle assets which the woman executive should use to her advantage.

Feminine intuition is a different way of the mind functioning. Intuition is a process of the mind by which we come to a conclusion without the intermediate steps of logical thought. We just feel that we know something, and we are satisfied that we are right. This conclusion may come to us in a flash, and we suddenly have some insight which we did not have before. Intuition is a non-logical function of the mind. It is not illogical which would be contrary to logical. It is paralogical, which really means that it is a process quite different from the logical one.

It is always hard to understand about intuition, so let me explain some basic principles. Over the ages the mind of man has evolved from relative simplicity to great complexity. In this process we have evolved the ability of logical thought. This has proved a great advantage to us as a species, so by the process of natural selection our mind has developed further and further along these lines, and other ways of the mind functioning have fallen into disuse. Intuition is one of the other ways in which the mind can work. But it can only work in this way when the logical function is relatively in abeyance. It is important to realize that intuition is a different way of the mind functioning, and is not just the logical way working unconsciously or in less degree. An example may clarify things. I do a lot of work with hypnosis, particularly in the way of helping patients to be more relaxed. I have frequently had patients wake from a deep hypnotic sleep and tell me that the answer to some problem has come to them. This is the result of the intuitive function of the mind, as we know that logical functioning ceases or at least is very greatly reduced in hypnosis. I mention this as additional evidence as to the reality of intuition.

Men are more gifted at logical thinking; women are more gifted with intuition. This of course is a generalization. Many gifted men, scientists, philosophers, poets, use intuitive thinking to full advantage. Many intelligent women have well developed logical faculties. But in general a woman has the advantage over a man in her capacity to think intuitively. The woman executive on the way up wants to be able to use this natural advantage.

Perhaps we should consider what intuition can do, and where it falls down. Intuition can make the breakthrough when we are unable to go further by the logical method. An analysis of many great discoveries shows that the final step, the ultimate breakthrough came in a flash of intuition rather than by some process of logic. We often lose sight of the extent to which intuition works. As soon as we come to a conclusion by intuition we go back and produce logical reasons for it. We then rationalize and come to believe that we came to the conclusion logically.

The disadvantage of intuitive thinking is that the process may go wrong, and we cannot check it over to be sure that it is right in the same way as we can with a logical conclusion.

How can a woman use her intuition in business? First let me say that I think that the scientific validity of this other way of thinking is beyond all doubt. Well, how do you use it practically? In an ideal situation it should be used to provide the breakthrough into new ideas when the logical approach is failing. The intuitive ideas should then be checked as far as possible by logically minded men. In other words an intuitive woman should be able to bring something to a group of logically minded men.

A woman has greater knowledge in certain fields. This principle is now widely accepted, and women are working more and more in these areas. For instance, a woman in medicine has distinct advantages in pediatrics and child psychiatry, as well as in obstetrics and gynaecology. The same applies in architecture, to interior decorating and kitchen layout. There is fashion, the clothing trade, and much of advertising in which a woman has greater personal experience than a man. And one can think of many other such areas. It is in these areas particularly that the female executive wants to work as a woman not as a man.

Feminine passivity can cope with some situations better than masculine aggression. Aggression is a masculine characteristic, and it provides the psychological drive that brings men to fight against a hostile environment, master it, and modify it to their own liking. Passivity is a psychological characteristic of the mature woman. By virtue of this she can cope with a hostile environment in a different way. This is a way which is difficult for the aggressive man. Through her passivity, she can go along with a hostile environment. By adjusting to it passively she can tolerate it better than a man. And rather than fight against it all, she can accept those elements of the hostile environment which it is possible for her to use. These two different approaches to life are of course related to our different biological roles as man and woman.

Let us consider these principles in relation to the practical world of business, and the woman executive on the way up. If the business situation is such that it can be altered to our advantage by an active and decisive approach, then the men with their masculine-aggressive psychological orientation are well equipped to deal with it. But if in our business we are up against some situation which cannot be improved by any action on our part, it is a question of adjusting to it and getting the best we can out of the existing circumstances. It is here that a woman with her traditional feminine-passive pattern of life should be able to help.

There is, however, a further complicating factor in this. In becoming an executive, a woman is breaking new ground. This requires determination and aggression on her part. In fact a woman lacking these qualities might find it harder than ever to succeed. The result is that many executive women have a greater masculine-aggressive bias to their personality than does the average mature feminine-passive woman. In consequence they do not bring this useful feminine attribute to the business, and in this respect they function like a man.

Don't base a career-girl image on false values. You have seen the woman executive on the films. She is a smart, well dressed young woman in a fashionable apartment, having drinks and bright conversation with sophisticated men companions. This is the image. It is a false one. The woman executive is a working woman, and she has to work hard.

Is there a conflict between career and marriage? Remember that there is no overall answer that applies to all of us. We are all different, and the right decision depends on our own particular circumstances and our individual personality. There are, however, some general principles that would apply to most of the young women who have consulted me in this situation.

Sometimes the problems seem to concern the choice between the real satisfaction of the present job, and the hope of still greater satisfaction in marriage. Are you deeply at ease with your man? Do you want him physically? Do you want to have his children? If you answer these three questions in the affirmative, and provided that there is not something clearly to the contrary, you should marry however much you like your present job. If you are often edgy together, and if you really do not care much about having a family, the situation is much more doubtful.

Don't forget that the young executive likes to flirt with business women. He finds you bright company because you are alert and are well versed in things that interest him. These are not necessarily things which would make him seek marriage. The danger to you is in allowing this situation to drift on indefinitely thinking that an offer of marriage will be made at any moment. This is still more likely to happen if the relationship has developed into an affair, and the man's motivation for marriage is so much reduced.

If you are a competent but rather bossy, masculine-aggressive type of career woman, you may not be well suited to marriage. Those elements of your personality will be of greater advantage in your career than in your home. Then of course there is also the future to look to. Marriage brings a different type of security to the firm's retirement fund.

Can you have the best of both worlds, successful marriage and successful career? Many women do. But these are gifted people. These are the elite. Can you aspire to this?

It is not just luck that some women are successful in their dual role of life. They know what they are doing, either by conscious reasoning or by intuitive wisdom. I do not think that they have two equal roles in life. I think the really successful ones all give their marriage first priority, and they still remain successful in their career. I have seen women as patients who have been failing in their two lives. These women have rather put their career first. The marriage has not gone too well. They have become tense and edgy so that their career has also suffered.

Is the woman executive Lesbian? When the cocktail party conversation is lagging, there is always homosexuality and Lesbianism as a topic. It is the same in the office; and the gossip turns to the woman executive. This type of talk is so prevalent, and often so misinformed that it deserves some clarification.

Perhaps it is well to mention that those who are most ready to gossip in this way are in fact revealing a latent tendency to homosexuality in themselves. This of course is why the subject is so intriguing to such people. A person's reactions always disclose what is going on in his mind beneath the surface. Thus the judge who is habitually severe with homosexuals is really protesting to the public that he abhors that way of life; and the reason he abhors it publicly is that he is secretly threatened by it.

It is well to remember that an individual is physically either a man or a woman. There are no halfway stages. But psychologically it is different. Every man has some female aspects to his personality, and these vary from very little to quite a significant degree. The same applies to women. Because the aggressive masculine element of the personality is of value in the competitive life of business, it is natural that we should expect women who enter business and the professions to have more masculine characteristics than the average. The great majority of these women have a normal heterosexual life. On the other hand there will be some who have made a Lesbian adjustment. An important point for those who would gossip and thus disturb the smooth running of things, is that it is not always possible to pick the Lesbian or the male homosexual simply on appearances.

The woman executive may have problems with her male subordi-

nates. This is only to be expected. The woman in business who assumes authority over a man is reversing their natural biological roles. We may talk a lot about equality; this may be well, but we must not forget the inherent differences of men and women. The woman in virtue of her passivity accepts his protection so that she can rear the family. You may say, 'What has this got to do with running a business?' It is this. These personality characteristics are deeply ingrained in us and, although we try to dissociate them from civilized business activity, they are still with us. Taking orders from a woman conflicts with a man's innate sense of masculinity. So he tends to feel threatened and ill at ease. Added to this there is a further psychological difficulty. As children we all accepted the authority of our parents, both mother and father. And the little boy accepts the authority of his female teacher at kindergarten and the early grades of school. To be under the authority of a woman in adult life unconsciously activates these memories, and the man has the uncomfortable feeling of being a little boy again.

You are a woman on the way up. I am not trying to discourage you from assuming executive office. I mention these things merely to warn you of possible difficulties, and to give you some idea of the psychological undercurrents on which they are based. By being aware how men may feel, these difficulties can be largely overcome.

Avoid the authoritative approach. This follows from what we have just been discussing. The danger is that the woman tends to be insecure in her role as executive. She may react to her insecurity by a very forthright attempt to establish an authoritative status. 'I will show them who is boss; then it will all be easy.' An insecure male executive can often use this approach successfully in the process of establishing himself. But with the woman executive it is much less likely to be successful because of the way that it arouses antagonism in the subordinate men.

In avoiding authority, don't turn to a seductive approach. It is easy for a woman to fall into this mistake. After all, how does a woman bring a man to do what she wants? She does it by making him like her. She may do it directly or indirectly but in either case it is essentially a seductive approach. This is sensible and natural; she is simply using her biological assets to advantage. Because she is a woman she has the ability for dealing with men. Don't forget that the seductive element in the approach may be very well disguised so that neither she nor the man really know what is going on. Nevertheless, it is a matter of using the sexual element of her personality to attain her ends. In business relationships this is dangerous on a long term basis because of the danger of emotional involvement on the one hand, or of provoking jealousies on the other.

Aim to use the feminine-passive element of your personality in managing subordinate men. It was easy to describe to you the authoritative approach and the seductive approach. This is more difficult. The authoritative approach is based on the power of the practical reality of your position in the firm; the seductive approach is based on the power of disguised sexual elements in your personality. This other approach is something different, and concerns a man's innate desire to please a woman. This is a part of his nature. If you can tap this hidden psychological trait in the men around you, then it is easy. There is no need to evoke authority or to fall back on a disguised seductive approach. You express a wish and they do it.

You may feel that this is all rather remote, and perhaps even a little romantic. But watch carefully and observe how some mature women get things done, and you will see this process in action.

6

How to obtain information from others who are reluctant to give it

Obtaining information from a reluctant subordinate

We must bring him to avoid holding back and lead him to abandon his natural restraint. We want him to be free and spontaneous with us, so that he will pass on information which might be of use to us although it is beyond the actual answers to the questions that we put to him.

The usual situation is that the other person is prepared to give us some information, but not all that he could. So our problem is how to illicit more information than the other person really intends to disclose.

Don't think that you can obtain all the information just because you are in a position of authority. People make this mistake time after time. We are likely to think that if we are in authority over the other person, all we need to do is to ask the questions and we will get the answers. This is not so. Our experience with naughty children should be enough to convince us that authoritative questioning can get us nowhere. It is too easy to answer 'I don't know.' 'I did not see it.' 'I don't remember.' If we use our authority by saying 'If you can't remember pretty soon I shall punish you', we rarely get any further.

The situation is just the same in obtaining information from a reluctant business subordinate only that his methods of evasion are rather more sophisticated than that of a naughty child. We can use our authority to ask questions which the reluctant subordinate has to answer, but somehow we do not obtain just the information that we require.

The use of authority makes the other person resentful. This reaction is so common that we must regard it as natural. I think the reason is that the subordinate unconsciously interprets the authoritative questioning by his superior as aggression. Our natural biological response is to meet aggression with aggression. This is a kind of built in protective reaction. In the particular circumstances of a business interview, the subordinate manifests his aggression as resentment. This provides the underlying psychological motivation which makes him unco-operative, and prevents us obtaining the information which he should be able to provide quite readily.

If you have any doubts about this, the next time you have occasion to question a reluctant subordinate, watch him closely. It is almost certain that you will see his aggression expressed in the tension of his face, the set of the jaw, the tightening of the lips, and the slight retraction of the upper eyelids. He unconsciously leans forward in his chair in uncon-scious preparation for action, and his fingers curl up as if ready to make a fist. His voice loses the easy rhythm of normal con-versation. It becomes harsher as his aggression produces an unconscious reaction to frighten his adversary.

If we rely on authoritative questioning, the other person will not volunteer any additional information. This is most important. When we seek information from someone who is reluctant to give it, the usual situation is that we are seeking something rather indefinite. This means that it is difficult to obtain the information from a person who politely answers just, 'Yes' or 'No'. To obtain the information that we want, the other person must volunteer something. This is exactly what does not happen when we question the other person authoritatively. He simply answers our questions, and because he feels unconsciously hostile, he does not volunteer that extra little bit of informa-tion which may be so vital to us. This is the reason why authoritative questioning so often fails. It is because we cannot use this approach to bring the other person to volunteer helpful comments.

Even when we are in a position of authority, we must establish rapport with the reluctant subordinate. This is the first step towards encouraging his spontaneous comments which are often so important to us. In other words we aim to change the reluctant subordinate into a friendly discussant. This must be done in a natural and easy way. There must be nothing about our behaviour to suggest to our subordinate that the boss is fawning on him. If this happens he will become supicious and still more unlikely to volunteer useful information. We are still the boss, but we can change our role from that of authoritative boss to that of friendly boss. This produces a reciprocal change in the role of the other person, from resentful subordinate to friendly subordinate. We are now in a position to form rapport by means of the communication of friendliness and trust which we have already discussed in some detail.

It may well be that the other person's reluctance to give us the information is simply due to his insecurity. With rapport he becomes reassured and the motivation for him to withhold the information is dispelled.

If we observe that the other person is withholding information, we must not let it make us hostile. This is quite a danger. The other person will not immediately start to volunteer the bits of useful information. He must first feel really secure with us; so it is natural at the commencement of the interview that he should withhold information. This is a tricky stage of the interview. His withholding is really a hostile act. If we let the hostile act make us aggressive, we lose everything. Instead of a friendly subordinate, we are back with a reluctant subordinate. Please note that I have said that his hostile withholding must not make us aggressive. To feel aggressive about it, and to cover it up is simply not good enough. The other person still senses our aggression even if he is not aware of it in full consciousness. So, like the psychiatrist, the successful business negotiator must be able to avoid letting his own aggression become mobilized when faced with the hostility of the other person .

Our own relaxation saves us from becoming hostile with the other person. This is the key to the situation in psychiatry. It is also the key to a successful business interview. By letting ourselves be really relaxed we do not experience these hostile feelings when we are thwarted by the other person. It is not a question of covering up our hostile feelings by presenting a facade of relaxation. Of course that is better than nothing, but it is not what we aim to do. We set out standard higher than that. We are relaxed, and because we are really relaxed, his hostile behaviour of withholding information simply does not worry us, and there is no concealed hostile reaction on our part. We are not really involved, and we are not emotionally disturbed in a way that would distort our preception and lead us to ill-considered reactions. Instead, through our inner relaxation we are free to respond in the way most appropriate to the circumstances.

We can increase rapport by communicating our relaxation, and so annul the other person's hostile reaction. We are not only relaxed but we communicate our relaxation. This means that the other person sees us as free from anxiety and without showing the ordinary defensive alertness which is a usual part of everyday life. This is tantamount to exposing ourselves psychologically to the other person. We are making no attempt to hide anything. He can see into us, and he sees that we are not in any way on guard watching him. This is passivity, and in the face of passivity the other person's hostility peters out.

We achieve this by letting the other person see our physical relaxation. Our posture in the chair is one of relaxation. Our wrists are flexed and our hands hang down. Our face muscles are relaxed and the lips slightly parted. It is important that the eyelids participate in this so that the eyes are only half open. In fact the eyelids come to close, quite slowly and naturally, and then open again equally slowly and naturally. Remember that with an experienced psychiatrist or skilful business negotiator, all this happens with complete naturalness and utter effortlessness. The other person's hostility disappears as there is nothing about us to make him hostile. We talk on in a relaxed way, and now it is likely that the other person will volunteer the useful little bits of information which he was previously withholding.

If necessary we can confuse the other person by increasing his anxiety and so bring him to disclose more than he intended. This is the common method used by police in interrogation and by barristers in questioning witnesses in the law courts. Almost every day one can read in the papers the evidence of some expert witnesses, which is clearly a half truth elicited by pressure of anxiety skilfully mobilized by the barrister in cross-examination. The same principles can be applied in an individual interview.

The other person's level of anxiety is increased by inducing an air of significance and uncertainty. Questions keep reverting back to some area in which he is uncomfortable. If there is something which the other person has cause to feel slightly guilty about, he is questioned at length around this point. This may be merely some minor aspect of his work which has not gone well; but in the circumstances it can be used to produce a sense of guilt. Persons with obsessive and introvert characteristics can be most easily manipulated in this way. As a result of this, the other person's anxiety is increased to a level at which he loses his ability for clear and considered thinking. In this mild confusion he tells us the things that he should, but which he had intended not to disclose.

The same principles can be applied in provoking a person to make him angry. Again, this is a technique frequently exploited by barristers in the law courts. It is most successfully used against people who are rather pompous and self opinionated, who regard themselves as experts, and who do not often have their opinions queried.

We can use the other person's personality characteristics either to form rapport or to increase his anxiety. We have seen how an individual's personality characteristics are really an expression of his habitual pattern of coping with life. When the individual is in a situation which gives full scope to his personality characteristics, the general level of his anxiety is reduced and he feels at ease. But if he is in a situation in which he cannot indulge his personality characteristics, his anxiety is increased and he feels tense and uncomfortable. The obsessive feels at ease in his meticulous routine of doing things, but is uncomfortable when he has to work in some large scale disordered environment. So with the introvert who is at ease when he can withdraw a little, but who becomes anxious if suddenly placed in the centre of attention.

We can use this principle to advantage in interviewing. If we want to form close rapport, we modify the interview to suit the other person's personality characteristics. This is not difficult. We go along with his approach to things; or if he is our subordinate we set the tone of the interview appropriate to his personality. If he is obsessive we deal with the matters, one, two, three, in orderly sequence. If he is hysteric we participate in his rather dramatic way of expressing his ideas. We show our own sensitivity to an introvert. We can do this by commenting how someone else must feel about the situation, then he knows that we understand how he feels. We have an open approach to extraverts. And if it is a woman of masculine-aggressive personality, we are passive and give her the feeling of being the boss.

On the other hand, if we want to increase the other person's anxiety, we proceed quite differently. We are casual, off-hand and haphazard with an obsessive. This makes him feel uncomfortable and increases his anxiety in a way that many people find it hard to understand. With a shy introvert, 'I shall have you explain this to those other people'. We make no response to the gestures of the hysteric. He feels he has fallen flat and his anxiety is increased. Our cold formality disarms the friendly and gregarious extravert, and he is immediately uncomfortable.

In reading this, please do not think that I am writing about exceptionally disordered persons. This is not so. Nearly all the people with whom you have contact have these personality traits in greater or lesser degree, and it is not difficult to use them to advantage in the ordinary discussions of everyday business.

Obtaining information from a reluctant superior

We can also obtain information from a reluctant superior. This of course is a more difficult task. The fact that the other person is our superior makes it improper for us to ask direct questions. So we have to rely on indirect means. Don't forget that the indirect method of obtaining information is often very reliable. Because the information is obtained indirectly it is not consciously censored by the other person. This is in contrast to the direct method, in which the other person answers a direct question. In this case the answer is censored critically and logically so that the answer given tends to be guarded. It may be only a half truth, or it may be truthful on its face value but presented to us in such a way as to mislead us. This degree of censoring does not occur in the indirect method. So, provided we can interpret the answer correctly, we have the real truth undistorted by the other person.

To bring the reluctant superior to give us the information which he should, we can first make contact by seeking his advice. Because of our inferior position we have to have some excuse to contact our reluctant superior. One of the easiest ways is simply to seek his advice on some matter. If this can be genuine, so much the better. Failing this, it is not difficult to find some matter in which we can seek a superior's opinion. The matter on which we seek advice should not be the subject on which he is reluctant to give information; but if possible it should be in the same field; so, when the time comes, it will not be too difficult to move on to the matter in question.

The approach by seeking advice has a number of advantages. It makes it hard for our superior to reject us. By seeking his advice we flatter him; we bolster his ego. This makes him feel good; and in consequence of feeling good, he unconsciously feels well disposed towards the person who makes him feel this way. This makes rapport come more easily.

Although we are in an inferior position, we can still form rapport with a reluctant superior. We have already discussed the various psychological reactions which are involved in the formation of rapport. When the other person is a reluctant superior we follow the same principles, but we proceed rather more cautiously. We cannot immediately make offers of friendship, as this would be sensed as out of place. But we can communicate trust; and this is completely appropriate, from a junior to a senior. It has the effect of bringing the reluctant superior to trust. us. We can do this by asking advice about some minor failure on our part. In this way we offer trust by expressing our weakness, and the reluctant superior unconsciously reacts by coming to trust us.

We can also aid the formation of rapport with a reluctant superior by communicating respect. When we do this, it must be a natural, man to man, respect, and not just the formal respect of good manners which is conveyed by a, 'Yes sir', 'No sir', type of attitude. The quality of the respect must be natural rather than formal, because the formation of rapport is essentially a natural emotional response. This type of natural respect is communicated by our attitude, our bearing and the way in which we conduct ourselves rather than by what we say.

It is only now, when we have communicated trust and respect, and when we are aware that the reluctant superior has made some favourable response to these communications that we are in a position to communicate the central theme of rapport which is friendliness. An offer to do something for the reluctant superior has this effect. Such an offer must be natural and carry the quality of being genuine. There must be no sign of ingratiation or trying to please.

Flatter his ego. Almost all of us are susceptible to flattery if the approach is subtle enough. The business executive, the big boss, is characteristically not a humble man. As a result of the executive position in which he is placed he is likely to have what is commonly called an inflated ego. We can work on this. And of course we do this in such a way that he is not aware of what we are doing. This is really not difficult. We slant our answers to his initial questions in such a way as to flatter his ego. If something is better, we link it in some way with our superior. We do not say that, 'It has been better since Bill Smith took over', but rather, 'It has been better since you arranged for Bill Smith to take over'. All sorts of events can be linked in this way with our superior. His ego is further inflated. He feels good. He unconsciously comes to have a liking for us. He is less on guard, and consequently so much the more likely to disclose to us what we want to know.

Bolster his feeling of power. Another useful mechanism is one which unconsciously appeals to our superior's sense of power. In addition to bolstering his ego, we can add to his feeling of strength by emphasizing our own lowliness in relation to his superiority. He comes to feel very strong, very superior. So strong and so superior that we are insignificant. Unconsciously he goes off-guard and with a little manoeuvring of the conversation on our part, he is likely to say things which he would otherwise have left unsaid.

If our moves to form rapport go well, we may be able to put indirect questions. In doing this we make a transition from seeking his advice. We started the interview doing this. But the emotional relationship between the two of us, due to our rapport, now allows us to continue the interview into a slightly different area. It is well to note that without rapport this is impossible. If we have failed to gain rapport, the reluctant superior gives us the advice which we seek and that concludes the interview. He just dismisses us, and that is that. But rapport allows us to prolong the interview, and change its character from the initial seeking of advice. When we have rapport we can continue along these lines, 'There is another thing I have often intended to ask you'. This type of phrase can serve to lead him into the area where he has been reluctant to help us.

We can sometimes soften up a reluctant superior by involving him in some emotional responses. If we have rapport, we can sometimes venture into telling a joke. 'What you say reminds me of such and such'. Of course, we must be sure of our man before we take such a step. There are many superiors to whom one should never venture a joke. But if the personality of the other person is suitable, it may not be too difficult to do this. The subject of the advice which we seek will concern something in the firm. In any firm there are always odd or humorous incidents taking place. If we can gain the opportunity to recount such an incident, the psychological effect is that we share the accompanying emotion with the other person. This is a kind of shared experience, and does much to bring us together and strengthen rapport. If such a story relates to people in the firm, we must be sure that the butt of the story is not some particular friend of our superior. It is by far the best, when possible, to relate some incident in which we ourselves are the butt. This has the additional advantage of also offering trust by disclosing our weakness.

If it is not possible to put indirect questions, we can still obtain information from a reluctant superior by observing changes in his

level of anxiety. This is a basic principle of psychiatry. I want to find out what is worrying the patient so that I can help him; but he feels so ashamed of what has happened that he cannot bring himself to tell me. I try to make it easier for him by doing all I can to strengthen rapport, but maybe he is a difficult and suspicious person, and he still cannot tell me. In these circumstances he is very like a reluctant superior in business; and I try the other way to obtain the information. It is rather difficult because I do not know in what direction his worry lies. So I allow our conversation to drift from topic to topic. In a relaxed kind of way I bring him to talk a little about his work and about his boss. Then I let the subject shift on to his home, his wife, their children, their finances, their friends, and their intimate life together. All the time I watch for changes in the level of his anxiety, as shown by his position in the chair, the tone of his voice, his rate of speaking, changes in the expression and colour of his face, the tension of his lips, the retraction of the upper eyelids, and the size of his pupils, signs of sweating, the position of his hands, and his rate of breathing. It usually happens that when I bring up some particular subject there is a sudden increase in his level of his nervous tension as shown by changes in these physiological accompaniments of anxiety. I then know in what area his trouble lies. I then let him settle down a little by introducing inconsequential conversation. Then I return to the trouble area again. If it should be thought of his work that increase his anxiety, I now talk of different aspects of his work. Is it too difficult; is the pay adequate; is the boss worrying him; is his wife pushing him for promotion? These matters are not put as questions, but are subjects brought into the conversation. The exact worry of the patient soon becomes obvious. I talk a little about it, and he soon comes to volunteer that this in fact is the matter which has been worrying him.

The business negotiator must train himself to observe minor changes of anxiety in the other person. In fact the successful business man is using psychiatric principles all the time. This is essential to the method which we have described for obtaining information from a reluctant superior. It is not difficult to learn. Young psychiatrists soon pick up it, and an astute business man can do so equally easily. It is largely a matter of continual practice in ordinary conversation with our friends. We soon learn that our friends respond differently to common subjects of conversation such as, women, politics, and religion, according to the individual's degree of emotional involvement. The business negotiator must not only learn to observe these minor changes in the other person's level of anxiety, but he must learn to do so in a natural way so that the other person is not aware that he is in any way being observed.

Obtaining information in negotiation

In negotiation we obtain information when the other is off guard. This follows the psychological principle which we have already discussed. Rapport is the essential factor. There is a tendency in business negotiations to get down to business very quickly. If we wish to obtain information from the others who are reluctant to give it, we must do what we can to avoid this rush to get started. We need a few moments for friendly and inconsequential talk to allow time for the emotional reactions which are the basis of rapport.

In our talk together before the formal business, we can often ascertain the other person's general attitudes. We may note that he displays spontaneous interest when we mention some subject near to the one on which we desire information. On the other hand, it may be clear that it is a matter of no concern to him at all

In these short conversations prior to the formal discussion, it is common for the conversation to switch on to mutual friends and acquaintances who work in the same field as ourselves. It is easy to bring into the conversation the name of someone who works in the area of the information which we seek. The other person's reaction to this may well give useful cues. Then we can put the casual question, 'How does he feel about such and such'. This being the problem in which we are interested, but the question comes up in off hand fashion as in polite conversation.

If we want to obtain information, keep the negotiations as informal as possible. It is much easier to bring the other person off guard in an informal atmosphere. In this respect a discussion at a formal conference table with a stenographer taking down the proceedings makes this very much more difficult. In these circumstances aim to establish rapport before the formal business.

7

How to bring other people to accept our ideas

When you read this, it may seem quite a tough assignment. But to bring someone to change his ideas is a common purpose of a business interview. We should note that this is also a common purpose of the psychiatric interview, in which I might aim to change the patient's ideas towards something more realistic or more ethical.

We can persuade people by logic

We can influence the other person either by logic or by suggestion. Ideas may be accepted into the mind by either of two different psychological processes, by logical evaluation or by the process of suggestion. An idea may be examined and critically evaluated by the logical functions of the mind. If from this examination, it is thought that the idea is a sound one, it is accepted into the mind, and becomes part of the individual's personal beliefs or attitudes. On the other hand, if the idea is found to be unsound, it is rejected. The individual may think about it and talk about it, but it is not part of his beliefs or attitudes. This is of course an entirely logical process, and we like to believe that most of the ideas which we hold have been accepted by us in this fashion. But I am afraid that this is not so.

In the logical approach we appeal to the other person's reason by the logical use of words. So it is essential for us to express ourselves clearly and concisely in a way that can be easily understood by the other person. We must remember that the other person may be less intelligent than we are, and he may not be able to comprehend complex propositions quite as clearly as we can. We must also remember that he may not have the subject matter at his finger tips in the same way as we do; and most important, he may not be as familiar as we are with the technical language of the subject. Psychiatrists often fall into this error of using their technical jargon when talking with doctors who specialize in other fields.

In using the logical approach to bring the other person to change his ideas, we not only take care to communicate clearly and logically, but we also pay attention to the various psychological mechanisms associated with anxiety and hostility which might work against his acceptance of our ideas, and which we have already discussed. As the logical approach is in fact logical, it is easily understood; so I shall devote most of my space to the discussion of the other, more elusive, approach to bringing the other person to accept our ideas.

We can bring people to accept our ideas by suggestion

Suggestion is the psychological process by which ideas are accepted into the mind in response to our emotional relationship with the other person. In fact the process of suggestion does not depend on the logical functions of the mind at all. This concept may seem strange to you at first. But we must come to accept the fact that a great many of the ideas of normal people like you and me have been accepted into our minds by a process which does not involve any critical evaluation at all. When the process of suggestion is operating the idea is accepted or rejected, not according to its logical merits, but according to our emotional relationship with the person who is presenting the idea to us.

Although the acceptance of ideas by suggestion is non-logical it is sounder than one might expect. We over-value our logical abilities and are rather inclined to minimise or neglect the importance of our other mental abilities. Of course, if the process of suggestion had not been of use to us, it would never have become part of our biological heritage. As a general principle it is sound enough to accept ideas from those with whom we have a good emotional relationship, and reject the ideas of those with whom we have a bad relationship. We accept the ideas of our friends and reject those of our enemies. We accept all that a loved one tells us. The child who cannot yet logically evaluate and criticise accepts the ideas of his parents by the process of suggestion.

Suggestion is a primitive function of the mind. It will help us to use the process of suggestion intelligently if we understand it in its proper biological perspective. In the long process of evolution, man's ability of logical critical thinking is a recently acquired function of the mind. Before primitive man acquired this logical critical ability there must have been some other psychological mechanism which determined the acceptance or rejection of ideas into his primitive mind. This of course was the process of suggestion. If the primitive liked the person offering the idea, he accepted it. We can see that although the process is not a logical one, there is still good sense in it. Through it we come to accept ideas which are offered by our parents and tribal leaders. By and large, ideas accepted from these sources should not lead us to much harm in the biological sense.

Primitive suggestion has been superceded by the logical process. Please don't think that I am being too theoretical. This is intended as an essentially practical book. It aims to explain basic psychological principles so that these can be used in a practical fashion by those on the way up. But to develop these practical skills and use them effectively we must understand the theory on which they are based.

The process by which ideas are accepted by suggestion is something which evolved with the dawn of the human race. More recently man learned how to think logically and critically, and came to use this new process to accept ideas into his mind. We have found that this is a better process, and we are gradually discarding the use of suggestion in favour of the logical process. In this respect mankind is in a state of flux. At one time we use the logical method, and at another we fall back on the older process of suggestion. This is going on every day with all of us.

When we accept an idea by suggestion, we rationalize and convince ourselves that it has been a logical process. The next point which we must understand is that we are thinking beings and are given to asking the question, 'Why?' We ask ourselves, 'Why do I hold these ideas?' This is a logical question, and we try to give ourselves a logical answer. So we find logical reasons as to why we hold any particular idea, and these usually seem convincing enough to us. The problem of course is that we may have originally accepted the ideas uncritically by suggestion in which case the logical reasons which we evoke are merely an excuse to ourselves for holding the ideas which were accepted by suggestion. This process of finding acceptable reasons for things is known as rationalisation, and it is very important in the matter of bringing someone else to change his ideas.

Suggestion works only in the absence of logical criticism. There is one more theoretical point which we must fully understand. Suggestion works in virtue of our emotional relationship with the person offering the idea. But if our critical faculties are fully active, it does not matter how complete or intense the emotional relationship may be, the critical faculties put a complete stop to the action of suggestion.

But there is a rather puzzling matter about this. Although the critical faculties put a complete stop to the acceptance of new ideas by suggestion, once an unsound idea has in fact been accepted by suggestion, the critical faculties are generally ineffective in helping us to get rid of the unsound idea. The critical faculties are only effective in preventing us taking in new unsound ideas. The unsound ideas which we have already picked up by suggestion have become a part of the general make-up of our personality, and are very successfully protected by the process of rationalization which we have already discussed.

An idea accepted by suggestion may be sound or unsound. We do not want to fall into the erroneous way of thinking that it is only unsound ideas which are accepted by suggestion. Quite the contrary. Most of the ideas which we accept by suggestion are in fact sound. This is what we would expect from our theoretical discussion. The ideas offered by those with whom we have a good relationship, parents and respected leaders, are in general sound ones

How can we apply these theoretical ideas in the practical world of business. There are three separate factors which determine whether or not an idea will be accepted uncritically. There is the emotional relationship, the prestige of the person offering the idea, and the absence of critical logical functioning of the mind. Let us translate these rather psychological concepts into the practical reality of coping with people. The emotional relationship, the love of the child for the parent, becomes the rapport which we establish with the other person as we talk with him. The respect with which the primitive regarded the tribal leaders becomes the status, social and professional, of the individual as he copes with other people. The absence of critical functioning is simply the relaxed, easy state of mind which we bring to the other as we talk with him.

There is a passive way and also an authoritarian way of using suggestion. The two approaches cannot be used together. We must use either one or the other. The passive use of suggestion depends upon the reactivation of the psychological mechanisms by which a mother passively brings her child to accept her ideas. In business life this method centres around our rapport with the other person. On the other hand the authoritarian use of suggestion depends upon the reactivation of the psychological mechanisms which are involved when a father authoritatively brings his child to accept his ideas. To use this approach in business, the effective mechanism is the assumption of prestige.

Rapport is essential if we are to bring another person to accept our ideas by passive suggestion. We have discussed the element of trust in rapport. We bring the other person to have rapport in the true sense. His trust is complete; and he just accepts what we say as a natural consequence of our relationship.

Rapport of this complete form is common between doctor and patient, between those who love each other, and between close friends. The rapport of business is a move in this direction, and although it is never so complete as in the cases cited, it can be used successfully to bring the other person to accept our ideas.

Rapport is the adult equivalent of a child's love of his mother. This is why it has such an important effect on our acceptance of ideas. In the adult situation, the old psychological mechanisms of bygone days are reactivated, and allow us to incorporate ideas which would otherwise be subject to logical scrutiny.

We can influence people more easily by suggestion if we have prestige. In psychology, prestige represents the exalted status of one individual over another. It represents the status of the tribal leader over the ordinary members of the tribe. This is the situation in which the primitive process of suggestion has evolved in times before the evolution of the logical faculties of the mind.

Prestige is the adult equivalent of the father's relationship to his child. This is different from rapport which involves a symbolic reactivation of the child's love of his mother. Prestige on the other hand involves the reactivation of the child's acceptance of the status and authority of the father. When a person has prestige in relation to another adult, he seems big and strong, wise and powerful, just in the same way as the father appeared like this to the child.

How do we establish prestige when we want to bring someone to accept our ideas by suggestion? How do we make ourselves appear like a tribal leader or a father to another clear headed businessman? Anything that impresses the other person helps to add to our prestige. Our professional standing, our business reputation, our position in the firm, the size of the firm, the importance of the task allotted to us, all these things add to our prestige. A big and expensively furnished office, an efficient secretary and receptionist are all matters which can give an individual status over another person. The things that I have mentioned appear rather trite. In fact, they are trite when we think of these in relation to any real sense of values. Prestige is a rather trite concept, but this does not lessen its psychological power.

In the ordinary affairs of business, the most practical way of using prestige is by personally assuming status. We can then use this to bring the other person to accept our ideas. We do this by assuming a mantle of importance and power in relation to the other person. Everything we do which adds to our status or detracts from the status of the other person will make it easier for him to accept our ideas by suggestion. We keep him waiting, we ignore him, we let the receptionist deal with him rather than talk to him ourselves; then when he finally gains our presence, he is seated in an inferior and uncomfortable chair. We hardly notice him. Before speaking to him, we finish writing on some papers on the desk. Then we look up, 'What is it? I only have a few minutes'.

Psychologically we gain prestige by establishing authority by extra-verbal communication. 'Put your coat there'. 'Sit down here'. 'I must just finish this first'. The skilful interviewer can establish prestige without offending the other person and without making him in any way feel hostile. We develop this status in which the other looks up to us just as the son looks up to the good father and the follower looks up to the good tribal leader. We tell him to put his coat there. We don't give him any choice. The extra-verbal meaning of the words leaves no doubt as to who is in charge.

There are innumerable variations to this opening gambit. We can ask him his name, even if we know it quite well; or if that would be too inappropriate, we ask what his position is or what he does. Even when he has informed us in advance of the purpose of his visit we ask, 'What have you come to see me about?' All such manoeuvres enhance our status at the expense of the other person.

The psychological effect of prestige is to make the other person regress. In psychology, regression is a return to childhood patterns of behaviour. When we assume prestige, the other person looks upon us as being big, strong, adult and powerful. In the face of this he himself feels small. He feels like a child again. More than this; the most important thing of all, he comes to function as a child again. This is psychological regression. It is just the way that his mental processes are working; and there may be many little outward signs of what is happening. Strange as it may seem, minor degrees of this process occur very easily and very frequently in ordinary everyday life, and pass quite unnoticed both by the person concerned and those around him. When we induce this state of mind in the other person by the assumption of prestige, he will then accept our ideas uncritically by the process of suggestion.

To influence anyone by suggestion we must communicate in a special way. This applies to both the passive and authoritarian use of suggestion; but it applies particularly to the passive method which is a very subtle procedure in contrast to the authoritarian method which is rather obvious and blatant.

If we use the logical approach to bring someone to accept our ideas, we must communicate in a way that suits the logical functions of the mind. On the other hand, when we use suggestion we must use forms of communication which suit his particular psychological process.

To influence anyone by suggestion avoid logical communication. It may not be possible to avoid all logical communication lest the other person should come to feel our conversation strange, and so be put on his guard. The reason for avoiding logical communication when using suggestion is that it alerts the mind, and the recently acquired logical activity inhibits the rather archaic process of suggestion.

We avoid asking questions or becoming involved in discussions which require the critical attention of the other person. The simplest way to achieve this is to do most of the talking ourselves. We do this in a relaxed manner, and we let ourselves ramble on about inconsequential matters which do not involve the other person in critical thought. We have already gained rapport, and we are mindful of the ideas which we want to bring the other person to accept. We present these to him when we are sure that he is relaxed and is not functioning at an alert critical level.

To influence a person by suggestion, talk around the subject rather than analyse it. We do this to avoid alerting his logical faculties. At all costs we avoid any step by step analysis of the proposition as this would stimulate his critical activity. By talking in a relaxed way about items peripheral to the main idea, the concept of the main idea comes to the other person without it being expressed in words. When this is possible, it is a very good approach, as the other person comes to accept our central idea without really being aware that he does so. This process by which the other person comes to accept some idea without it ever being expressed in words happens quite commonly in every day life, and is a routine technique of psychotherapy. I recently saw a woman who was going to leave her husband and children to go off with her lover. In fact she had made all the arrangements although she had been urgently advised against it by a number of people. I talked to her in this way without reference to the central problem, her husband and children. Next day she came back saying she had changed her mind, and how glad she was she had done so. This was just the outward manifestation of the complex psychological reactions which had enabled me to bring her to accept my idea although I never expressed it in words.

To influence anyone by suggestion, talk in a way which assumes he believes the things which he does not believe. I must stress that these principles which we are discussing are matters which we all use in our everyday life without thinking about it. They come quite naturally to us. For instance, if a little boy is tearful and refusing to go to school, his mother may start talking about what she has given him to take with him for lunch, and something she has added that he can give his friend. In other words she is influencing him by suggestion by assuming as a fact the matter which he is denying; she simply assumes that he is going to school while he maintains that he is not.

Another example occurs when a sick patient refuses advice that he should go into hospital. We can just talk on in a relaxed way about the hospital, where it is and how one gets there. 'Don't forget to bring something to read'. We assume what the other person is denying, and so influence him by suggestion.

In a rather more sophisticated way we can use the same principles to influence people in business. We may know that the other person is opposed to an idea which we ourselves favour. We talk around the subject, and refer to things which he will be able to do when the idea to which he is opposed is put into action. In this way we influence him by suggestion.

When we assume what the other person denies, we must avoid direct confrontation. The importance of this is obvious. If we have a direct confrontation we precipitate a logical discussion which is just what we want to avoid, if we are to influence the other person by suggestion. In actual fact it is not as hard to avoid a confrontation as one might expect. Our own relaxed attitude is important. After we have made the difficult point, we talk on in a relaxed way without pause. In this way we avoid the idea of challenging or contradicting the other person. A pause invites the other person to talk. In this case it would only invite him to disagree with us; so we deny him this opportunity by talking on for a moment or two after we have made the untrue assumption.

The danger of a confrontation is further reduced by expressing the difficult assumption rather vaguely and indirectly. This is best done by the indirect use of words so that the idea is conveyed by the extraverbal meaning rather than the logical meaning of the words.

When we have rapport and prestige, and we offer ideas indirectly, the other person accepts them automatically. However strange it may seem, this is a fact of life. It seems strange only because it does not follow the logical principles to which we have become so accustomed, but of course from the other point of view it is the natural and logical outcome of our biological development as human animals.

These three things, the rapport, the prestige and the indirect presentation of ideas, come more easily to me as a doctor than they do to you in business; but don't forget that the same psychological principles are equally valid in both circumstances. It only requires the thoughtful manipulation of the interview for these principles to be just as effective in business as they are in medicine.

Ideas are accepted more readily by suggestion if we first offer ideas that are very easily accepted. By this means we accustom the other person to the acceptance of our ideas. The psychological process of suggestion becomes facilitated by repetition. We then suggest propositions to the other person which are increasingly difficult for him to accept. This is quite an important principle of psychiatry, and is known as grading the suggestions. When the other person has accepted some very simple propositions, then some more difficult ones, we are then in a position to offer the central idea which we want him to accept.

In the passive use of suggestion the whole approach is friendly and leisurely. The acceptance of the idea depends on our emotional relationship with the other person. In the passive approach good rapport is essential. Psychologically this represents the child's love of his mother. So we act towards the other person in a way that is calm and sympathetic symbolizing the qualities of an idealized mother.

In the authoritative use of suggestion the whole approach is one of bullying command. In this case prestige is the important psychological mechanism. It represents the feeling of the child towards his father or tribal leader. So we do everything we can to enhance our status in relation to the other person, and we offer him our ideas loudly, firmly and with the utmost authority.

We can influence people by adopting roles. In the medical interview, I am the psychiatrist and the other person is the patient. In other words we both accept roles, I as the psychiatrist and he as the patient, and we act in a way that is consistent with those roles. This makes the use of rapport, prestige and the indirect communication of ideas so much the easier. But this tendency to adopt roles is something which is quite deeply ingrained in us. In business it is not too difficult to use it to help us to bring other people to our way of thinking.

We can use the other person's natural tendency to role-playing to influence him by suggestion. In ordinary life we all know people who assume the role of givers of advice. They give advice about likely changes in the weather, about the best way to dress and about future trends in the stock market. Despite the fact that these people often get caught without an umbrella, do not dress very well themselves, and have not made a fortune out of stocks and shares, in spite of this, other people still take their advice. The bald barber still sells bottles of hair restorer. These are incidents of everyday life, and few of us examine them critically; but if we do, we see that if a person assumes the role of adviser, other people very easily fall into the role of being advised.

If we consciously assume a role, the other person unconsciously falls into the reciprocal role. This is quite simple. One person assumes the role of leader, and unless he does it too blatantly or incongruously, the others fall into the role of followers. There are many simple examples of the same principle in which we can impose a role on another person. Quite commonly friends come to me professionally to seek my advice on some matter. They usually come in and start talking as friend to friend. But it is very hard to advise or treat a friend. So I quite quietly assume the role of doctor. This comes easily and quite naturally by my asking a few medical questions. My friend unconsciously slips into the role of patient and one who accepts advice. He is not aware of the changes of roles. But I can help him much more effectively as doctor to patient than I could as friend to friend. Similarly, in many business situations it is possible to assume the role of a giver of advice. If this is done in a natural, unhurried way, the other person quite unconsciously falls into the recipiocal role of the receiver of advice.

The whole manoeuvre has to be carried through without alerting the other person's critical faculties. There must be an air of naturalness. This is most easily attained by communicating our own leisurely relaxation. And when assuming the role of adviser, we must first consolidate our role by giving some advice in an area in which we are knowledgeable and the other person is not. This sets the process going, and we follow up advising on matters peripheral to the main topic before coming to the central idea itself.

The degree to which another person accepts our ideas is influenced by his expectancy. This is quite an important principle. Let me explain what I mean by giving an example of what happens with me every day. Patients are usually referred to me by another doctor. When he is making arrangements with the patient, the referring doctor often adds some comment, 'He recently helped another patient of mine who had trouble rather like your own'. The patient then comes to me with expectation of help, and he readily accepts what I say. On the other hand, there are still some doctors who have some kind of prejudice against psychiatry. If such a doctor eventually finds that he himself is unable to help the patient, he may in desperation refer the patient to me; but in doing so adds, 'See how you get on with him'. This patient comes to me with little expectancy of help, and does not readily accept my advice. To help him I have to use these psychological mechanisms which we have been discussing in order to bring him to my way of thinking. Now, please don't think that I am always quoting medical examples, rather than business ones. Medicine is my life, and medical examples are always ready in my mind. The point that I wish to make is that the same basic psychological principles apply in any situation, medicine or business.

How can we increase the other person's expectancy? One way is to use a kind of team approach in the way of the medical example which I have just quoted. Our subordinate sees the other person first, just for a moment on the pretext of apologizing for his being kept waiting for a few minutes. 'You are going to see Mr. X about such and such. He is our expert in this field'. You will note that such a comment also adds to Mr. X's prestige. Expectancy and prestige are psychological mechanisms which work closely together.

In the interview itself we must conduct ourselves in such a way as to enhance the other person's expectancy. This applies particularly to our initial meeting with the other person and the early part of the conversation. This is so because expectancy is essentially an anticipatory feeling about something in the future. So any moves to increase the other person's sense of expectancy must be completed before the main part of the interview is commenced. The way in which we communicate our natural ease and our natural confidence is important. This unconsciously leads the other person to fall into the role of listening to what we have to say; he is prepared for our advice and is ready to accept our way of looking at the problem.

If we express our ideas with casual certainty, they are more readily accepted. Our casualness communicates the idea that we ourselves have no doubt about the proposition whatsoever, and as a result of the certainty of our own mind, we naturally assume that the other person feels the same way.

With this approach there must be no attempt at all to convince

[214]

the other person. Any move to strengthen the situation by further reassurance has the opposite effect. Any extra argument weakens the proposition by indirectly indicating that there is at least a possibility that it could be wrong. At all costs avoid any phrase such as, 'Now you understand, don't you?' This of course invites the other person to examine the proposition logically. Although our proposition is logically sound, it is easier to bring a difficult person to accept it by the paralogical process of suggestion rather than a logical approach in which the difficult person will query every step that we take.

In the same way it is well to avoid asking, 'Are there any questions about it that you would like to ask me?' This has the same alerting effect on the other person. We always ask questions when we are using the logical approach, but never when we are using suggestion to bring the other person to accept our ideas. Our casual certainty assumes that the other person sees the proposition just as we do, and thus denies the possibility that he might wish to question it.

If the other person is tense, he is on guard and is consequently critical of what we say. During our discussion we have seen over and over again how a person's acceptance of ideas is influenced by his level of anxiety. Anxiety alerts the critical faculties of the mind, and we have seen that activity of the critical faculty, which is biologically a recently acquired ability, immediately puts a stop to the much more primitive function of suggestion.

If however the other person is anxious to a marked degree so that he is really extremely tense and jittery, then his perception is reduced by his acute anxiety, and he is less likely to notice subtle moves that we might make. Extreme anxiety of this nature allows ideas concerning the safety or health of the individual to be accepted by suggestion, but because of his anxiety his thinking is too reduced to accept significant ideas of a business nature.

We can use suggestion or we can use the logical approach, but we cannot use both. This is very fundamental. Activity of the logical element of our mind always puts a stop to ideas being accepted by suggestion. Yet people, and doctors and psychiatrists are

P   [215]

included in this, very frequently try to help along the process of suggestion by adding a few logical arguments in favour of the proposition. But instead of helping the situation, this only makes things worse. If we give some sound logical argument to support our proposition we necessarily bring the other person to function at a logical and critical level, and as a result the process of suggestion ceases to function.

If we are using the logical approach, and if we foolishly try to add further conviction by suggestion, the other person immediately perceives the lack of reason in the suggestion, because we have made him alert from the logical approach. He becomes suspicious, and re-examines all our logical arguments in an over critical fashion.

Although the proposition may be sound logically, it may still be better to present it by suggestion. This applies when we are dealing with over-critical and suspicious people, and also those who are negativistic. We are all familiar with such people. They are inclined to say 'No' before they have heard what our proposition is. With a logical approach, rather than keeping an open mind, these people are inclined to be thinking how they can best counter our logical arguments. In all business dealings of a technical nature in which the other person is not familiar with all the technicalities, the final acceptance of the proposition is by suggestion as the other person's lack of technical knowledge prevents the full use of the logical approach.

8

Morale

Morale in your business

Morale is more than just being contented in the job. We must not get into the way of thinking, 'There are no strikes; so morale is all right'. No. We must aim much higher than that.

Good wages, good working conditions, good amenities, good chances of promotion, good retiring allowances, all these things help our employees to be contented in their job. These are matters which are within our general competence and we deal with them in practical and realistc fashion. But morale is something much more complex.

Morale is a state of mind which brings us to do things beyond the normal call of duty. Most people who are successful in business have the ability to induce this state of mind in others. If you are on the way up, this is something very important to you.

The essential part in morale is identification with the firm. The staff come to feel that it is their firm. It is really quite easy to estimate the morale of any organization. Just listen to a couple of employees talking. If they talk about what 'we' are doing, meaning what the firm is doing, the morale is all right. This means that the staff identify with the firm. To them it is 'our firm'. If the staff feel that it is their firm, they take some kind of personal interest in it. This is the basis of morale.

How can the executive bring his staff to identify in this way? This of course is the essence of leadership. The psychological principles involved are simple and straight forward. There are three steps each of which is quite clear. First the leader himself must identify with the organization. Secondly, the leader's identification with the firm must be apparent to the staff. Thirdly, the staff are brought to identify with the leader which automatically involves identification with the firm. Let us discuss each of these steps in rather more detail.

The executive himself must identify with the firm. 'Of course, I have my money in it. If anything goes wrong, I lose my money'. Not good enough. The executive who will inspire morale in his staff must identify on a much more personal basis. This is very important. Don't disagree with me here. Don't just brush off the idea with the thought 'How I feel about it doesn't affect the staff'. Quite wrong. It does affect the staff because your feeling in the matter seeps through into your actions and unconsciously influences those around you. You are not aware of the ways in which you betray your feelings; and the staff in their turn are not consciously aware of picking it up from you. But these things happen every day, and morale is a very subtle, emotionally determined phenomenon which is easily affected by these intangible influences.

The executive's identification with the firm needs to be real. There needs to be a feeling of being personally responsible for things that go on in the firm, so that you feel that it is genuinely your firm.

The staff must be aware of the executive's identification with the firm. The fact of being seen on the job, both early and late, communicates this idea. When talking with members of staff, the executive can demonstrate his identification by saying, 'We are going to do this or that', when he means it is the firm that is going to do it. There is more than this. When we identify with something, it is ours, and we have concern for it, genuine concern. This genuine concern is sensed by the staff, and they come unconsciously to regard the executive and the firm as one.

We cannot appeal to our staff for morale in a logical way. We must constantly remember that identification is an unconscious process. So we cannot appeal to the employee's reason. It is no good saying to him, 'It is to your advantage as well as ours that morale in the firm should be high'. This is a completely logical and truthful statement. But it does not have any real effect on morale because this is developed by psychological processes of which the individual is unaware. A group of people cannot decide to have good morale. It is just something that happens.

You, the executive, are accustomed to dealing with problems factually and logically. You may find it hard to go along with me in this. But what I say is true. In fact, if you try to make a logical approach on this matter you will almost certainly do more harm than good. The very fact of such an approach being logical means that the proposition will be examined critically. Doubts are raised, and suspicions which were dormant before, are now brought into clear consciousness. The employee just wonders what you are getting at.

We improve morale by making it possible for unconscious processes to operate. We must approach this aspect of the problem from basic principles. This means understanding something about identification. All the psychological mechanisms like identification are abilities that we have inherited which help us to cope with life. Identification is very important to us when we are children. We identify with our parents, and this helps us in the biological sense in our struggle to adult life. In later years identification comes easiest with some person who in some way resembles or symbolizes our parents. In this way we identify with our teachers, political leaders and those who have authority as our parents did. The process spreads so that we identify with our family, our school, our city, our country, our church, and our firm. We can see that in each case these organizations are related in a symbolic way to our family and hence to our parents.

Morale comes more easily if the executive in some way can symbolize our parents. Please don't think that I am becoming too airy-fairy as psychologists and psychiatrists have such a habit of doing. I am talking practical business. This idea of the firm's executive symbolizing our parents is not quite so remote as you think. In our eyes as children our parents had status and we looked up to them. The executive has status and we look up to him in a similar way. Our parents had authority and disciplined us; so does the executive. Most important of all our parents provided for us; and so does the executive. So at an unconscious level the employee looks at the leader or the executive as a parental figure. The more this can be developed, the more it paves the way for the type of identification which builds morale.

But we identify with real, live, living, people; not with the signature on a pay cheque. Children in the war years had this difficulty. But in favourable circumstances we can identify with parent substitutes. The teacher often fills this role. A similar process can take place in business so that employees identify with the department manager and not with the top executive. This occurs in the same way as the soldier identifies with his company commander and not with his C.O.

What are the qualities in an executive or leader which make identification easier? We identify with someone whom we would wish to be like. We would not want to be like someone who is anxious, hostile, suspicious or too uncertain of himself. We want to be like someone who is kind and considerate, but at the same time firm and strong. We cannot identify with anyone who seems too perfect. That would be like trying to identify with a Saint. The good leader is not afraid to let his subordinates see minor imperfections in himself. This is frankness, a kind of openness. It makes him more human, and they can go along with him so much the better.

The way in which orders are given is quite important. He must not be offensively authoritative, as this would separate him from the men too much. He must not give orders in a half hearted way so as to curry favour. If he does this the quality of leadership is lost. Nor should he try to be just one of the men. This may appeal to our democratic ideal, but it lacks all the force of unconscious parental identification.

'We are in this together.' This is the feeling that leaders must inspire in others to build morale. But it must be a feeling that comes, and not a logical instruction, or the whole intangible quality of morale will just disappear. In the first place, from his efforts, his purpose and his devotion, we see that he is indeed in it. If we like him as a person, and if we trust him, and if without our knowing it he symbolizes a parental figure to us, then we unconsciously identify; and we are in it together.

Morale is better if the firm has some symbolic resemblance to the family. Our sense of security is very important in this. The family provided this. When we were young, we would return to the family circle, and our fears of the outside world would melt away. We could rely on the family. They would not let us down. Can your firm provide some kind of equivalent to this? Security is a major factor. If the employee is frightened that he may lose his job at any moment, he may work very hard to try to keep his job, but his morale in the true sense will be poor.

But security in itself does not make morale. Think of the low morale of many government departments which offer very complete security of employment. Security is important in building morale only when it has the unconscious psychological effect of helping the individual to look upon the firm as a symbolic home and so leading him to identify with it.

The employee can come to regard the firm as a symbol for his home more easily if some material comforts are provided. But somehow these comforts should have a homely quality about them. An elaborate new factory building may lack this homely quality although it may cater very well for the employees' material needs. When a move has been made to new and better premises it is not uncommon to hear both executives and employees say, 'Somehow I liked the old place'. This of course is evidence of the type of identification which I am trying to describe.

Our family cared for us. If the firm somehow gives us the feeling of caring for us, it is so much the easier for it to symbolize the family. In this way, good working conditions, facilities for recreation and retirement allowances are a help towards the unconscious formation of morale. This is something quite distinct from the rational effect of good conditions of employment on the staff. This rational effect brings employees to be loyal to the firm out of self-interest which of course is something quite different from morale.

You can't buy morale; high wages don't make it. This is a mistake made by many executives. We should not really expect it to be so. After all the morale of many poor families is much better than the morale of many rich families.

On the other hand, low wages reduce morale because they bring discontent. If high wages are interpreted by the staff as spontaneous generosity on the part of the executive, then morale is increased; but high wages in themselves have little effect.

Some executives try to identify with their staff. This is an aspect of the togetherness in commerce and industry which seems to be encouraged by some management consultants. The attitude is expressed in such sayings as, 'The firm has set this for us to do'. In this situation the leader makes it clear that he identifies with the staff and not with the firm. In this way he gains favour with his subordinates, and may be able to use this to encourage production. But it is really a short cut aimed to achieve immediate goals. It is a second class approach and effectively prevents the development of real morale in the sense that I have described it.

Morale in business follows the same general principles as army morale. We all need to have the feeling that there is some purpose in what we are doing. This applies equally to soldiers in the field and to the industrial army. This feeling is quickly destroyed by countermanding orders. Any reversal of policy, or 'stop-go' decisions by the executive quickly reduces morale. 'It does not matter to them, they still draw their wages', is only a silly rationalization of the incompetent executive, because it does matter psychologically; and the bad psychological effect will reduce efficiency and production.

Fatigue is likely to reduce morale in both army and industry. So that men working long hours of overtime may be happy with the wages they earn, but at the same time may lose morale through inward fatigue. Nervous stress has a similar effect. This may arise at work through a monotonous or dangerous job, or from stresses of family life.

Insecurity has an important but varied effect on morale. Sometimes morale is reduced; but as in war, sometimes the insecurity precipitates a wave of identification with a leader, and morale is greatly enhanced.

A report that everything is going smoothly may simply mean that the organization is dying on its feet. Life is not smooth. If the firm is really living, it must be subject to continual changes. Otherwise the dynamic quality of life is missing.

A few months ago I attended a meeting of existentialist

philosophers. One of the points which seemed to keep recurring in the discussion was that life was continually subject to change, and if the individual becomes static in his outlook and thinking, and ceases to change, he in fact ceases to live in the real sense, and might just as well be considered as dead. I believe this to be true; and I believe that the same principles apply to the firm as they do to the individual.

If we aim to have everything going smoothly, we inhibit change which gives the firm life. Primitive man had to adjust to a hostile and changing environment, so does the present day individual in a competitive society. In the same way a modern business organization has to keep making changes to adjust to the changing and competitive circumstances in which it operates. As changes rarely go completely smoothly, we should not put too much emphasis on the smooth running of our enterprise. Rather we should strive to adjust to the continual changes of the society in which we live without too much upheaval in doing so.

The desire to have everything running smoothly is promoted by anxiety. Please do not think that I am over emphasizing the importance of anxiety as a motivating factor in our everyday life. It is easy for you to say, 'It is natural to want things to go smoothly'. Of course it is. I agree with you completely. It is natural to want things to go smoothly because it is natural to avoid anxiety as it makes us feel uncomfortable. This is the nature of anxiety.

Changes are always associated with some increase in our general level of anxiety. This is so because we are changing from circumstances with which we are familiar to those which are strange, or at least less familiar. So we tend to shun change so as to avoid the feeling of disquiet associated with anxiety. This type of reaction is commonest in older executives, as avoidance of change and doing things by routine are defences against anxiety commonly used by older people.

In considering these matters, please remember that a psychological reaction never operates in a vacuum. It is always complicated, modified or distorted by other reactions which influence the individual in other ways at the same time. For instance people also seek change because of the stimulating effect that it provides. Again, this is part of our biological heritage; but it is seen mainly in younger people who can often manage the anxiety associated with change by the physical and mental activity that goes with it. Nevertheless, this does not in any way negate the general principle that we also tend to avoid change to save ourselves the experience of anxiety, and this has a general tendency to reduce morale.

A lack of trust destroys the morale of employees. There can be no real identification with management if the employee feels that he is not trusted. If this occurs the employee unconsciously feels that the firm is just the place where he works. He takes home his pay and spends it to what advantage he can; and that is that. The executive who runs the firm on these lines may be effective enough, but he is not on the way up because the real spark of morale which makes things go is lacking.

A lack of trust provokes some people to act in an untrustworthy fashion. This is one of the quirks of human nature. In discussing the management of others, we have seen how people unconsciously take on our own attitude of mind. The tense and anxious person will take on our calm and ease. In a rather similar way, if we are untrusting some people react against it. 'If this is what he expects of me, this is what I shall do.' If great precuations are taken over the expenditure of petty cash, there will always be some who regard it as a personal challenge, and as a result are provoked into petty thieving in a way which would not occur with more liberal management. If we seek a psychological explanation for this rather perverse reaction, it is probably associated with the individual's early resentment of over strict parental supervision and his rebellion against it as a child.

Trust builds morale. I doubt if many employers fully realize the extent to which this operates. I have become very aware of it through talking with patients at all levels of employment. It would seem to me that in most cases the senior would have been quite unaware of the significance of some action which the junior has interpreted as a matter of trust. In psychiatry the situation discloses itself this way. The patient complains of being tense, and I seek possible causes for his anxiety. 'How do you get on with the boss.' 'Oh fine. Last week he gave me such and such to do.' In the factual sense, the task he was given seems insignificant. But the employee has interpreted it as a matter of the boss trusting him. 'He has faith in me.' From the way that he recounts the matter, it is clear that the incident, which may be pathetically trivial in itself, has had quite a profound effect on his attitude towards the firm.

There are other things besides money, which are subject to trust. Money for which the individual does not have to give accurate account is the everyday matter of trust. In this way a few cents is as significant to the office boy as is a considerable sum to a junior executive. In both cases they feel that they have been trusted, and morale is increased. But there are many other things with which we can trust a person, and these other matters have the same effect on morale. To leave a person with any decision which is not a matter for confirmation is a matter of trust. The office boy is trusted to get you some lunch without specifying what, and the junior executive is trusted to make some significant purchase on behalf of the firm. Confidences are a matter of trust and promote morale at all levels. In this respect the confidence must never concern another member of the firm in a derogatory way. 'He says this about so-and-so; what does he say about me.' Incidental confidences of one's own personal doubts expressed in a natural way to a junior are a communication of trust and increase morale.

Trust which amounts to lack of supervision also destroys morale. 'They have so much money, they don't care what happens to it.' 'If they don't care why should I care?' These are attitudes of mind which are reactions that one can easily understand. They are most common in extraverted people whose pattern of life is to accept things in a matter-of-fact, uncomplicated fashion. Because of this matter-of-fact attitude the extravert does not have scruples, and does not feel that his attitude to the firm in these matters is in any way dishonest.

Too great trust may make introverted employees anxious. This is really a matter of putting stress on individuals who are not quite robust enough in their personality to take it. The introvert is so preoccupied with the subtleties of interpersonal relations that he begins to ask himself if he is worthy of the trust that is given him. And because of his sensitivity he worries that he may not be able to fulfil this trust; and as a result his level of anxiety is increased and morale deteriorates.

Your own morale

You might well ask me. 'If you have seen a number of executives as patients, what are their common troubles?' Anxiety is the common trouble. This has been the case with more than ninety per cent of the executives who have consulted me as patients. But their anxiety has shown itself in a variety of different ways. Some come to me complaining of a sense of increasing nervous tension and irritability. When things go wrong they are put out of their stride more easily than they should be. They are inclined to flare up in a bad temper, and then feel sorry for it afterwards. They complain that they are more sensitive to noise than they used to be. The clatter of the typewriters or the noise of machinery, or simply people talking in the passage or the rumble of the traffic outside disturbs them in a way that it did not do before. With other executives the nervous tension has shown itself more at home. The marriage is not going as well as it was. Tensions arise over matters which in retrospect are recognized as trivial. Instead of enjoying the exuberant behaviour of the children, it irritates him, and the children are scolded and perhaps punished for things that are really no more than the normal behaviour for their age. Sometimes the executive patient has been accompanied by his wife, and she has told me that things have changed. She used to look forward to his homecoming, but now he is so tense and irritable she does not know what to expect. With other executives the anxiety has shown itself as a sense of apprehension. It is experienced as a kind of foreboding. There is a feeling that something bad is going to happen, but the patient does not know what it is, or what he might expect it to be. With others there has been a disturbing lack of concentration. There is not much nervous tension or apprehension, but the anxiety is sufficient to make concentration impossible. He brings the work home thinking that he may be better able to do it in the quiet of the evening. But it is no good. It is not uncommon for such people to confide to me that they have a vague fear of impending insanity.

With others the anxiety is channelled into psychosomatic symptoms. There may be palpitations, a thudding feeling in the heart and a general sense of discomfort on the left side of the chest. The feeling of an impending heart attack is constantly in mind, and has not been relieved by a normal electrocardiogram. Dyspepsia is another common symptom of anxiety. The executive is aware of the high incidence of ulcers in others who do similar work. It seems that his stomach trembles or turns over. Impotence, either partial or complete, has been another common symptom. Anxiety always tends to inhibit sexual function in both men and women. It is not uncommon for the impotence to be associated with some foolish extramarital affair which has added to his anxiety. Headache and blurred vision, and with it the fear of a tumour of the brain is another frequently occurring symptom.

The anxiety may be accompanied by depression. Things look gloomy. It is hard to see the bright side of things. The executive often complains that he has achieved material success, but it is really pointless and meaningless. A common complication of the executive's anxiety and depression is that he comes to me saying, 'Yes, I feel so bad I have just resigned my position'. I must stress the point again; we must all be very careful about any decision which we make when we are not completely well.

Anxiety saps morale. The executive who has developed anxiety may be able to hide his symptoms from his colleagues, and it may be that the first thing they notice amiss is a failure of his morale. Anxiety disrupts the state of mind in which we do things beyond the mormal call of duty. There is a quality in morale which transcends anxiety. If anxiety has become uppermost morale has gone. This state of affairs is well demonstrated in war. When morale is high there is a conspicuous absence of overt anxiety.

[227]

Hard work and long hours by themselves rarely cause serious anxiety. There is almost always some other factor. At first the executive patient is always inclined to deny this. He tells me, 'I work too hard, and it has made me tense and anxious'. But it is never as simple as this. With a little probing the other factors are disclosed. It frequently turns out that there is some element of uncertainty as well as hard work; and it is this which is the primary factor in producing the anxiety.

In other cases the uncertainty has concerned the executive's relationship with his immediate superior or perhaps the board. He does not know how he stands. This plays on his feelings of insecurity which we have all inherited in greater or lesser degree from our days of infancy and childhood when we were insecure in fact. His uncertainty with his superior can stir up this latent insecurity. Of course this is much more likely to happen if the individual was usually insecure as a child through feelings of uncertainty with his parents.

With executives I have seen, changes due to computerization have been a common cause of anxiety. These situations produce the uncertainty to which we have referred. The executive has to deal with something new and something with which he is unfamiliar. It is not the long hours and hard work which produce the anxiety, but it is the uncertainty of the new situation.

I have seen this happen on many occasions with the installation of computers. As one would expect, the older executives are most vulnerable to this type of stress. I would offer some advice here. If you are in the older bracket of executives you simply cannot become expert in all the technicalities of computerization. So don't try. Get the advice of younger experts; hear what they have to say, and make your decisions accordingly. If on the other hand, you are on the way up in the younger bracket of executives, it is obvious that you should do all you can to master these new techniques so that you have as full an understanding of them as possible.

The stress of take-overs often produces severe anxiety and has a bad effect on the morale of all concerned. Judging from patients whom I have seen, the threat of a take-over with all its uncertainty would seem to be almost as stressful as the take-over itself.

Executives in the firm which is being taken over fear that they will be considered redundant and will be paid off. A man in this position in his late fifties came to me crippled with anxiety. Fortunately, he was able to use the relaxing mental exercises which I have described so effectively that he was able to reduce his anxiety in quite a remarkable way. With his reduction of anxiety his effectiveness in the firm has so increased that he has been kept on by the new management.

There is another aspect to take-overs and morale. The executives of the take-over firm are often very competent men, aggressive and quite ruthless. They take over the weaker firm and dismiss the executives and redundant employees. This may seem good business; but this display of ruthlessness has a disastrous effect on the morale of the staff.

Promotion to the limit of one's ability is a common cause of breakdown. We all need a little reserve. Then if things go wrong, our anxiety can increase, but it still does not reach the dangerous level of getting out of hand. This is most clearly seen in unintelligent persons who can often work satisfactorily in unskilled jobs; but when they are given a semi-skilled job they immediately breakdown because they cannot cope with the additional stress. The same principle applies at a much higher level with the executive who is promoted beyond his capacity.

Personal problems are a more important cause of anxiety than business stress. The business executive always starts off talking about the stress of his work. This is a kind of cover-up until he feels that he can trust me with the real problem. The most common personal problem is an extra marital affair; and the person most commonly involved is the secretary. There are three common situations. He is either in an acute panic because he thinks she may be pregnant, or he thinks that his wife will find out, or the wife has found out and the affair is over but she is using the situation as a kind of permanent blackmail. Of course, there are many variations. Each requires both practical guidance and help in reducing the level of anxiety.

Of the patients whom I see, another common source of anxiety is the matter of indiscretions on overseas trips. If the executive has obsessive traits in his personality he is inclined to ruminate over the indiscretion. This often progresses to the stage in which he cannot stop himself thinking about it. This persistance of an idea in the mind against the wish of the subject is known as obsessive thinking. The usual sequence of events is that he comes to feel that it would help him to get the idea out of his mind if he were to tell his wife. So he tells her. Then the wife is not as understanding as he had hoped, and his anxiety is further increased.

The executive's anxiety may result from simple family problems. I explained earlier that anxiety results from the summation of stresses from different sources. Many executives have a high level of anxiety as a result of multiple stresses at work. This may be the reason why they seem to be particularly vulnerable to stresses arising within the family circle. Infidelity or the threat of infidelity may cause anxiety and psychosomatic symptoms. But so may surprisingly simple stresses in the home. Many executives seem to be over ambitious for the success of their children. To many it is desperately important that the children should pass their entrance examinations for the university. A rather ridiculous situation develops. As the time for the examination approaches, the parent suffers more anxiety than the student! This happens most acutely in persons who have placed too high a value on the material aspects of their own success. It is often aggravated by doubts and concern in the mind of the parent about a daughter's relationship with boys. Concern of this type is usually greatest in parents who have themselves sown some wild oats in their own youth.

'It would count against me if it were known that I attended a psychiatrist.' Young executives on the way up have often said this to me. It is a real problem, both for them and for myself. A man may attend a gymnasium to help him maintain good physical health, and nothing is thought of it. Similarly, he can attend the priest to maintain spiritual health. But if he see a psychiatrist like myself to help maintain mental health, people talk, and it counts against him. This is obviously wrong.

In general, executives like yourself do not make full use of people like me. You feel quite well; but if you go to a gymnasium now and then, you will feel better still. Many people who feel quite well go to church, and are the better for it. This same principle applies to visiting a psychiatrist. An occasional visit can do much to reduce your nervous tension. If you feel better; you work more effectively; life is better.

'There is nothing wrong with me; perhaps I am a little tense; I would just like to talk things over with you.' This is the introduction of the man who is all right; he is in no way sick; but he has the insight to realize that he may be capable of functioning even more effectively. What is more, he has the enterprise to investigate the possibility of help in this direction. Over the last few years an increasing number of people have approached me in this frame of mind. I believe that they have all gained from the venture.

Although they come saying that they want to talk things over, when it comes to the point they are never quite sure what it is that they want to discuss. It seems that there are vague uncertainties that they hardly like to put into words. Although it is vague, they feel this uncertainty niggling them. Sometimes it concerns things at work, sometimes things at home. If it is work, it is not so much the technical side of the job, but it is rather the personal aspects. 'Is this really what I want of life? Is there something else that would better satisfy my inner longing?' These are the vague ideas that are given expression. Then they have often added, 'Or is it just that I am a romantic fool, seeking something in life that does not exist.' 'I know I must work to support my wife and kids.' These are the manifestations of the vague uncertainties of which I speak.

How am I going as a man? Is this the question that underlies these vague uncertainties? I think it is. We can tell pretty well how we are going on the way up in the material sense. In this there are definite signposts, the rungs on the ladder. But in this other matter there is little to guide us. In fact we do not want an outside guide. All we want to know is that our inner methods of self assessment are working smoothly and effectively. This is what talking things over with the right kind of person does for us.

There is a further point, and I would like to stress this as I believe it to be very important. Sometimes when we are very relaxed in our body and mind, the truth of these things comes to us. This is not a logical process. It is another example of the intuitive functions of the mind. So I do not presume to attempt to guide people who come to me like this, but instead I show them how to relax deeply. This helps to relieve their tension, and sometimes brings understanding of those problems that are too deep for words.

Some practical considerations

Square pegs in round holds develop anxiety. I know this to be true because they come to me on account of it. They are stuck in their present job, so I help them to reduce the general level of their anxiety by showing them the relaxing mental exercises which I have already described. I can think of many examples of square pegs in round holes who have consulted me on account of their nervous tension; an introvert too sensitive to manage a factory; a dirt conscious obsessive who bought a dairy farm; a sensitive man who could not bear the exploitation of housewives in his house to house sales business; a doctor too sensitive to cope with suffering people; a professor too self conscious to give lectures; an accountant who could not stand up to clients who wanted to dodge tax; a clergyman with no faith; and dozens of others, all square pegs in round holes. It would have been much better for all concerned if they were working in a job more consistent with their personality. The trouble is that the individual disguises his corners from others and tries to deny them to himself. It may take an unusually alert employment officer to perceive these personality traits in an applicant.

The conformist is well placed as an executive of a large firm. I know that some top executives will not agree with this. They are inclined to pride themselves on the way that they encourage new ideas and new approaches. But this in fact is lip service rather than reality. The very structure of the big firm makes conformity essential. A person who does not conform is a constant worry to others, and general efficiency is reduced. The non-conformist individual is well suited as top executive of his own little business. He can then use to full advantage the enterprise of mind which his non-conformity brings.

The dependent individual is best placed in a large firm or government service. The dependent person needs some emotional support from a senior in order to work at his optimum capacity. This does not mean that the senior has to mother him. In fact the senior may not be aware of the degree to which he supports a dependent person who is working as his subordinate. But the dependent individual feels that the other is there, and if the occasion should arise, he would help him. In most cases the occasion does not arise, but the dependent person still needs the shadow of the other to work effectively.

In contrast, those of an independent nature are best advised to work in a small firm where the chance of using their independent attitude to advantage is so much the greater.

There are different ways of taking risks. Success on the way up demands risks of certain kinds. There are really two types of risk. There is the calculated risk. In it we have some other plan to fall back on, if the project should fail. The other type is the gambling risk. In it everything is at stake, and if the project fails it is a disaster. The obsessive is the master of the calculated risk while it is mainly psychopaths and sometimes extraverts who indulge in the gambling risk. If one has the gambling tendency, employment in a large firm has a restraining influence which may lead the individual to greater maturity in the future.

How accessible should we be? This is something which must come to the mind of every thoughtful executive. It is obvious that if subordinates have free access to us, they gain a feeling of security, and of really being part of the concern. In consequence their morale is so much the better. On the other hand it is equally obvious that these matters can waste time which should be spent on high level planning which after all is our primary function. From this it would seem that each of us must make some wise balance as to how to proportion his time according to his individual needs. But it is not quite so simple as this, as unconscious psychological factors often come to mislead us.

To make oneself inaccessible may be simply a defence against one's anxiety. When this happens, as it quite often does, the executive is acting not in the interests of the firm, but in response to his own inner anxieties. As we would expect, this type of reaction is more common in introvert executives. The introvert would prefer to be in his office quietly working things out, rather than dealing with the problems of some other member of the firm at a personal level. He finds the demands of these situations difficult because he does not have the knack of making an easy friendly relationship with the people who come to see him like this. So he avoids it, even when the others have legitimate reasons to come to him. He thinks, 'So and so can look after him. I have more important things to do.' And we, of course, can see that he is rationalizing.

Extravert executives may fulfil their gregarious needs by being too accessible. The other side of the picture is that the extravert likes a chat with people. It is a part of his nature. So he makes it easy for juniors to come to him with their problems. He does it well because he gets on easily with them. But he is really spending the time in response to the drives of his own personality rather than in the interests of the organization. One sees this most commonly in the older, benign extravert executive who is everyone's friend, and who does much to maintain smooth working relationships in the organization; but at the same time may not be putting his talents to their best use for the firm.

Obsessive executives may make themselves too accessible because of anxiety. We have seen that the obsessive is a very conscientious person. He is really over conscientious, in fact pathologically so. When someone wants to see him, the obsessive executive may find it very hard to put him off. He is plagued with the feeling, 'Perhaps I ought to'. He becomes tense about it. Then in response to his tension he agrees to see him, 'Just for a few minutes'. This type of short interview of a few minutes rarely solves the problem. It only relieves the executive's anxiety which has arisen on account of his obsessive conscientiousness.

To protect themselves against this type of situation, obsessive executives commonly establish a very rigid hierarchy so that an individual must always make any approach through the person immediately above him on the hierarchial system. This of course is current practice in many large organizations. It is effective, but it loses both the flexibility which can lead to greater enterprise, and the personal touch which can do so much for morale.

How much should we delegate to others? 'Delegate as much as you possibly can.' 'You cannot run the business single handed.' 'The more you delegate, the more successful you will be.' This is the simple, straight forward, rational advice that one hears in lectures on management. But in fact the matter is neither simple nor straight forward nor completely rational, for the reason that psychological mechanisms tend to influence us unconsciously when we come to delegate our authority to others.

Obsessive executives have difficulty in delegating. The obsessive executive has the greatest difficulty of all. His habitual way of coping with his anxiety is to try to have everything just right. He then unconsciously feels that there can be nothing to worry about. So he keeps checking things over to be quite sure that everything is just right. But if he delegates the task, he has to leave it to someone else. He can't keep a check on it any longer. He does not like this, and the level of his anxiety is increased. So he unconsciously tends to avoid delegating work that should be delegated. He says, 'I would sooner work back and do it myself'. This is true. He does prefer to do the extra work himself rather than suffer uneasy feelings of anxiety.

The obsessive also has another problem about delegation. He is very conscientious. When he goes to delegate some work he suffers pricks of conscience, that perhaps he really should be doing it himself. Then when the obsessive executive does delegate the task, he is inclined to supervise the job too much. This is a part of his checking over to be sure that everything is right. By over supervising the work in this way he irritates the man to whom the work has been delegated and makes him anxious. The answer to all this is simple. If in fact you have obsessive traits in your personality, make yourself delegate what is necessary, and leave it with the other person without undue supervision.

Insecure executives don't like delegating. They just don't like it. Hence they avoid it, as it makes them feel uneasy. This is what we should expect. The insecure person is frightened to give away any of his authority or power as he fears that in so doing he will feel still more insecure. If you yourself are a little insecure, make yourself delegate. You will find that your apprehension about it is only temporary, and as a result of the experience you will become a little less insecure, which will help you to do the same on future occasions.

Some executives delegate too much. These are mainly extraverts. Their matter-of-fact approach to things makes delegation easy. It is the sensible thing to do. They are not held back by any complicated psychological doubting. It is all easy and straight forward. And because it is so easy, extraverts often fall into the way of doing too much of it, and so avoiding work which in reality they themselves should be doing.

There are often complicated psychological reactions about training an understudy. We grow old and retire; but the firm goes on. It is essential that we train people who can take our places. It is easy to see the necessity for this, but the process often evokes psychological reactions beneath the surface which the individual does not understand. In a general way these follow the psychological reactions concerning delegation. Obsessive executives are inclined to irritate their understudy by supervising him too much and by demanding an unnecessary attention to detail. On the other hand extravert executives may be too casual about it, and fail to give their understudy the degree of help and training which he requires.

Insecure executives try to make themselves indispensable. They do this unconsciously in an attempt to gain greater inner security. In other words it is a psychological defence. But when the time comes for them to train an understudy their defence crumbles, the presence of the understudy is a constant reminder that in fact they are not indispensable. Their inner feeling of insecurity is increased and the general level of their anxiety rises. We become hostile to those who make us anxious, so instead of having an easy friendly relationship with his understudy, the insecure executive is unconsciously hostile to him. This shows itself very clearly when the understudy makes some minor error. The insecure executive takes it out on him by being quite unnecessarily aggressive about the incident. This helps to bolster his own morale by pointing out to himself and to others that the understudy is really only a fool of a boy and could never replace him. In fact his behaviour clearly communicates the message, 'You can see I am indispensable'.

'He works hard and plays hard.' They say this about a lot of executives. What do they mean by it? It is the image that these men wish to create for themselves. It means, 'I work all day, and I drink until morning with girls in night clubs. You can see what a strong and masculine man I am'. Of course it is only the man who has his own doubts on these matters who needs to proclaim it in this way. Then at another level this behaviour means that he works so hard that he gets so tense that he needs regular sessions at a nightclub to unwind himself.

The work hard and play hard concept is a tawdry image for the second-rater who finds himself further up the ladder of material success than the true way up would have taken him. Any discerning outsider sees this. But young men in the firm identify with their seniors. They accept this as the behaviour of the man who is a success. They try to emulate him, thinking that if they are seen at nightclubs their friends will believe that they too are a success.

The senior executive has a responsibility to his juniors beyond the scope of business. This is so whether we like it or not. It arises through the tendency of young people to identify with older people who are in an authoritative position in relation to themselves. This reactivates the boy-father situation; and the young executive comes to identify with his senior. This is a fact of life. It is no use trying to rationalize. 'My responsibility to these young men ceases when I walk out the office door.' However much you might like this to be the case, it is just not so. They identify with you in what they know or imagine of your private life, just as much as they do with your life as a business executive. I have seen other examples of the same principle. A university professor indignantly stated that he was no longer responsible to his students once he has left the campus. But of course he is. If he expresses antisocial views, his students tend to take on these ideas by the simple process of unconscious identification. It is the same with you, and they will take on aspects of behaviour and morality which they believe to be yours.

What do you regret most in life? I have put this question to approximately one hundred executive patients and have tabulated and analysed their answers. Of course many spoke of incidents in their personal life, of youthful indiscretions, of the girl they could have married but didn't, or the girl they 'got into trouble'. But the greatest regret in the life of a great number of executives is simply that they had not gone further in their education. Considering the very great number of things that one can regret in life, the frequence with which they regretted their lack of education really astonished me. And the most interesting part is that men of vastly different levels of education express the same regret. Thus it is easy to understand that the man who has made good without much formal schooling should regret his lack of education. But the man who did well at school but went into business instead of going to the university says the same thing; and the greatest regret of many executives who had obtained a bachelor's degree at the university was simply that they had not gone further with their studies and obtained a higher degree. One man with a Ph.D. said the same thing. His regret in life was that he had not done some postdoctoral study!

What is the meaning of the great importance which the executive class of individual places on education? I do not think that it is simply a matter of gaining professional qualifications or additional skill, as all these men had made good in the material sense. There is clearly some other factor as well. It would seem in the business world that education brings advantages beyond material competence. If these are of a cultural nature which might lead the individual to a fuller life, then their lack is indeed to be regretted. But I do not think that this was in the mnd of the majority of the executive patients who discussed these things with me. It seemed that most of them regretted the rather tawdry social advantages which higher education offers in the 'one-upmanship' of everday interpersonal relationships. It would seem that the businessman is very self-conscious in this area. This is only an outward manifestation of the inner insecurity of many apparently successful people.

9

Retirement

The way up ends in retirement. It can be a fitting finish to a full and useful life, or it can be a miserable prelude to death. It is what we make of it. Adjustment to this last phase may not be too easy. People of retiring age have lost some of their flexibility, and changes are all the more difficult. On each of the other important steps through life, such as on first going to school, our first job, marriage, our first executive appointment, we are younger and more adaptable to change, and there are others near at hand to help us. But this last hurdle, adjustment to retirement, is often faced alone.

Retirement can be a disaster. We need only look about us to see the truth of this. A senior executive still functioning effectively reaches retiring age, and within three months we see him just a shadow of his former self. There is no real cause in the way of physical illness. It is purely a psychological reaction. He has failed to make the last step in his otherwise successful life.

A man who is suddenly cut off from active participation in his life's work may find himself in an emotional vacuum. His world has gone, and there is nothing left. If he has been an habitually anxious person with a high level of nervous tension, he has almost certainly looked forward to retirement as a chance for greater mental and physical relaxation. But all too often his anxiety is suddenly increased. He is apprehensive, and his world that was so full, is now filled only with emptiness. Commonly the anxiety that causes his apprehension suddenly affects his body with the development of psychosomatic symptoms. It is not always a relaxing experience for the man who has led a full and active life suddenly to find that he has nothing significant to do. It is the apparent lack of significance of anything they do in retired life which seems to destroy these men. In the past all their activity was directed to great purpose, and now in contrast, it seems to have little meaning. Men of obsessive personality suffer most in this way, and extraverts suffer least because they can more easily fill in the void with gregarious activity with their friends.

The prevention of this type of disaster depends on two factors in the life of the individual while he is on the way up. He must aim to cultivate a way of life in which he can cope with stresses and strains without too much anxiety. He then copes with the transition to the last phase without too great upset. The other factor of course is the gradual development during life of some inner personal philosophy, so that when this last transition brings him a step closer to death he is able to face the situation calmly and realistically.

'They pension you off before you die.' This is true. Let us not delude ourselves about it. We have known all this for many years; we are calm; we understand; we are all right in our inner selves.

But the man who has failed to develop his inner resources on the way up may find himself at a loss. He is likely to become obsessed with the idea 'If I am too old to work, it must be near the end for me'. This state of mind provides preoccupation with one's body, and hypocondriacal attitudes soon develop. This type of hypochrondriasis is quite common in retired anxious patients who consult me professionally.

Some do better than this. They try to adjust to retirement, but fail in the attempt. They tell me, 'Charity work seems so feeble after doing the job I have been doing'. This of course reflects the individual's state of mind, it comes with people who have over-valued the power and the status of their previous executive work, and the loss of position hurts because of the loss of pride.

Now I have the time to do all the things that I have wanted to do. This is only a different way of looking at the same situation. But this different orientation makes a profound difference to the psychological balance of the individual. Instead of increased anxiety with its physical accompaniments, this man leads out to greater ease and maturity of personality; and he may well say,

'This is the best period of my life'. He has the experience of having lived and learned, and still has sufficient flexibility to develop new activities. The role of older statesman among his friends comes easily and fittingly. He can indulge his interests and hobbies. He finds an increasing interest in his children and grandchildren of which his business life had previously denied him. Perhaps even more important and more satisfying, he finds time for some kind of leisurely contemplation, and reconsideration of values, religious, philosophical and spiritual.

When should I retire? Patients ask me this, and I am sure the answer should depend on the particular circumstances of the individual concerned. If the individual on the way up has been able to develop worthwhile interests outside of his business, he should retire early enough to obtain benefit from these. This means retiring while he still has reasonable flexibility and drive. On the other hand, the man whose whole life has been his business, and who has little or no outside interests should continue in his job as long as he can because he has nothing on which to fall back. For this man the only alternative is a very early retirement, while he is still full of vigour, so that he can make a complete change and take up a completely new way of life.

'How should I prepare to retire?' If we have made the way up in any real sense we are already prepared for retirement because we have gained a degree of inner success which will make successful retirement a certainty. If, as you read this, you have doubts, then it is essentially a matter of letting yourself drift into interests outside of your work. Don't suddenly say to yourself, 'I must get more interests'. If you set out purposely to get other interests, you will almost certainly be too logical about it. An interest is something emotional, something that you like.

You cannot impose an interest on yourself. I have seen people who have tried to, and it simply does not work. It becomes a burden, a chore which the individual makes himself do. He becomes frustrated. His anxiety increases; and he deteriorates. No. It is not like this at all. There is something that you have an inkling

[241]

for, perhaps something a little different from the general pattern of your life as it has been, something that you have hardly admitted to yourself because you did not want anything to interfere with your work. Now is the time to let yourself drift towards this. It is effortless; this is your interest.

Retirement comes easier if it is not too abrupt. It is the same with any psychological adjustment. A little time helps. It gives the psychological processes of the mind a better chance to develop new patterns of functioning. So if we can ease ourselves out of our job into retirement over a period of a few months, the process is all the more likely to go smoothly. I know that this is not always possible. When it is not possible, I think it is a help to get started on some of the new interests of retirement before the actual day comes. Then the sense of sudden emptiness is avoided.

10

What is success

It feels good to be successful. This is something rather different
from the practical rewards of material success. There is satisfaction in success itself. This is a psychological reaction. It is an
important one, and most of us need to experience it from time to
time to keep going. Let me explain by an analogy. Many
golfers like to play for a small wager of a few cents. The pleasure
in collecting the few cents from a friend exceeds perhaps a
thousand times the material success of winning the wager. It
just feels good. There is a similar psychological counterpart to
material success in business. We are often not quite aware of it,
as we attribute our feeling of pleasure to the material gain we
have made, but this is only one aspect of it. We forget too easily
our biological nature. We are competitive animals. Without
this quality we would not have survived as a species. This is
part of us. It is something that idealist planners of the socialist
state often overlook. If such plans are to work effectively, there
must still be some outlet for our drive to beat the other fellow,
which finds such easy expression in the ordinary life of competitive society.

Why seek to be successful? It seems a silly question, but people
answer it in different ways. To some it is a simple biological
drive. 'It is natural.' Others think more of the ethical side. 'It
is the decent thing to do, to use the talents committed to my
charge.' Practically minded people say, 'To support my wife
and family.' Those with more psychological insight answer, 'It is
the feeling of power that it brings.' Other rationalize, 'By being
successful I help others'. As with most things, when there are
many good reasons, it is probable that none of them is true.
    Perhaps we can look at it this way. We live in the hard
practical world of reality. At the same time we are complex

psychological beings beset by doubts and satisfactions some of which we can understand and some we cannot. The seeking of success is intimately concerned with both aspects of our life, the outer reality and the inner which is also a reality. Looked at from this point of view, success, instead of being something which distorts and corrupts, may be seen as something which integrates and gives full expression of the best that is within us.

There are dangers in success. These are essentially dangers to our personality. There is the insidious development of chronic nervous tension from the stress of executive work. Success breeds on success, but it is really motivated by increasing enterprise, push, drive and aggression. People who are becoming increasingly successful may at the same time become increasingly aggressive; and this may extend into the home in such a way as to disrupt family life. The isolation and lack of normal criticism can breed an arrogance. If there is no real criticism, the executive can easily come to believe that he is always right, and this feeling soon extends beyond his business where his competence lies. Because of the isolation and lack of frankness from the 'yes-men' around him, the top executive can easily deteriorate into an unpleasantly suspicious person.

Paradoxically enough, instead of great happiness, success may bring a sense of depression. There are guilt feelings that success has been achieved at too great cost to others. I have seen this reaction many times.

Must success corrupt? Success brings power. Even the psychological manoeuvres which I have described bring power to those that use them. Must this corrupt? If we look about us, what do we see? The petty civil servant full of the insolence of his office. It is all around us, even the doctor is corrupted by his power, and keeps his patients waiting without consideration. So it is with the executive who is on the way up on the larger scale. There can be no doubt that power often corrupts. But is this necessarily so? Is the way up, also the way to inner dissolution? If this be true we should have none of it.

This is a question of the moral dangers as opposed to the psychological dangers which we have just discussed. In talking with successful patients I have observed a tendency for them to set themselves apart from others, and to set their own standard in morality, not only in an unconcern for promiscuity, but also in the way in which many successful men use their mistresses with little or no consideration for the feelings of the other party. If the impersonal attitude of the executive creeps into his love life, then success has corrupted.

Is it power that we seek? Success and power go together, and the desire for power is certainly a motivation for success. This is natural enough. As children we were weak, and our parents were powerful. We wanted to be powerful like them. This is often the reason why people seek power when there would seem no real reason for them to do so. The exercise of power may bring material rewards, but it also brings psychological satisfaction. That is why we like doing it. This satisfaction may become so strong, so demanding, that we lower our moral standards to achieve it.

There is a further point. Many successful men seem to have an unusual power of rationalization. This means that they can produce reasons which are convincing to themselves that their corrupt action is really good. This attitude is often maintained by a successful man by an emphasis that the corrupt action will benefit others besides himself. At the same time he is able to make himself psychologically blind to the fact that the action is harmful or unjust to others.

What is your scale of moral values? The basis of our moral standards is evolved by our identification with our parents or others around us when we are children. But the social milieu in which we are placed also has quite a surprising influence on our moral standards. An example will make the point clear. During the war it was the recognized behaviour of soldiers to acquire odds and ends which would be useful in their camp from people in the district. This was known as 'scrounging'. A man would be proud to be known as a good 'scrounger' by other men of his unit. Yet scrounging is nothing but thieving, and was done by thousands of men who in other circumstances were completely honest. There is an element of this with many successful people about their income tax. Conduct is gauged by a differenet set of moral values. However much we like to rationalize it, the situation is a corruption of basic morality. It shows through under most flimsy disguises. My friends talk of tax avoidance as opposed to tax evasion as if they were different things. In this way success corrupts. To say, 'Everyone does it', is little justification.

There is a sexual element in the drive to success. We see this very obviously at simple levels. The lad wants to get on so as to attract his girl. Later he wants to get on to provide for her and his children. And there is also a deeper sexual motive. The boy wants to be a man, a grown up sexual man. Success becomes a kind of symbol for masculinity. In being a success the young man in an indirect way fulfills his need to express his adult male status.

Our success may bring danger to our children. 'But it is really my children that I work for.' Yes; but this and your success may still endanger them. We know that many children suffered by being brought up in the absence of their father during the war. Some executives live in the house, but might just as well be away as far as the children are concerned. But there are other even more important reactions. You have made the way up. Good. You expect your son to do the same. That seems fair enough. But the problem is that he may not be as competent as you are. He feels this pressure from you to do well. 'Not from me. I don't say a word.' No, of course not. You are too perceptive and sophisticated for that. But you still indirectly express this idea to the boy by the very circumstances of your life. In actual fact I see a case like this almost every week. The boy has done well in the past, but now he seems apathetic, he can't concentrate, he can't get on with his studies. He is usually accompanied to my consulting rooms by both parents. This in itself is an expression of their concern that he should do well. The boy talks. 'They don't say anything, but I feel the pressure is on me. They make study easy for me. But I can't concentrate. They expect too much of me.' I have heard the story many, many times. This is one way in which our success endangers our children.

There is also another danger. In general the successful man is competent, decisive, and clear cut in his ideas. These are things which have helped him to be successful. In psychiatric terms we consider him as having a well integrated personality. His friends regard him as a strong character. Now, the boy's character, because of his youth, is not strong like this. It is pliant, flexible, incompletely formed and vulnerable to outside stresses. It often happens that the impact of the strong well integrated character of the executive has a disastrous effect of the still unformed character of the adolescent boy. The executive unconsciously expects the same decisiveness in the boy as he has himself; and the boy in his turn feels overpowered by the forceful personality of his father. I have seen many examples of this situation in which the force of the father's personality has brought the boy to withdraw into a state of quite extreme introversion. All the time the father has been unaware of what was happening. The answer is to be psychologically gentle with the boy. If the problem should be arising in your household, it is a help to let him see some of your weakness. Talk to him a little about something that has gone wrong, about some matter in which you have failed. Then the gulf between you is not so great, and he feels less overpowered by the strength of your personality.

The way up, to where? I have been talking about the way up as if it were the ladder to top executive status. I have done this purposely, so as to make it easier for you to go along with me. But the way up is more than this. I am sure you have sensed this already. But it has been rather vague; and I think the time has now come for us to try to be more precise about it.

Is material success a worthy goal? I expect that there are many who have never paused to doubt it. But some do, and they would seem to be an increasing number. There are the hippies, who would abandon material things for the pleasure of the senses. Students the world over are protesting that they want something better in life, that the materialistic standards of our generation have brought nothing but war, corruption and moral degradation. And in their view much of this has come about as a result of the pursuit of material success. So they say the idea of work and material success must be wrong. It is only a part of a rat-race invented by man. They feel it is a kind of universal delusion. So they will have none of it, neither work nor success. And in its place they try to experience the happiness of the moment while they can.

But there is another way of looking at it. We live in a world of reality. Material success means wealth, power and status. These are not wrong in themselves. It is only their misuse that is wrong. But their misuse can come about insidiously and without our awareness. That is why, if we are on the way up, we must evaluate these things.

Is material success enough? Material success is not enough unless we also acquire the state of mind to enable us to use the fruits of success wisely. But what seems wise to one, seems foolish to another. One successful man buys a steam yacht and a string of racehorses; another gives all his wealth away again. Is there real wisdom in either? If we are really on the way up we must do better than this. Material success of itself is not enough.

If material success is not enough, what else is there? There is the success of yourself as a person. This must include the full integration of our personality as a unity. If the stress of the way up has made us tense and anxious, we have not achieved this type of integration, and our success is incomplete. But if the way up demands success as a person, there must be still more than an integrated personality. We must have certain attributes of the mind.

We must have a mature sense of values. It is difficult for a psychiatrist to write on this. The materialistic concept of success has also invaded psychiatry, and today's psychiatrist is liable to say, 'You are working well, you have a full sex life; you are all right'. But there are levels of living, and if we are on the way up we must bring ourselves to live at a high level. But what is a high level? Is it caviar and smoked salmon or is it personal austerity? Here we are putting a judgement on values. This is something which is frowned upon by modern psychiatrists. But such judgements are real. They are a part of life, so somehow we must learn to come to make them wisely. But we have already hinted that there is no objective criterion for this kind of wisdom. Your thoughts may be running on ahead of me. 'I have made the way up. But where am I? You are telling me that I am in the wilderness, in the void.' No, that is not it.

Material success is good, but it is not enough. On the way up we also attain an inner success. Without this, material success is no success at all.

What is inner success? It is simply that state of mind which allows us to live with our full human potential. To be calm, to be able to love and to be loved, to understand, to experience our sense of being, and to know that we are part of it all. But these are only some of the attributes of inner succes.

You are a practical business man. I have seen people like you as patients so I know how you feel. 'He was all right when he was writing about the practical psychology of business, this is what I wanted. But this mixed up philosophical and religious stuff is not for me.'

Let me explain. This inner success of which I speak does not always come to those who would seem to seek it most diligently. Vicars, ministers, priests, rabbis, and nuns, have all consulted me as patients. I have sat with yogi mystics in the Himalayas, and I have lived with Zen practitioners in a Buddhist monastary. I have mixed with the existentialists and have learned what I can from Hippies. These are people who have abandoned all that is material in the hope of attaining inner success. But only a few, very few had attained it. Now, what has this got to do with you, the man of business. It is this. It at least shows that the denial of material success in itself does not lead to inner success.

Well, what is success? I had written a couple of pages under this heading setting out logically the material, psychological and spiritual attributes of success. But on re-reading the manuscript I have deleted it. We have agreed that some communications are best made by the extra-verbal rather than the logical meaning of words. If this be so, the message that I would give has already been spelled out in all that has gone before, and you will have read it. That is all.